150 DUTCH & BELGIAN RECIPES

DISCOVER THE AUTHENTIC TASTES OF TWO CLASSIC CUISINES

150 DUTCH & BELGIAN RECIPES

EXPLORE THE INGREDIENTS AND COOKING TECHNIQUES, WITH REGIONAL DISHES SHOWN STEP BY STEP IN MORE THAN 750 STUNNING PHOTOGRAPHS

JANNY DE MOOR AND SUZANNE VANDYCK

HERMES HOUSE

This edition is published by Hermes House,
an imprint of Anness Publishing Ltd,
Hermes House, 88–89 Blackfriars Road,
London SE1 8HA;
tel. 020 7401 2077; fax 020 7633 9499
www.hermeshouse.com; www.annesspublishing.com

If you like the images in this book and would like to investigate
using them for publishing, promotions or advertising, please visit
our website www.practicalpictures.com for more information.

Publisher: Joanna Lorenz
Senior Editor: Lucy Doncaster
Copy Editors: Catherine Best, Jan Cutler and Jenni Fleetwood
Designer: Nigel Partridge
Illustrators: Anthony Duke and Rob Highton
Photographers: William Lingwood and Debi Treloar
Food Stylists: Lucy McKelvie and Sunil Vijayakar
Prop Stylist: Helen Trent
Production Controller: Mai Ling Collyer

ETHICAL TRADING POLICY
At Anness Publishing we believe that business should be
conducted in an ethical and ecologically sustainable way,
with respect for the environment and a proper regard to the
replacement of the natural resources we employ.

As a publisher, we use a lot of wood pulp to make high-quality
paper for printing, and that wood commonly comes from spruce
trees. We are therefore currently growing more than 500,000
trees in two Scottish forest plantations near Aberdeen – Berrymoss
(130 hectares/320 acres) and West Touxhill (125 hectares/305 acres).
The forests we manage contain twice the number of trees employed
each year in paper-making for our books.

Because of this ongoing ecological investment programme, you, as
our customer, can have the pleasure and reassurance of knowing that
a tree is being cultivated on your behalf to naturally replace the materials
used to make the book you are holding.

Our forestry programme is run in accordance with the UK
Woodland Assurance Scheme (UKWAS) and will be certified by
the internationally recognized Forest Stewardship Council (FSC).
The FSC is a non-government organization dedicated to promoting
responsible management of the world's forests. Certification
ensures forests are managed in an environmentally sustainable
and socially responsible basis. For further information about this
scheme, go to www.annesspublishing.com/trees

© Anness Publishing Ltd 2010

Previously published as *Dutch Cooking* and *The Food and
Cooking of Belgium*.

PUBLISHER'S NOTE
Although the advice and information in this book are believed to
be accurate and true at the time of going to press, neither the
authors nor the publisher can accept any legal responsibility or
liability for any errors or omissions that may be made nor for
any inaccuracies nor for any loss, harm or injury that comes
about from following instructions or advice in this book.

NOTES
Bracketed terms are intended for American readers.

Quantities are given in both metric and imperial measures and,
where appropriate, in standard cups and spoons. Follow one set
of measures because they are not interchangeable.

Standard spoon and cup measures are level.
1 tsp = 5ml, 1 tbsp = 15ml, 1 cup = 250ml/8fl oz.

Australian standard tablespoons are 20ml. Australian readers
should use 3 tsp in place of 1 tbsp for measuring small quantities.

American pints are 16fl oz/2 cups. American readers should
use 20fl oz/2.5 cups in place of 1 pint when measuring liquids.

Electric oven temperatures in this book are for conventional
ovens. When using a fan oven, the temperature will need to
be reduced by about 10–20°C/20–40°F. Check with your
manufacturer's instruction book for guidance.

The nutritional analysis given for each recipe is calculated per
portion (i.e. serving or item), unless otherwise stated. If the
recipe gives a range, such as Serves 4–6, then the nutritional
analysis will be for the smaller portion size, i.e. 6 servings.
Measurements for sodium do not include salt added to taste.

Medium (US large) eggs are used unless otherwise stated.

Cover shows ZeelandMussel Soup, for recipe see page 55.

CONTENTS

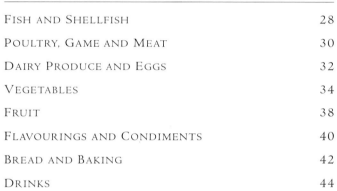

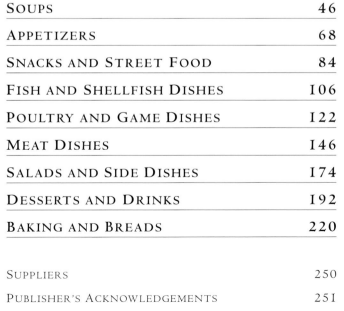

INTRODUCTION

Situated in north-western Europe, the Netherlands and Belgium were once part of the same state. They share a common history and language, Flemish, although French is also spoken in Belgium. In addition they have similar topographies and climates, and produce many of the same crops. Although each country has its own iconic foods, such as *frites* in Belgium and pancakes in the Netherlands, many dishes can be found in both countries, albeit with slight regional variations. This informative book contains a selection of the very best recipes from both countries, providing a tantalizing taste of these sophisticated cuisines and an insight into their development over the ages.

SHARED HISTORIES

Given that the two countries have a common past, it is perhaps not surprising that their cuisines and cultures have marked similarities. Linked to their European neighbours both geographically and by a shared Roman heritage, the region was strongly influenced by French, and to a lesser extent Italian, culinary traditions during the 15th and 16th centuries, and this is particularly evident in Belgium, where French is still widely spoken.

The Golden Age in the late 16th and 17th centuries had an even greater effect. This was a period of power, with exploration, colonization and trading at its peak. The Dutch East India Company (*Vereenigde Oost-Indische Compagnie* or VOC in Dutch), for instance, was especially dominant on a global scale and was the first multinational corporation. In addition to its colonial activities in Asia, it was a key player in the spice trade, competing against the hitherto dominant Portuguese and successfully claiming the monopoly on spices produced in parts of Indonesia. Dutch colonies were also to be found as far apart as Sri Lanka, South America, the Caribbean and South Africa.

The impact of such activities on the cuisine was two-fold: an increased awareness of the importance of a healthy diet, which meant that more fresh fruit and vegetables were eaten by the general populace; and the introduction of new ingredients (most notable of which was spices), and cooking techniques, some of which were embraced and assimilated, producing such delicacies as *pepernoten* and *speculaas*.

Despite their eventual split into two separate countries in 1830, the regions continued to share a common fate: both

Above: Bread plays an important role in Dutch and Belgian diets, and there is a wide selection of artisanal products on offer in many towns.

were blighted by famine in the 19th century; and both faced a slow descent from power as industrialization gripped the rest of Europe and other countries, such as Great Britain and France, gained the upper hand. Both countries flourished in the latter half of the 20th century, however, and remain key players in modern Europe, with Brussels being at the heart of the European Union, and exports and trade remaining important industries.

REFINED CUISINES

Dutch and Belgian cooks are notable for their use of extremely high-quality produce and refined techniques. Although the premise of most meals is a simple one, comprising meat, potatoes and an accompaniment of vegetables or salad, the dishes themselves are far from basic. Great care is taken when it comes to pairing ingredients and

Left: Amsterdam is famous for its many waterways, which in the 17th century helped establish the city as the world's commercial centre.

Above: Belgium is home to many ancient abbeys, some of which still contain the Trappist breweries that continue to make world-class beer.

marrying flavours to create the ideal balance, while sophisticated techniques and attention to detail ensure that the most is made of every component, be it fresh asparagus or endives or a fine cut of prime beef.

The Dutch and Belgians take great pride in their food. Traditions that date back to the Middle Ages, and in particular the period of monastic influence, are still upheld and nowhere is this more apparent than in Belgium's brewing industry, which is famous throughout the world. Cheeses, breads, mustards and fruits are also still made in both countries using age-old techniques, and an in-depth knowledge about local produce and its uses are very important for home cooks as well as chefs.

As a result of the attention to detail and care taken to select the best ingredients, the gastronomies of both countries are sophisticated and it is perhaps time that they were recognized more widely. It is with very good reason that, until recently, Brussels had more Michelin-starred restaurants per capita than any other city.

NATIONAL DISHES

Although the two countries are renowned for their world-famous classics, such as the *moules-frites*, waffles and chocolates of Belgium and the meatballs, *stoemp* and pancakes of the Netherlands, there are also many more lesser-known delicacies.

Of key importance are vegetables, such as white asparagus and Belgian endive, which are transformed into appetizers, salads, soups and side dishes, while potatoes – the staple accompaniment – are mashed, gratinated and, of course, fried to make the *frites* that are consumed so avidly by the Belgians.

Fish and shellfish, including the beloved herrings, mussels and shrimp, appear in many guises, both at the start of the meal and as the star feature, while meat, game and poultry are roasted, grilled (broiled), stewed with beer or shaped into meatballs or croquettes.

Desserts, many made with fruits, chocolate or dairy products, are very popular, and are often followed by coffee, chocolates and regional liqueurs. Away from the table there is a dazzling array of street food, pastries, cakes and breads, which are enjoyed as snacks or in the countless cafés and restaurants.

All of these foods and more are explored in this comprehensive new book, which provides an insight into the traditions surounding the dishes as well as more than 150 classic recipes, enabling the home cook to discover for themselves the gastronomic delights of two ancient and delectable cuisines.

Below: There is a huge range of speciality regional cheeses in the Netherlands and Belgium.

THE GEOGRAPHY OF THE NETHERLANDS

The Netherlands did not exist as a political entity until 1581 when the seven northern provinces founded a new republic, independent from Spain. Endless battles, treaties and alliances meant that the borders were constantly redrawn until they were finally settled in 1830, and the area was split into the separate states of the Netherlands and Belgium. The Netherlands today consists of 12 provinces: Friesland, Groningen, Drenthe, Utrecht, Overijssel, Flevoland, Gelderland, Zeeland, North Holland, South Holland, North Brabant and Limburg.

A LOW-LYING LAND

The country is bordered by the North Sea to the north and west, Belgium to the south, and Germany to the east. It is a densely populated and geographically low-lying country, with its name translating as 'low countries' or 'low lands'. The plural form is used because the Netherlands has its origin in the unification of the seven northern provinces, hence 'lands'. The Dutch

Below: The dunes are a method of protecting the Low Countries against the North Sea at high tide, shown here by the 'Slufter', a trench cut through the dunes on the island of Texel.

distinguish between the name of their country (Nederland, singular) and the kingdom (Nederlanden, plural).

The region to the south and east of the country consists mostly of plains and a few high ridges, whereas the western and northern region is lower and includes reclaimed land (polders) on the site of the Zuiderzee and the delta of the Rhine, Meuse, and Schelde rivers. Coastal areas are almost all below sea level and the land is protected from flooding by dunes and artificial dikes.

Above: Large numbers of windmills were traditionally used for effective land drainage. While their task has now been taken over by pumping stations, working mills are still a common sight. Countless canals and ditches divide the Dutch polders into neat rectangles.

Below: The belts of canals around the centre of Amsterdam are a favourite destination for sightseers wanting to view the city by boat. The canals were formerly used to supply the homes and storehouses of rich merchants.

Holstein Friesians. Pigs and chickens have also been a traditional source of protein and, until recently, were very intensively farmed and exported.

As well as being a country of rich pastures for raising cattle and, therefore, a producer of high-quality dairy products and good beef and veal, the country also cultivates a wide range of vegetables and fruits. These include the potato, which has been a Dutch staple for centuries, and apples, which have been cultivated since at least the Middle Ages. Cereals, such as barley and rye, have played an important role in the development of Dutch cuisine, both in bread-making and baking and in their world-famous brewing industry, and continue to be a staple crop.

Products grown using more modern methods under glass or in polytunnels include flowers, tomatoes and, more recently, (bell) peppers. Flower bulbs such as tulips and daffodils are cultured on the fertile land behind the many dunes, and the sale and exportation of cut flowers and potted plants is a leading national industry.

Below: Bulbous plants, especially tulips and daffodils, are grown primarily on the mixed soil of low fen and sand directly behind the dunes.

Above: The flatness of the country and the rich soil make the Netherlands an ideal place for cattle breeding and agriculture. Cheese, vegetables and fruit are key export products.

INLAND WATERWAYS

Controlling the water flows around the country has always been key to its safety and prosperity. As far back as the Middle Ages, peasants drained peat bogs to make them into fertile agricultural areas. The drainage canals created to achieve this also provided an excellent method of commercial transport. This, combined with broad rivers such as the Rhine and Meuse, which provided access to the remotest parts of Europe, led to rapid urban and commercial development and in the

17th century Amsterdam was seen as the world's commercial centre. Rotterdam harbour is still one of the biggest in the world, and commerce, transportation and agriculture are still essential to the Dutch economy. The negative aspect of the waterways has been frequent floods throughout the country's history, and these still pose a threat in many areas.

A PRODUCTIVE NATION

Because the country is bordered by the North Sea, the Dutch have always been excellent fishermen and entrepreneurial international traders. The flat soil and the mild maritime climate make it ideal for agriculture and cattle-breeding. In fact, one-third of the world's dairy cattle are the familiar black-and-white Dutch

THE DEVELOPMENT OF DUTCH COOKING

Some 10,000 to 12,000 years ago, the area now called the Netherlands was a tundra stretching as far as England. Hunters from Hamburg and Ahrensburg roamed there, eating reindeer and fish. Archaeologists have discovered that the first great culinary revolution took place 7,000 years ago when the first Dutch farmers settled on the 'Löss' grounds of Limburg, clay grounds highly suitable for agriculture.

Their diet was oriented around sheep, cattle, goats and pigs and cultivated produce such as emmer wheat, peas, lentils, linseed and poppy seed. About 500BC, the coastal areas of the middle (Holland) and the north (Friesland and Groningen) also became farmland. Archaeological finds prove that as early as about 150BC cheese was being made in earthen moulds.

THE ROMAN ERA

Roman cuisine was introduced around the beginning of the first century. At that time, Dutch was not a written language, so everything known about that period comes from the Romans, especially the historian Tacitus. In his book *Germania*, written in AD98, he describes the tribes of the Batavians and Caninefates, or 'rabbit catchers', who lived in those regions, 'Their food is very simple; wild fruit, fresh venison, or coagulated milk. They banish hunger without formality, without curious dressing and curious fare.' (Tr. Thomas Gordon.)

Not only did the Dutch derive the word *koken*, to cook, from the Romans, they also learned how to prepare food the Roman way, with the introduction of new ingredients and flavour combinations.

THE MIDDLE AGES

In the period around AD400, the climate of the Netherlands became colder and wetter, large areas of land were washed away and vast marshes were formed. This was when the Dutch started to reclaim land from the sea. Churches and monasteries, the centres of learning in the Middle Ages, also became the focus of culinary culture.

Records from monasteries and city archives, as well as medieval paintings and miniatures, provide information about how the rich ate. They were served a lot of game and poultry, including swans, peacocks or herons. In the same period, the more common people ate simple stews, although there were periods of famine as a result of war or poor harvests, as in the disastrous years 1315–17.

FOREIGN INFLUENCES

In the early 15th century, the counts, dukes and bishops who had ruled the Low Countries in the Middle Ages had to come to terms with the growing influence of the dukes of Burgundy, powerful princes of the French royal house of Valois. When Charles V, who was also Duke of Burgundy, became Holy Roman Emperor in 1530, French

cultural influences, including culinary style and habits, became more evident throughout the Netherlands.

In 1588, Carel Baten's 1000-page *Medicine Book* was published, containing for the first time written mention of exotic ingredients not grown in northern Europe, such as lemons and oranges, and also some vegetables, such as spinach, stewed with wine, apples and sugar. European influences are also evident in recipes for such Italian imports as cauliflower and Savoy cabbage, which were served with ground ginger.

The importance of eating healthy foods such as fruit and vegetables was fully recognized in the Netherlands of the 16th century, although many were hard to get hold of and had prices that made them only accessible to the privileged classes. Paintings by Dutch artists such as Joachim Beuckelaer (1533–73), Jan Victors (1620–76) and Jan van Huysum (1682–1749) show an abundance of vegetables and fruit on the tables of the rich, commissioned to display the luxury of the owners' lifestyles.

THE GOLDEN AGE

Towards the end of the 16th century, a period of economic prosperity and cultural growth began in the Netherlands, now known as the Golden Age. The Dutch became a major economic power and colonies and trading posts were established worldwide, including the Dutch East Indies (Indonesia), Suriname in South America, Dutch Ceylon (Sri Lanka), the Netherlands Antilles in the Caribbean and South Africa. Remaining under the Dutch Empire until the fall of imperialism in the 20th century, the food culture of these colonies became well assimilated in the Netherlands. Spices from South-east Asia in particular are to be found in cakes and biscuits such as *pepernoten*, and traditional dishes from these countries, especially Indonesia, remain very popular in the Netherlands.

Left: Centres of learning, such as the abbey depicted here by Jan van den Hecke, kept records of the eating habits of the Dutch in the Middle Ages.

Right: This painting of The Fruit Seller, *by the 17th-century Dutch painter Jan Victors (1620–76), shows fruit being sold directly from the farm.*

The introduction of the brick oven in the houses of rich merchants, especially those of the powerful East India Company, resulted in a dramatic change in Dutch culinary techniques. One-pot cooking became a thing of the past for such families because more dishes could be prepared at the same time.

Vegetables, salads and fresh fruit became ever more popular as doctors emphasized their health benefits. Breakthroughs in the treatment of scurvy on the nation's trading vessels supported this movement, as did the increasing availability of fresh produce. Other changes included sugar being banished from savoury foods, and a corresponding rise in the number of desserts.

ARISTOCRATIC TASTES

Almost all provinces of the Netherlands published their own cookbooks in the 18th century. The recipes were mostly written by ladies who then read them out loud to their maids.

While the lower classes in the country were poor, the well-to-do continued to enjoy French cuisine, using books written by French chefs. The bestselling French cookbook was *Alice the Perfect and Thrifty Kitchenmaid*, first published in 1803.

Despite the adjective 'thrifty', the recipes follow the previous century's rich cuisine, using lots of eggs, expensive butter and wine. It includes the first mashes and the combination of potatoes, vegetables and meat that are still the foundation of Dutch daily meals.

19TH-CENTURY HARDSHIP

Industrialization dawned slowly in the Netherlands of the 19th century in comparison to the rest of Europe, and the country's economic power was undermined by Great Britain's sea forces and the French army under Napoleon. Famines in the Netherlands, Belgium and other areas of Europe also had an impact, with peasants only surviving thanks to the potato. This is shown in Vincent van Gogh's (1853–90) sombre painting, *The Potato Eaters*.

Several domestic science schools were opened in the late 19th century, irreverently called Spinach Academies. Most of them produced rather dull, healthy recipes. Intended to teach the

Left: Numerous Dutch still lives, such as this one by Jan van Huysum (c.1725), were intended to show off the opulence of their owners' lifestyles.

poverty-stricken working class how to cook properly and frugally, they were (and often still are) widely regarded as middle-of-the-road cuisine. However, the traditions of the true Dutch cuisine continued to make themselves felt at home, where mothers taught daughters how to make their favourite dishes. This 'secret cuisine' of the Netherlands was recorded in handwritten notebooks that now command steep prices.

A NEW PERSPECTIVE

Two world wars left scars on the infrastructure and economic prosperity of the country, and these required much effort to heal. After World War II, however, cooking became democratic, men acknowledged their interest more openly, and cooks became famous chefs.

In the Netherlands of today, this change of perspective is making itself felt as distinguished chefs, such as Jonnie Boer, are developing Dutch cuisine around the world, inspired by home-grown foods and almost-forgotten local dishes. This, together with restaurant-led campaigns and promotions of regional products, led to a revival of the 'secret cuisine' in the 1990s, which continues to this day.

DUTCH EATING HABITS

Like all nations, the Dutch have their own eating habits, mealtimes and table manners. The main emphasis in the Netherlands is always on a main meal that combines vegetables, potatoes and meat, although the Dutch are also fond of sweet and savoury snacks and take frequent coffee breaks.

Many visitors to the Netherlands judge the cuisine and food culture solely on the basis of its restaurants, which is misleading because these represent so many national cuisines. The traditional diet and eating patterns are best seen in the Dutch home, where mealtimes remain social occasions when friends and family gather and share their news.

BREAKFAST AND COFFEE TIME

Ontbijt, or breakfast, is taken between 7 and 9 a.m. In its most luxurious form it consists of white, brown, rye, currant and sugar bread, rusks, spice cake, a boiled egg, cheese and cold cuts. Jam and chocolate sprinkles are provided for the white and brown bread or rusks; sweet breads and spice cake are eaten just with butter. In addition, there will

be orange and grapefruit juice, tea and coffee. However, during the week, one slice of bread with jam or cheese is more normal.

At about 10.30 in the morning, it is coffee time. This is mostly drunk with milk and sugar and accompanied by spice cake or cookies.

LUNCH, COFFEE-TABLE AND TEA

Middageten, lunch, often consists of a few sandwiches and a glass of milk, although the French custom of a heavier main meal at lunchtime is gaining ground, especially at weekends. If you have reason to celebrate or want to discuss business, you may be invited to sit at a *koffietafel*, or coffee-table between midday and 2 in the afternoon. The Brabant *koffietafel*, consisting of brandy with sugar, buns, sausage buns, brawn (head cheese) and everything you also get for a festive breakfast, is especially famous.

Tea is normally served between 3 and 4 p.m. but it is not as elaborate as traditional English tea. Children usually have biscuits (cookies) and a drink.

Above: Currant Bread is served with a boiled egg, cheese and cold cuts at special breakfasts.

DINNER

Avondeten, dinner, is served between 6 and 8 in the evening, although it is common to arrive at restaurants between 7 and 8. This is the most important and largest meal for most Dutch people and consists of soup or a salad, a main course and a dessert.

FOOD ETIQUETTE

The Rotterdam scholar, Desiderius Erasmus, wrote about table manners in 1530, when people still ate with their hands from a common dish. He advised against spitting, blowing your nose in your napkin, licking your fingers or drinking wine more than twice during the meal. While Erasmus's advice became a general convention, the Dutch also like to break these rules; they eat with a knife and fork, but will say that nothing tastes as good as a piece of smoked sausage or a chunk of cheese eaten with your fingers.

Left: The Dutch still love to eat raw matjes *(fresh herring) by dangling the fish from their hand, preferably immediately after the fish have been brought to shore.*

Right: Although there are numerous international restaurants in the Netherlands, ones serving regional foods, such as oysters, remain popular with Dutch families for special occasions.

The Dutch are hospitable and love to invite guests to a meal, although uninvited guests are generally not welcomed as hosts like to be prepared. A birthday, however, means an open house and visitors are encouraged to drop in throughout the day. Treats are sweet tarts and pies, coffee, tea, cookies, and savoury snacks, after which the adults are offered a *borrel*, or drink. This convention is summed up in one word, dear to all the Dutch – *gezellig*, or cosy.

EATING OUT

Dutch families go to restaurants less frequently than other Europeans, but when they do go out, it is often to eat non-Dutch food, with more than 80 countries represented in the restaurants of Amsterdam. Such venues typically represent the cuisines of nations such as China, Indonesia, Suriname, Italy

Below: Poffertjes, traditional small, spongey, sweet pancakes, are prepared using a cast-iron or copper pan with shallow indentations.

and Greece. Chinese restaurants are a perennial favourite, and most of them offer a mixture of Chinese and Indonesian dishes – Indonesia was a Dutch colony until 1949 and the Dutch remain fond of Indonesian food.

As well as restaurants, there are many cafés in every town, usually serving both coffee and alcoholic drinks. Snacks, such as *bitterballen*, are also frequently available.

There are cafeterias, snack bars, with a choice of fast food, such as salads, chips (French fries), Indonesian-style *loempia*, *nasi* or *bami slice*, croquettes, 'bear claws', sliced meatballs with onions in between, and *belegde broodjes*, filled soft buns. The best place to find these buns is a *broodjeswinkel*, which is a bun store, not a sandwich bar. At the famous deluxe lunchroom Amsterdam Eetsalon van Dobben, they serve buns with incredibly indulgent fillings. It's also certainly worth trying *pekelvlees*, a typically Dutch kind of pastrami.

In numerous *pannenkoekenhuizen*, or pancake restaurants, all over the country, you can order inexpensive pancakes with a wide variety of fillings. The Dutch like to eat them with golden (light corn) syrup, even if the filling is savoury, such as cheese and bacon.

In a traditional pancake restaurant in Leiden they are served on enormous Delft blue plates that evoke scenes of rural life in the Netherlands.

STREET FOOD

If there is a smell of freshly fried fish at the fish stall, the Dutch love to take their children with them to buy and eat *lekkerbekjes*, deep-fried breaded whiting, hake or pollack. Another favourite is *kibbelingen*, formerly made of breaded salted cod cheeks, but nowadays using pieces of cheaper white fish. The Dutch will eat these with their fingers, standing together at the stall before taking home smoked mackerel, herring, salmon, eel or whatever fresh seasonal fish is available. Alternatively, they may decide to eat a herring at the *haringkar*, herring cart, which specializes in fresh herring and pickles.

New exotic specialities from Taiwan, Vietnam and other parts of South-east Asia available in Dutch marketplaces have not yet supplanted the *stroopwafelbakkers*, bakers of caramel waffles and the *gebakkraam*, literally meaning 'pastry booth', where you can buy *oliebollen* all year round, as well as thick Belgian waffles and *Berliner bollen*, 'balls from Berlin', deep-fried puffs filled with vanilla pudding.

DUTCH FESTIVALS <u>AND</u> CELEBRATIONS

Nowadays a huge number of holy days is celebrated in the Netherlands throughout the year, including those of various Christian denominations, and Buddhists, Hindus and Muslims. It is not feasible to mention them all here, so the following is confined to the officially recognized festive days – not all of them religious celebrations – when almost everybody gets a day off to celebrate. The days described often have a special food or drink traditionally associated with them.

NEW YEAR'S DAY

The year starts and ends with home-made *oliebollen* and *appelflappen*, which are these days usually accompanied by champagne or other sparkling wine. Some people prefer an old-fashioned mulled wine, called 'bishop-wine', made by simmering red Bordeaux with a lemon decorated with cloves and sugar. Other New Year dishes include Hussar's Salad, Herring Salad and other small salads (*slaatjes*), which the Dutch share with their neighbours when setting off fireworks at midnight.

Below: Carnival celebrations are popular all over the Netherlands, with most cities and villages organizing their own carnival over three days just before Ash Wednesday.

CARNIVAL

Every spring, just before Ash Wednesday, a nationwide carnival is celebrated in the Netherlands for three days. While now only remotely connected with the Catholic Church, those who have fasted during Lent still welcome the return to normal food. Cities and villages have their own carnival clubs, headed by an elected 'prince'. Floats parade the streets, special carnival hits are sung and beer is consumed in large quantities. Many people open their doors for guests who are treated to tubs full of soup and herring.

Above: Queen's Day is celebrated on 30 April, the anniversary of Queen Beatrix's (b.1938) succession and of her mother's birthday. Large crowds typically gather to greet her, or even shake hands with her personally.

PALM SUNDAY

On the Sunday before Easter, the custom is for children to carry a palm cross (*palmpaasje*) decorated with ribbons, strings of dried fruit, and small bread figures in the shape of swans or cockerels, called *palmpasenbrood*.

EASTER

During this Christian celebration, coloured eggs, symbols of new life at the beginning of spring, are seen everywhere, with sweet eggs consumed in large quantities. Beautifully decorated chocolate eggs are offered for sale by pâtissiers, together with chocolate hares (jack rabbits), chosen because of the fertility of the species. Bakers also sell *paasmannetjes*, Easter men, little bread men clasping a cooked egg in their arms, and the sugared *paaskrakelingen*, Easter cracknels, made from bread dough or puff pastry. The shape of these cracknels is thought to be a symbol of life and death, following the cycle of a seed sown in the ground, then the shoot growing above ground, then withering and, finally, 'dying' for a short time.

QUEEN'S DAY

In the past, the birthday of the Dutch monarch was celebrated on the birthday itself, but nowadays, 30 April is the fixed day of celebration. Early in the morning the national tricolour is flown, with an orange streamer symbolizing the House of Orange, the Dutch royal family. Bands march in the streets and almost every city and village organizes a fair. The royal family visits a different city or village every year, mingling freely with the crowds. People eat orange-coloured cakes and drink *oranjebitter*, an orange liqueur made specially for the occasion.

HALLOWEEN

This celebration on 31 October is now established in most parts of the Netherlands. Pumpkins are hollowed out with cut-outs for eyes, nose and mouth, and a light is placed inside to shine at night. The flesh can be used to make a delicious soup.

SAINT MARTIN'S DAY

Celebrated on the Friday or Saturday preceding 11 November, children used to dress up and go from house to house with a candle in a hollowed fodder beet, singing special songs, whereupon they were rewarded with sweets (candy) or cake. Nowadays, children walk the streets with Chinese lanterns, mostly

accompanied by adults. At home, a hearty Saint Martin's soup with a Dutch rusk awaits them.

SAINT NICHOLAS

This saint is the Dutch equivalent of Santa Claus, a benevolent Christmas figure who distributes gifts on 5 December. During the preceding fortnight, children place small presents for the saint in their shoes each evening with some hay and a carrot for his horse.

The story of Saint Nicholas, or *Sinterklaas*, says that he travels to the Netherlands by steamer from his home in Spain. When he arrives, he stands there in his bishop's robes, surrounded by his servants, all called 'Black Peter', armed with sacks full of sweets for all good children. These include chocolate letters, puff pastry filled with almond paste, marzipan, *taaitaai* – 'chewy chewy' – and *speculaas*, an almond paste cake (*see* page 228).

On the evening of 5 December, the whole family gathers to receive presents. At the start of the evening, a Peter's black hand throws 'pepper nuts', tiny balls, made from *speculaas* dough,

Left: Even in small villages, Sinterklaas *is said to arrive by boat, from his home in Madrid, Spain. He is always accompanied by his Black Peters who distribute 'pepper nuts' to the children.*

Above: Sinterklaas, or Saint Nicholas (280–342), is the patron saint of children in the Netherlands and Belgium. His arrival in mid-November attracts large Dutch crowds, both young and old. His story tells of him riding a white horse over the rooftops. Saint Nicholas' Eve, on 5 December, is when gifts are shared, each one with a poem from the saint.

through the half-opened door into the room. This traditional Dutch feast now competes with the more modern Santa Claus who appears on 24 December, and is viewed as a pagan intruder by most Dutch people.

CHRISTMAS

The whole country celebrates Christmas with enthusiasm and with the associated preparation of exquisite food. Traditional main dishes are beef roll, turkey and often game. To satisfy the Dutch people's sweet tooth, *kerstkransjes*, round biscuits (cookies) with a hole in them, are bought from the baker and are sprinkled with flaked (sliced) almonds and pearl sugar. Other baked treats are *kerstkransen*, puff pastry rings filled with almond paste and decorated with cherries, and the special currant bread filled with almond paste that was adopted from their German neighbours.

THE GEOGRAPHY OF BELGIUM

Roughly triangular in shape, Belgium – known as België in Dutch or Flemish and Belgique in French – is located at the crossroads of north-western Europe. It shares borders with France, the Netherlands, Germany and the Grand Duchy of Luxembourg, with access to the North Sea in the north-west.

A tiny, densely populated country, it is blessed with fertile soil and ideal growing conditions. Farmers produce an abundance of fresh foods, ranging from meat and dairy to fruit and vegetables, and, combined with the culinary influences from its neighbouring countries, this has helped to shape the country's superb gastronomy.

CLIMATE

Belgium's climate is moderate, with regular, gentle rainfall throughout the year. Conditions on the coast are milder and more humid than those found farther inland. This temperate climate provides ideal conditions for agriculture: a long growing season during which farmers can grow high-quality produce over a sustained period. New agricultural techniques for growing under cover have also now prolonged the season for delicate crops, such as strawberries and tomatoes.

Below: The beautiful port town of Ostend is famous for its fish markets and restaurants.

THREE DISTINCT REGIONS

The terrain of Belgium can be divided into three categories: coastal plains, fertile central areas and the highlands of the Ardennes. Each of these is especially suited to growing and rearing different foods, which has given rise to regional specialities made from ingredients that are available locally.

Situated along the short North Sea coastline are the two main fishing ports, Zeebrugge and Ostend, which receive abundant daily catches of plaice, sole, herring, cod, grey shrimp, oysters and mussels from the North Atlantic Ocean boats that trawl the waters of the North Sea.

Surrounding these towns are flat coastal plains that are dominated by sand dunes; then, moving inland from the North Sea coast are the polders, a low but fertile land that was once flooded by the sea and rivers but is now protected by dikes.

Farther inland are fertile valleys with clay and sandy soils, irrigated by a number of waterways. The area of Flanders is mostly dedicated to intensive cattle breeding, dairy farming, rearing calves for veal, and pig-keeping. A range of crops also flourish in this region, including oats, rye, wheat, spelt, sugar beets, Belgian endive, hops and flax, as well as potatoes and other

Above: Several rivers, including the River Semois, meander through the verdant uplands of the Ardennes, which are prime hunting and hiking territory.

vegetables, fruits and a range of ornamental plants. Many of these are exported to other parts of Europe.

Hageland, the verdant area surrounding Brussels and Leuven, is called the Green Belt because of its many beautiful natural parks, meadows, gardens and characteristic villages, including the Brussels-Mechelen-Leuven triangle, which is the centre of Belgian endive, asparagus and Brussels sprouts production.

The major fruit-growing areas of Belgium are Henegouwen in the west and Haspengouw in the east, where Jonagold and Boskoop apples and Conference and Comice pears are widely grown. As a result of these fruits' abundance, artisan ciders and speciality fruit syrups, such as sirop de Liège, are also produced in these areas.

Between the rivers Vesder and Maas (Meuse) in the province of Liège lies Land van Herve, a region renowned for its historic caves, as well as the production of mushrooms and a number of types of unpasteurized cheeses that are aged in the humid cave conditions or in cellars.

Above: Bruges is situated on the extensive network of waterways in Belgium, and is often called 'The Venice of the North'.

Rising from west to east is the higher plateau of Belgium, the Ardennes. This hilly landscape of forests, streams and steep river valleys is home to a wealth of indigenous animals, making it prime hunting and fishing territory. The highest point in Belgium, the Signal of Botrange (694m/2,277ft above sea level) is found here, and offers ample opportunities for hiking and hunting around and within the valleys of the rivers Maas and Ourthe.

POLITICAL AND LINGUISTIC BOUNDARIES

In addition to the three geographical areas, Belgium is divided into three main political regions: Flanders, Wallonia and The Brussels Capital Region. Both Flanders and Wallonia are further subdivided into ten provinces, each of which has its own capital city. Brussels is the federal and regional capital of Belgium, as well as being home to the EU and NATO headquarters. Best known as the administrative heart of Europe, it is also a centre of gastronomic excellence, with a range of multicultural restaurants and markets and some of the best chocolate stores in the world.

In addition to the geographical and political regions there are also four main language divisions in the country: the community in Flanders who speak a dialect of Dutch called Flemish; the French speakers in Wallonia; a bilingual enclave of people speaking both Flemish and French in the Brussels Capital Region; and a small community of German speakers in eastern Wallonia.

WATERWAYS AND RAILWAYS

The principal rivers in Belgium are the Schelde and the Maas. Both are important arteries with their tributaries gradually running through the central plateau to the sea. Located on the main river Schelde are the ports of Antwerp (which is the farthest inland port and a major European sea port) and Ghent (which was once the centre of the Flemish lace and textile industries) with its many bridged waterways. These waters are home to several species of relatively rare river fish, such as pike, carp, perch, grayling and barbel, which appear in local dishes.

Belgium was the first European country to build a railway system, in 1831, which was used to export its abundant vegetable and fruit crops quickly and easily to neighbouring countries. Over the years fruit and vegetable production developed into a highly competitive sector, and today it has one of the highest productivity levels in Europe.

Below: Bordered by four countries and with access to the fecund North Sea, Belgium is perfectly situated for lucrative trading with its neighbours.

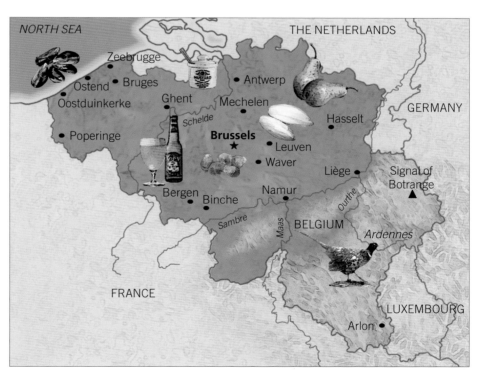

THE DEVELOPMENT OF BELGIAN COOKING

The region that comprises present-day Belgium has been invaded and ruled throughout the centuries by various powers, including the Celts, Romans, Vikings, Spanish, Austrians, French, Dutch and Germans. In addition to the cooking techniques and ingredients introduced by these invaders, returning Belgian Crusaders brought with them a wealth of knowledge and foods, in particular spices, from faraway lands. These were subsequently absorbed and adapted by the local population, resulting in the distinct cuisine that exists today.

EARLY HISTORY

During the Neolithic era (5000–2500BC), tribes lived in small-scale communities, and are known to have farmed cattle, pigs, sheep and goats, as well as growing einkorn wheat (an early, wild form of wheat), millet, barley, lentils, emmer (another early form of wheat) and spelt.

Around 1000BC–AD1, however, the ferocious Celts took over, emerging as a recognizable culture in Gaul (the area that now comprises France, Belgium, Luxembourg and parts of Germany), and imposing their more advanced culture on the indigenous tribes. A powerful nation, these *Belgae* traded freely with Greeks, adopting their coinage and sharing similar polytheistic views.

Below: Wheat and other crops have been grown in Belgium since Neolithic times. Today, arable farming remains one of the country's key industries.

Despite the prowess of its warriors, Gallia Belgica (Belgian Gaul), as Belgium was called by the Romans, was conquered by Julius Caesar around 56BC, and became the Roman province of Belgica. The region flourished under the rule of the advanced Romans, who constructed roads, enabling free trade, especially of foodstuffs, and making Belgium one of the great crossroads of Europe. In addition, the application of Roman planting patterns, designed to maximize the potential yield of an area of land, increased both the amount and the variety of foods that could be grown.

While allowing the *Belgae* to govern themselves, the Romans introduced a system of local control, whereby each tribe was given a city and an elected representative who, in conjunction with a central Roman civil service in Reims, regulated local authority building schemes and the maintenance of bridges and other thoroughfares.

Although the natives adopted many Roman customs, some culinary traditions survived. These include their method of preserving fruits, such as grapes, plums, apples and pears, by exposing them to the sun or drying them in ovens, the result of which was a fruity treat that was highly prized on winter banqueting tables.

THE MIDDLE AGES

Following the collapse of the Roman Empire in the 5th century AD, Germanic tribes, and in particular the Franks, came to power and Belgium became part of the Merovingian dynasty under Clovis I. This Frankish King introduced Christianity to the region and started a wave of conversion, which continued to spread when Charlemagne took over in the 9th century and the country became the centre of the Carolingian dynasty.

During this period, Benedictine and Cistercian monasteries became centres of economic and cultural life, and the monks developed model farming methods from which peasants could learn about agriculture. Monks were also great bread bakers, and led the way in developing cereal cultivation. Bread became something of a status

Above: This 19th-century painting depicts a romantic view of Saint Clotilde watching over the baptism of her husband King Clovis I.

symbol at this time, with sifted white flour being used to make loaves for the elite, and rye being made into the daily bread for the peasantry.

The monks also developed the tradition of brewing beer, which was used medicinally and in cooking. Milk from the monastery farms was used to produce cheeses, which matured in the cellars of their abbeys. Today, beer- and cheese-making are still popular traditions in the monasteries across the country.

More advanced methods of fish farming were also developed during this period, in order to supply sufficient fish for eating on Christian fasting days when meat was prohibited for religious reasons.

SPICES FROM THE EAST

The Crusades (AD1095–1272) led to a revolution in medieval cooking, and the distinctive cuisine of modern Belgium first started to emerge. The leader of the First Crusade, Godfrey of Bouillon, Duke of Lower Lorraine, and his men brought back spices – nutmeg, cloves, ginger, saffron, cinnamon and peppercorns – from the Holy Land. These were incorporated into local Belgian dishes, including *peperkoek*, a delicious spice cake and *speculaas*, an iconic spice cookie.

Above: Belgians are proud of their cuisine and most people enjoy visiting a traditional eatery serving much-loved classic dishes.

Belgium went on to become the centre of the northern European spice trade, with spices increasingly used by royalty and the nobility in cooking and as gifts, or for trading. Condiments such as mustards and vinegars were combined with dried fruits in recipes, giving a sweet-sour flavour to many dishes that are part of Belgian cuisine to this day.

The 12th and 13th centuries were a period of intensive commercial development throughout the southern Low Countries, and cities flourished. Merchants became very prosperous, and powerful guilds erected majestic belfries, guildhalls and churches, which can still be seen in many cities.

A GOLDEN AGE

When the Low Countries became part of Burgundy (*c.*1369), wine from the region was introduced to the Belgian upper classes, who held sumptuous banquets as a major part of the celebrations for ducal weddings and meetings of the chivalric Order of the Golden Fleece, and this affinity with Bordeaux and Burgundy wines remains strong today.

Great prosperity in industry permeated to all levels of society, with plentiful food for all, and the arrival of ingredients such as tomatoes, sugar cane, rice, potatoes, coffee and cacao from the newly discovered Americas resulted in a more sophisticated cuisine. The love of the culinary arts is much in evidence in the paintings from the 14th–17th centuries, during which time Belgium became a centre for intellectual, cultural and artistic activity in cities such as Ghent, Antwerp and Brugge. Among the many great artists of the time are van Eyk (d.1441), Pieter Bruegel the Elder (*c.*1525–69), his son Jan Brueghel the Elder (1568–1625), Rubens (1577–1640) and van Dyck (1599–1641).

FOREIGN DOMINATION OF BELGIUM

After the Burgundian rule there was a period of foreign domination by Spain that lasted until Napoleon Bonaparte came to power and Belgium became part of the French empire at the start of the 19th century. During this time, Belgian cooks adopted and adapted cooking styles from the French, integrating them as part of their culinary repertoire.

Following the defeat of Napoleon at Waterloo in 1815, Belgium was ceded to the newly formed kingdom of the Netherlands. Catholic, French-speaking Belgians fiercely resisted the imposition of the Dutch and Flemish languages and Protestant religion and, in 1830, Belgium declared its independence from the Netherlands, adopted a constitution, and chose its first king: Leopold I.

TOWARDS MODERN BELGIUM

The neutrality that had been granted to Belgium following its independence in 1830 lasted until the country was occupied by the Germans during the two World Wars. During this time the local population suffered much hardship, with food becoming scarce and people existing on a meagre diet of potatoes, herrings and porridge.

To meet the demand for coal workers in an increasingly industrialized nation after World War II, many immigrants came to Belgium from Italy, Turkey and North Africa. These people brought their cuisines with them – and today Italian cuisine is the second favourite type of food in Belgium.

Present-day Belgium has an open outlook, although classic Belgian food is still extremely popular, and the nation's devotion to its culinary traditions remains strong. In this spirit of taking pride in their cuisine and enjoying food, Belgians bring a certain *joie de vivre* to the family table, where the importance of friends, family and a good meal prevails.

Below: This detail of a section of the painting The Battle between Carnival and Lent *by Pieter Bruegel the Elder shows a woman carrying a table bearing waffles, revealing the existence of* wafla *or* wafel *in Belgium as long ago as 1559.*

BELGIAN REGIONAL DISHES AND SPECIALITIES

The common characteristics that unite the ten provinces in Belgium are the national love of breads in all their forms and an abundance of sweet and savoury baked pastries, and chocolates and sweets (candies). Aside from these ubiquitous foods, the origins of many of Belgium's dishes can be traced to individual villages or provinces, such as the Matten tartlets, which are made only in and around the area of Geraardsbergen. Because of the different historic influences and the various dialects spoken in these locations, regional foods often have whimsical nicknames or contain an unusual ingredient.

FISH AND SHELLFISH

Although most of the salt water fishing takes place out in the North Sea, an ancient method of shoreline fishing is used in Oostduinkerke. Here, fishermen drag their nets close to the shore at low tide behind their legendary Brabant draft horses, scooping up grey shrimp. These are then sold to the coastal restaurants in Flanders to be cooked in the classic dish of tomatoes filled with shrimps, *tomate crevette*.

Freshwater fish appear in various local dishes, such as eel in green chervil sauce – a speciality of both East and West Flanders, and *truite à l'Ardennaise* (Ardennes-style trout). In Brussels, the ancient tradition of eating *caracollen*, tiny sea snails in court bouillon, continues, and the snails are sold as street food at fairs and markets.

POULTRY, MEAT AND GAME

Chicken is a favourite ingredient all over the country, although Brussels still bears its nickname *kiekefretters* ('chicken eater') due to its inhabitants' love of a range of dishes made with the meat. There is a range of breeds available to buy, but the Coucou de Maline, a speciality breed from Mechelen, is considered the best.

East Flanders and the Ardennes are renowned for their smoked hams, *jambon d'Ardennes* and *vlaamse been hesp* or *ganda* ham. Flanders' pastures provide pigs that produce a ham that is more tender and milder in flavour than

the ham from the Ardennes, which has a smoky taste and a dry texture. These differences are due to the feed the pigs are given, as well as the method of hanging the hams over smoking juniper wood that is used in the Ardennes.

Certain areas in Belgium are notable for horsemeat, a tradition that harks back to the eating habits of the Celts. The city of Vilvoorde (Brabant) is most famous for its horse markets, where 'horse steak' is cooked in horse fat and served with *frites* and mayonnaise. *Schep*, a horse stew from the area of Willebroek (Antwerp), is served at special festivities.

VEGETABLES

Belgian endives and white asparagus are especially popular in Kampenhout (Brabant), where specialist restaurants offer menus featuring these star ingredients. Dishes range from soups and appetizers to main dishes, with *endive au gratin* (endive gratin) and *asperges à la Flamande* (asparagus served with butter and chopped hard-boiled eggs) being among the top choices.

Deriving their name from the region in which they were first cultivated, Brussels sprouts are now enjoyed all over Belgium. Another speciality from the Brussels region, *stoemp* (mashed potato mixed with other vegetables) is often served with blood sausage and a local beer, and makes a frequent appearance on cold winter days.

Above: Smoky, flavoursome Ardennes ham is a much-loved regional speciality in south Belgium.

Hop shoots (sometimes called 'hop asparagus') may be served as part of either hot or cold dishes, and are one of the priciest vegetables on earth. Cultivated only in the areas of Poperinge and Asse, they make a star appearance for just four weeks between March and April.

Below: The fishermen of Oostduinkerke are famous for dragging nets for grey shrimp along the shoreline on horseback.

FRUITS

The Haspengouw region is a fruit-growing area *par excellence* that produces many fresh fruits and fruit products, including apple ciders and *sirop de Liège* – a sweet, thick syrup made from cooked-down pears, apples and dates, which can be spread on pancakes or breads or added to sauces to accompany game or meat. Today, sadly, only a few enterprises making such regional syrups are left, so it can be hard to find.

DAIRY

Every city has a speciality cheese store (*fromagerie/kaaswinkel*), offering hundreds of different regional varieties, ranging from fresh white cheeses to mild or strong, matured types. In addition to Brussels *hettekees* and the ancient-style Herve cheeses, others are often named after specific regions or castles, such as Wynendale, or abbeys such as Chimay, Maredsous, Westmalle, Orval, Corsendonk and Postel.

BREAD AND PASTRIES

In addition to the two types of *pistolets* (crunchy round bread rolls and soft, slightly sweet, oval-shaped rolls called

Below: The popular sirop de Liège *is one of the few regional fruit syrups still made in Belgium.*

sandwich) that are found throughout the country, each region in Belgium has its own speciality bread. These include *cracquelin* from Liège (a soft white bread made with pearl sugar, eggs and butter) and *mastellen* (cinnamon rolls) from Ghent.

A key feature of Belgian's gastronomy is its pastries and its reverence for the fine-quality pastry shops (patisseries) that are present all over the country. Local delicacies such as *speculaas* (spice cookies) are sold nationwide, although there are some regional twists on the classic recipe. These include the famous *speculaas* from Hasselt, the recipe for which is linked to local genever production as it uses the burnt sugar left over from the process of making the drink.

As well as the spices used in *speculaas*, almonds are a key ingredient in many pastries, including a delectable almond tart from Diksmuide. Savoury pastries, such as the ancient *tarte al djote* from Nivelles (made with pungent fermented cheese and chard or beet leaves) are also much enjoyed.

MUSTARD

Ghent is home to one of the oldest mustard manufacturers, Tierenteyn, which has been in operation since 1790. In addition to this company, a small number of artisan mustard manufacturers still remain throughout the country.

SWEETS

Brussels is the birthplace of the praline, a luxury chocolate-filled sweet that was introduced by Jean Neuhaus Jr in 1912. A true Belgian speciality, it is found in more than 2,000 chocolate stores all over the country. Stylishly packaged ballotins include round or square pralines filled with liqueur and a variety of chocolate flavours. There are also numerous regional sweets (candies) and biscuits (cookies) with amusing names, such as *babbelaars* or *babelutten* ('someone who talks a lot'), a caramel-like sweet made in Ieper and Veurne (West Flanders).

Above: Speciality cheese stores stock a wide range of regional cheeses, such as this one from Bruges.

DRINKS

Belgium is world famous for its beers. Among the countless regional varieties there are a few that stand out, including Gueuze and Lambic. Brewed only to the west of Brussels, the most significant characteristic of Lambic is that it is allowed to ferment spontaneously by being exposed to the unique microflora from the Senne Valley, called *Brettanomyces bruxellensis*. It is then fermented for a second time in oak barrels, which lends it a sweet-sour taste, infused with sour cherries.

Other beers include the legendary rich, dark Trappist varieties, including Chimay, Orval, Rochefort, Westmalle, Westvleteren and Achel, and abbey beers, such as Leffe, Duvel, Corsendonk, Kwak, Karmeliet and Affligem. These beers were originally produced by monks as part of their ancestral tradition of brewing. Each should be drunk from a specific glass, the shape of which is said to enhance the beer's characteristics.

Several medieval brewed liqueurs are still produced. These include Elixir d'Anvers (Antwerp), a herbal liqueur for nightcaps and medicine, and Elixir de Spa, a drink composed of more than 40 plants and herbs.

BELGIAN EATING HABITS

From a culinary standpoint, Belgium has always been unfairly placed in the shadow of its French neighbour and it is a little known fact that Belgium has more Michelin-starred restaurants per capita than France. Belgians enjoy their culinary heritage, and if a person has a reputation for enjoying good food, drink and life in general they will refer to themselves as 'Burgundiers' or with a 'Burgundian lifestyle'. This reference alludes to the Burgundian era when art and food were especially celebrated in Belgium, and is a philosophy of fine dining that is very much alive among every generation, including the young.

FAMILY LIFE

The family plays a vital role in Belgian society. Since most people continue to live in their hometown upon reaching adulthood, weekends are usually dedicated to visiting family members for lunches or dinners to catch up on the past week's events.

Below: Assorted breads, including soft white loaves and rustic granary versions, are sold in bakeries and eaten with every meal.

BREAKFAST

For most Belgians, breakfast usually starts with a *boterham* or *tartine*: two slices of white or wholegrain bread spread with *chocopasta* (chocolate paste), or filled with a slice of *speculaas* (spice cookie) or *peperkoek* (spice cake). Also on offer are an assortment of cold cuts (charcuterie), cheeses and jams, accompanied by coffee, tea or milk. During the weekends and holidays the breakfast table extends itself to a variety of breads, *pistolets* (bread rolls), sugar, raisin and chocolate breads and *koffiekoeken* (breakfast pastries). Belgians enjoy taking time for their meals, and a Sunday breakfast can last at least an hour.

LUNCH

The midday meal will begin between 12 p.m. and 1 p.m. and traditionally consists of soup, followed by potato, vegetable and meat dishes and a dessert or some fruit. However, because of modern working patterns, weekday lunches are more often a sandwich taken to work or school and perhaps combined with soup or a salad. Bottled sparkling or spring water and a range of other drinks are usually served with lunch.

Above: Soup, such as this one made with watercress, is often served for lunch and/or supper, followed by a potato dish accompanied by meat or vegetables.

SNACKS AND STREET FOOD

Afternoon snacks play an important role in a Belgian's daily life, as they love to socialize around a small bite to eat. In the afternoon many people take a coffee break and enjoy a pastry, pie, waffle or pancake with friends and colleagues in a coffee salon or patisserie. On sunny days, terraces of brasseries fill up with people buying a refreshing Dame Blanche ice cream (ice cream with a chocolate sauce), or indulging in a *toast cannibale* (toast with a raw meat topping) or croque monsieur (a grilled ham and cheese sandwich). These are usually accompanied by a cold drink. Waffles, ice creams and *frites* are also sold everywhere on the streets for those in a hurry, and a *frietkot* (*frites* booth) or warm waffle stand will never be too far away.

SUPPER

Between 6 p.m. and 7 p.m., depending on the quantity eaten for lunch, a warm three-course menu will be prepared, traditionally starting with soup and followed by a meat, potato and vegetable platter, and dessert – mostly enjoyed with wine or beer. If a hot lunch was eaten, however, a simple meal with

Above: Frites *are a favourite food and can be eaten as an accompaniment to other dishes, or on their own as a snack, served in a paper cone or tray, often with a dollop of mayonnaise.*

bread, cheese and cold meats will suffice. Consequently, bread is eaten at least twice a day, a habit that suits the bread-loving Belgians.

SOCIALIZING AND EATING OUT

Going out for dinner to a restaurant is a social event, and a table will usually be booked for the entire night. Dining is still the preferred way of meeting friends and family, allowing hours of quality time over good food and drink. Diners usually start with an aperitif, which can vary from cocktails to beers and wine, accompanied with appetizers or *amuse bouches* (tiny morsels to eat), which allow the diners time to decide upon a selection of first courses, side dishes and desserts. Although beer is widely consumed, good-quality French wines are still the drink of choice for elegant entertaining.

The entire menu selection is most often dictated by the seasons. During the winter months, hearty dishes such as stews, game and winter vegetables (such as *endive au gratin*) will be offered, whereas a spring and summer menu will feature the assorted delights of vegetables and fruits or seasonal fish, including the many mussel dishes.

Above: Ice creams, such as the traditional Dame Blanche, provide a refreshing snack at any time of the day, and are often sold in the bustling brasseries and cafés.

For those who prefer not to spend their entire night dining in a restaurant, 'going for a drink' to a local café or tavern at around 9 p.m. is a popular weekend activity. Here people meet friends and enjoy a few drinks and a small bite to eat. Later, many stop at

one of the innumerable snack bars for a cone of *frites* or another hot treat to satisfy late-night hunger pangs.

Socializing at home with intimate dinners for friends and family is also very common. Cheese and wine evenings, where a tray of various breads and cheeses is offered with complementary wines or beers, are popular entertaining events. Bringing a ballotin of pralines as a gift for the host is the most common gesture when invited to someone's home.

TABLE ETIQUETTE

Belgians take great pride in their appearance, their cuisine and the impression they give to others, and this is reflected in their eating styles and decorous table manners. Good table etiquette is expected both at home and when dining out, and using the right cutlery with each course and the correct glass with the appropriate drink is of utmost importance for an enjoyable meal.

Below: Friends and families enjoy socializing over a meal consisting of their favourite foods, such as mussels or steak served with frites *and beer.*

BELGIAN FESTIVALS AND CELEBRATIONS

Although there are now many other religions, Christianity remains the predominant faith in Belgium, and the holy days for this faith tend to be celebrated on a national scale. Many regional festivities celebrating ancient pagan events also still take place in every part of Belgium, reflecting the strong national identity and determination to protect and preserve their history. For hundreds of years these festivals have involved lavish food events with many speciality foods on offer, such as *smoutebollen*, *pepernoten*, *moppen*, *nic-nacs*, *speculaas* and other delectable items.

VILLAGE FAIRS

Kermis is an annual village festival tradition that dates back to the 16th century, when it originated as a religious event to commemorate the patron saint of the city or village. The celebrations included a procession and a *kermis* (fair) that lasted eight days. Although the processions have mostly disappeared, the *kermis* is very much alive. This excitedly awaited event features food stalls selling typical fair produce: *frites*, sausages, shrimp

Below: Wooden speculaas *moulds are often used to make the traditional spice cookies that are served at* Sinterklaas *and were once used as a way of proposing.*

croquettes, *smoutebollen* (fritters dusted with powdered sugar), apple beignets, light and airy waffles from Brussels, or sugary and dense ones from Liège – and much more.

PILGRIMAGES, PROCESSIONS AND CARNIVALS

Christian devotion and pageantry is very much alive all over Belgium and there are numerous events during the year. These include a candlelit procession for Our Lady of Scherpenheuvel, which dates back to the Spanish occupation of the 16th century. This takes place in the small town of Scherpenheuvel on the Sunday after All Saints' Day. However, because thousands of pilgrims visit the town throughout the year, there is always a celebratory atmosphere, with stalls selling souvenirs and typical sweets such as *pepernoten* (a cookie-like confections).

The Procession of the Holy Blood is another important event, and it has taken place in Bruges each May since 1303. During the religious pageant, the relic of the Holy Blood is carried at the head of a mile-long procession of more than 1,500 Bruges citizens, who dress up in medieval garb.

One of the most famous festivals is the Binche festival, which has been classified by UNESCO as part of the world's cultural heritage. Dating from

Above: Waffles, such as these ones from Liège, are among the many treats on sale at food stalls at a kermis.

1549, the three-day carnival take place in February. During the festivities, men called *gilles* dress in bright costumes and some wear high, plumed hats. Having eaten a breakfast of oysters and champagne at 4 a.m., they then take part in parades, letting off fireworks and throwing small blood oranges into the crowd on the Grand Place, while spectators feast on local double-buckwheat pancakes filled with melted Herve cheese, called *les doubles de Binche*.

SAINT NICHOLAS

The legendary bishop *Sinterklaas*, or Saint Nicholas (AD270–343), is the patron saint of Belgian children and makes his entrance every year on 6 December. He brings presents and sweets (candies), including moulded hollow chocolate and figures made from sculpted marzipan, *nic-nacs* (tiny biscuits dusted with icing (confectioners') sugar), *guimauve* (soft candy shaped in the form of St Nicholas or Mother Mary), gold-wrapped chocolate coins, and mandarins.

In addition, spice cookies, *speculoos*, or *speculaas*, are eaten for this celebration. The name derives from the

Above: Children cut off the head of the lamb-shaped cake made from ice cream that is served at their first communion.

Latin *specula*, meaning mirror, because the cookies were originally pressed into wooden moulds of various designs showing pictures of people or animals. In medieval times doll-shaped *speculaas* were given by men to girls as a way of proposing.

CHRISTMAS, NEW YEAR AND THREE KINGS' DAY

Families share special meals at home during Christmas. They will start with aperitifs followed by an appetizer, which may be fish or shellfish, and then the main course, which is often game, goose, duck, turkey or roast lamb accompanied by a variety of vegetables and a potato dish (such as potato croquettes). For dessert many choose a *bûche de Noël* (Christmas log). For New Year the ritual is similar, although it is often celebrated with non-family members in restaurants and combined with dancing parties.

For Three Kings' Day (Epiphany) on 6 January, children dress up in costumes and go from door to door singing and receiving money and sweets (candies). This custom dates back to the 19th century, when the peasants were given waffles and cookies by the rich, and bread by the monks at the local monastery. In recognition of this, rich foods such as pancakes, waffles, crown-shaped king cakes, apple dumplings and sausage breads are enjoyed.

EASTER

On Easter morning children participate excitedly in Easter egg hunts. The story goes that the church bells leave for Rome on the Saturday, returning on the Sunday with chocolate eggs, which they drop into the children's gardens. The Easter bunny then helps to hide them for the children to find.

According to traditional religious beliefs no animal products can be consumed up to 40 days before Easter, so Easter itself is a time for the celebration of food. Breakfast will start with soft sugar breads, often enclosing boiled eggs, and lunch and dinner usually consist of poultry or lamb and egg dishes, such as *vogel nestjes* (bird's nests). The consumption of eggs symbolizes the victory of light over the long dark winter and the beginning of the fertile period of spring.

BIRTHS, CHRISTENINGS AND WEDDINGS

Other events during the year are also celebrated with food. Friends and families visiting a newborn baby are welcomed with *suikerbonen* – small decorated packages of pastel-coloured, sugar-coated pastilles filled with almond paste or chocolate. Weddings and christenings are celebrated by throwing elaborate parties with multiple and varied buffet menus.

For a child's first communion an *ijslam* is made. This is a cake in the shape of a lamb formed out of ice cream. The child traditionally cuts off the lamb's head so that a grenadine syrup or raspberry coulis that is inside drips on to the ice cream.

After a funeral service mourners are invited to attend a *koffie tafel*, where an assortment of breads, cheeses and cold meats will be offered as a last farewell to the departed.

Below: On Easter morning Belgian children hunt for chocolate eggs, said to have been brought from Rome by the church bells and hidden by the Easter bunny.

THE DUTCH AND BELGIAN KITCHEN

There is a phenomenal range of ingredients available to Dutch and Belgian cooks, and seasonality, freshness and quality are of paramount importance when they are shopping for food. Most people have well-educated palates and can distinguish between the many regional varieties of products such as cheese, beer or mustard on offer, and know how to combine and cook ingredients in order to maximize their potential. The result is wonderfully diverse and flavoursome food, which is enjoyed with gusto.

FISH AND SHELLFISH

Belgium has only three main fishing ports on its short coastline – Zeebrugge, Oostende and Nieuwpoort – and most of the fish eaten in Belgium is imported from other European countries. The Dutch coastline is relatively long at 451km (280 miles), and includes the Friesian Islands that meander out along the country's northern edge. Numerous fishing communities of all sizes inhabit these regions. The fishing industry here is tightly regulated and extremely efficient, with trawler captains, auctioneers, processors and scientists working together to produce the best quality fish for export as well as home use.

It is always best to check the sustainability of fish before buying and consider using a substitute if you are unsure. Line-caught fish are more expensive but the method used to catch them is much more eco-friendly.

SEA FISH

In both Belgium and the Netherlands, sea fish play a major role in the traditional national cuisines. Herrings, cod and flat fish such as sole and plaice are especially popular.

Below: Belgian and Dutch fishermen catch a range of fish in the cold waters of the North Sea.

Above: Raw herrings marinated in brine are an age-old speciality of the Netherlands.

Herrings are small coldwater fish, eaten both cooked and raw, soaked in salty brine. Raw herrings are marinated for a few days, traditionally in an oak cask but nowadays more often in special cooling vats, then filleted and served as a simple treat with raw onion slices. The Dutch love to eat whole fillets of new-season herring bought from street booths, holding each one by the tail in traditional fashion.

Cod is the ubiquitous white fish beloved by most northern Europeans, although stocks are now under threat and other alternatives such as pollack should be considered instead. Belgians cook their cod in beer or wine, while the Dutch have a fondness for stockfish (salted cod) served on a base of red cabbage and apples with mashed potatoes. Monkfish are usually pricey, but are becoming more popular, and have a meaty texture and fragrant flavour.

The most common kinds of flat fish are sole and plaice, both of which are found in the North Sea and can be used in all kinds of baked dishes, or plainly poached or grilled (broiled) with a simple salad and some fries.

Below: Freshwater eels are transformed into delectable dishes throughout Belgium.

Above: Monkfish, despite their ugly appearance, have plenty of delicious meat in their tails.

Many other kinds of fish are found around the coast, such as red gurnard, turbot, whiting and haddock, all of which have their place in Dutch and Belgian cuisines.

FRESHWATER FISH

In past centuries, inland areas did not have very good transport links, so sea fish was not available farther than a few kilometres (miles) from the coast. Fortunately, plenty of freshwater fish such as salmon, trout and eels are found in the rivers and lakes of these low-lying regions, supplying the majority of the population with a reliable source of fish.

Wartime privations, particularly in World War II, meant that local people had to make the most of everything they could find, including freshwater eels. These unprepossessing creatures make a good stew, and Belgians love eels dressed with their favourite herb, chervil, in a fresh green sauce.

River trout and salmon feature in many dishes from Belgium and the Netherlands, in both fresh and smoked forms. The Dutch are particularly fond of smoked salmon and smoked trout as appetizers, served with a piquant horseradish dressing and salad leaves.

As in other northern European countries, the tradition of abstaining from meat during Lent used to be very strong in Belgium and the Netherlands. At this time of year, during the months of February and March, a dish of freshwater pike or carp made a warming centrepiece for a Sunday dinner or the Good Friday celebration.

SHELLFISH

The shallow coastal waters along the sandy beaches of Belgium and the Netherlands are teeming with shrimp, oysters, scallops and mussels. Every Belgian or Dutch cook has a favourite recipe for these delicious morsels that brings out their salty, fresh flavour.

One of the most typical dishes in Belgium and the Netherlands is fresh mussels cooked in stock or wine and butter, and this is nearly always accompanied by fries with mayonnaise and a cold beer. Devotees will pay large sums of money for the best-quality specimens, many of which are farmed around the Dutch coast. As with all types of shellfish, they require careful preparation, the trick being to eat only fresh molluscs, tapping them on a hard surface and discarding any that fail to shut. If any of the remaining ones stay shut once cooked discard those too. Then simply scoop out the flesh using an empty shell.

Below: Brown shrimp are fished in deeper waters than the grey type. Both are popular in Belgium and the Netherlands.

Above: Top-quality scallops are a luxurious delicacy, best served simply.

On the short Belgian coast of Oostduinkerke, the small boats that go out into the shallow water to catch shrimp are still complemented by part-time fishermen on their sturdy horses, pulling their nets behind them through the waves at the edge of the beach. The tasty little shrimps, each one only around 5–8cm (2–3in) long when it is caught, come in two varieties: grey from the shallow waters, and brown from the deeper sea. Both are ideal for use in appetizers and light dishes, accompanied by a few salad leaves, or for flavouring a fishy soup, as they are relatively inexpensive and taste wonderful.

Scallops and oysters also feature in many Dutch and Belgian recipes, both as appetizers and as main courses. They can be simply dressed with butter and herbs and served grilled (broiled), or baked in a gratin dish with a creamy sauce to bring out the salty flavour.

Below: Mussels are the primary ingredient in the iconic Belgian dish Moules à la Marinières.

Buying and cleaning mussels
Bivalves such as mussels, clams and oysters should contain plenty of sea water and feel heavy for their size. Do not buy any that have broken shells. If the shells gape, give them a sharp tap on a hard surface; they should snap shut immediately.

1 Wash the mussels in plenty of cold water, scrubbing them. Scrape off any barnacles with a knife.

2 Give any open mussels a sharp tap; discard any that fail to close.

3 Pull out and discard the fibrous 'beard' that sprouts between the two halves of the shell.

POULTRY, GAME AND MEAT

Belgian and Dutch people love meat in all its forms. While there are vegetarians in both countries these days, the tradition of eating a substantial amount of meat persists. For instance, many soup recipes contain at least some meat such as bacon pieces, or are based on meat stock. The Dutch, in particular, have a reputation for eating simple, solid food throughout the day, and particularly in the evenings, when dinner at home is still likely to focus on meat and potatoes in many families.

PORK

There are almost as many pigs as there are people in Belgium and the Netherlands. The pork industry is a major part of the economy and has been so for centuries, since the days when small mixed farms covered most of the available land, each with a few pigs, cattle and poultry. Nowadays, pork production is on a vast scale, but more interest is currently being shown in free-range and organic pork where the animals have room to move about freely and live in small groups in the open air, rather than in huge factory sheds.

Many traditional recipes for pork dishes arise from the old days, when almost every household would have kept at least one pig in the back yard, and every part of this precious animal would have been eaten, including the trotters. Anything that could not be made into a main-course dish such as a roast or stew would end up in the

Below: Every part of the pig is enjoyed in Belgium and the Netherlands, including leg of pork, which is often roasted.

Above: Outdoor markets, such as this one in Han sur Less, Belgium, provide a great range of meat and charcuterie.

delicious sausages made in both Belgium and the Netherlands; even the pig's blood was saved for blood sausage, a great favourite with fried onions and a good helping of mashed potatoes. Numerous pork dishes can be found on the menu today, including pork chops, sausages, terrines, hams and the traditional pressed brawn mixture known as *kip-kap*.

BEEF

More than four million cattle graze contentedly on the lush green grass in the low-lying fields of Belgium and the Netherlands. The black and white cows that can be seen everywhere in Europe were originally Friesians, from the northern Netherlands, and were interbred with Holsteins from the United States to produce a cow that gives a great milk yield and good-quality beef. Beef is eaten in many ways, from the best steak that only needs a bowl of fries as accompaniment, to the

Minced (ground) meat

The Belgians and Dutch have a particular thrifty fondness for lesser cuts of meat made into tasty patties, meatballs, croquettes and other shapes. The meat used can be pork, veal or beef – singly or mixed together in varying quantities – with plenty of salt and pepper, some breadcrumbs to thicken the mixture, and a few herbs. Traditional mouth-watering snacks of croquettes or *frikandel* (skinless sausage), deep-fried and often eaten with fries and mayonnaise, crop up at every outdoor booth in the big cities and at major outdoor events such as summer fairs and harvest festivals. Little savoury *bitterballen*, shaped like a smaller croquette, are served as snacks with a beer or at parties. At home, many families still eat such traditional dishes as *blinde vinken* (blind finches) – parcels of thinly cut beef steak stuffed with minced meat and herbs, and served with vegetables as a main course.

lesser cuts that are made into stews, soups, meatballs and croquettes. The Belgians add beer to their stew to make a strong dark sauce in *carbonnades a la Flamande* – a recipe that dates back to medieval times – and this delicious stock demands potatoes or bread to mop it up. The Dutch like their beef steaks well done, served with vegetables and potatoes in a plain but satisfying plateful. Another real favourite in the Netherlands is *rookvlees*, smoked beef that is served cold and sliced very thinly on white bread and butter.

CHICKEN, DUCK AND GOOSE

The poultry industry in the Netherlands and Belgium is another huge affair, which, like pork farming, is now branching out into free-range and organic. Belgium exports a large amount of its poultry. At home, chicken meat is often made into delicious pies and casseroles, such as the creamy *waterzooi*, or simply flash-fried and served with salad. The rich flavour of duck also seems to suit the braised dishes with vegetables that are so popular in Belgium and the Netherlands. Goose is traditionally served for the main Christmas meal, but turkey is also becoming popular for special occasions.

GAME

Game animals and birds have been eaten in Belgium and the Netherlands since the early Middle Ages. The kinds of game available vary from forest

Below: Duck is used to make rich and warming slow-cooked dishes in Belgium and the Netherlands.

*Above: Ghent-style Chicken Stew (*waterzooi*) is just one of the many popular chicken dishes on offer.*

animals, such as wild boar and venison, to those from the open fields, such as rabbit and hare (jack rabbit). A wide variety of animals and birds are hunted during the season in the forest region of the Ardennes, including pheasant, partridge, capon, deer and wild boar, and classic as well as newly created game dishes are plentiful on the autumn menus there. Rabbit and hare dishes are often prepared with the addition of speciality beers and combinations of berries and spices, which complement the succulent meat perfectly. Game meat is not just found in hot stews; some is made into delicious cold mixtures such as wild boar pâté.

Below right: Oxtail is a cheaper cut of meat that is full of flavour and makes a sustaining and delicious stew.

Above: Venison is one of the many game animals that have been hunted and eaten since the Middle Ages.

OTHER MEAT

Veal is one of the top choices in Belgium and the Netherlands, savoured for its delicate flavour in dishes such as *blanquette de veau* (veal ragout in white cream sauce). Lamb is perhaps less popular than beef or pork, as sheep are found more often in upland areas; although some sheep thrive on the moorlands of both countries, grazing on the fragrant heather, and are found in celebratory dishes such as roasts. The lesser cuts such as oxtail and tongue are part of the thrifty lifestyle of most Belgians and Dutch, although these days not many cooks prepare them from scratch. Oxtail does make a very tasty and nutritious stew or soup, and prepared cooked tongue is part of the range of charcuterie to be found in every butcher's shop.

DAIRY PRODUCE AND EGGS

The Dutch and Belgian diet would be unthinkable without dairy products, which are commonly eaten throughout the day. Most people start the morning with a buttered slice of bread and cheese, drink milk with their lunch and end their dinner with yogurt, rice pudding or one of the many varieties of milk dessert that are nowadays available in supermarkets.

MILK, YOGURT AND QUARK

The millions of cows grazing in the Belgian and Dutch fields give a lot of milk, which is happily consumed in many different forms by the local people. Fresh milk is drunk cold for breakfast or with a sandwich for lunch, not just by children but by adults too. It makes the basis for hot desserts such as rice porridge, cooked gently on the stove with cinnamon and topped with fruit, or cold dishes such as ice cream or rice pudding, which in the Netherlands is usually served chilled. Both fresh and sour cream are added to many soups, or poured generously over apple pie for dessert.

The next stage of thickening is yogurt, which has been a favourite dessert in both countries for generations and has great nutritional qualities. A

sweeter dessert is the Dutch *vla*, a kind of custard mixture that is served on its own or with fruit and is available in many flavours from vanilla to chocolate. Lastly, the Dutch and Belgians are very fond of soft cheese such as quark, and the Dutch *kwarktaart* (cheesecake) is found in every bakery. This is usually served as a dessert or as a mid-morning treat with coffee.

CHEESE

Most Dutch and Belgians are experts in the various types of cheese produced in their countries. These are not only distinguished by their place of origin but also by the various stages of ripening. Many people still buy their cheese direct from a farmhouse, where it is produced according to age-old recipes; otherwise the cheese will be carefully chosen from a supermarket cheese counter or one of the many specialist cheese shops in every town.

Dutch shoppers know exactly what kind of cheese they require for each meal and to suit the tastes of each family member. Cheese is usually cut

Below: A glass of cold milk is commonly drunk by everyone at breakfast and lunch, as well as being used in desserts.

Below: Cheesemongers still carry Gouda around on hurdles at the Alkmaar cheese market in the Netherlands.

Above: Gouda and Edam are two of the most famous Dutch cheeses.

with a special cheese slice, a spatula with a sharp-edged slot, leaving the inedible rind behind.

Gouda is by no means the only cheese from the Netherlands, but it is one of the best known and has been made there since at least the Middle Ages. Ancient traditions persist to this day, and the famous cheese market at Alkmaar, where cheesemongers in traditional costume carrying hurdles piled high with the heavy, round, yellow cheeses, is still as popular as ever. Gouda is sold at four main stages of ripening: young, ripe, mature (sharp) and extra mature, when it has a very hard texture and a strong flavour that is similar to Parmesan.

Other well-known Dutch cheeses include Edam, with its distinctive red rind, and Friesian *nagelkaas* (clove cheese) studded with cumin seeds and cloves. Maasdam is a relatively recent addition to the country's cheese repertoire, but the best-known brand of Maasdam, Leerdammer, is now popular around the world. Known as the 'Dutch Emmenthal', Maasdam has a mild, nutty flavour and large holes throughout its flesh.

Belgians enjoy more than 300 types of artisan cheese, many of which are named after specific regions or castles, such as Wynendale, or abbeys, such as

Left: Maredsous cheese is named after a Belgian abbey.

Right: Maasdam is a relatively new cheese in the Netherlands.

Chimay, Maredsous, Westmalle, Orval, Corsendonk or Postel. Most of these are very strong, even acquired tastes for those not brought up on their pungent aroma and flavour, and never reach the export market since they are best eaten soon after purchasing with the local fresh bread and a glass of beer.

They are often made of sheep's milk, giving a distinctive sharp flavour to the cheese, which is either sold young and fresh or refined by ageing with a marinade of Belgian blond beer. Artisan blue cheese is made by carefully moulding the curds and allowing the mould to spread throughout the cheese to form a random pattern of blue cracks. Goat's cheese is rarer but is now being made by several specialist farmers and sold in small portions, dusted with a rind of herbs or even ashes to give a grey/black bloom.

Some of the best-known Belgian cheeses include Brussels cheese and the ancient-style Herve cheese, which

is made from unpasteurized cow's milk and traditionally aged in the caves sited around the town. Pungent and soft, it has a strong flavour and is best eaten with dark bread and beer. It is sometimes flavoured with herbs. Maresdous, Rubens and Limburger are also popular.

EGGS

With so many chickens in residence in the Netherlands and Belgium, it is not surprising that eggs feature in hundreds of local dishes, often combined with dairy products such as cheese or milk. The most famous egg sauce is, of course, mayonnaise, which is a vital part of the steak, fries, mayo and beer combination so beloved of the Belgians.

But eggs are also stars in their own right in such delicate recipes as poached eggs with hop shoots, or in a more robust form, topping a bread, ham and cheese *uitsmijter*. They make part of a nutritious breakfast menu, served with bread and cheese for an excellent start to the day. Hard-boiled eggs are chopped finely as a garnish for savoury dishes such as freshly cooked asparagus, and of course combined with flour and milk in the form of fantastic Dutch pancakes.

Finally, the starring role of eggs in the traditional Belgian drink Advocaat should not be forgotten. This alcoholic mixture consists of brandy, sugar and egg yolks, and in its country of origin it is sometimes served with whipped cream on top and even sprinkled with chocolate and eaten with a spoon like a dessert.

Left: Extremely versatile, eggs are used to make a wide range of traditional dishes and drinks.

Mayonnaise

Potato chips or fries are always served with mayonnaise in Belgium. The famous concoction of eggs, mustard, vinegar and seasoning can be plain or flavoured, and is also the basis of a wide range of dips, sauces and salad dressings. It is quick and easy to make. The secret of success is having all ingredients at room temperature. Makes about 250ml/8fl oz/1 cup.

1 fresh egg yolk
5ml/1 tsp mustard powder or made mustard
15ml/1 tbsp lemon juice or white wine vinegar
salt and ground black pepper
120–200ml/4–7fl oz/½–scant 1 cup vegetable oil or sunflower oil

1 Mix the egg yolk, mustard, lemon juice or vinegar, salt and pepper in a bowl placed on a wet towel to prevent it from moving while whisking. Pour the oil into a jug (pitcher).

2 Whisk the mixture vigorously with one hand while adding the oil drop by drop with the other. When it begins to thicken, the oil can be added in a thin and steady stream. It may not be necessary to add all the oil. Stop when the mayonnaise is thick and creamy.

3 Check the seasoning, then serve.

VEGETABLES

The Dutch and Belgians are famous for their vegetable growing. Farmers benefit from a temperate climate with predictable rainfall throughout the year and few variations in temperature, which is ideally suited to growing hardy root vegetables such as onions and potatoes, and leafy green varieties such as cabbage and sprouts. This is a tradition that goes back to at least the 16th century, as we know that many other European countries imported vegetables from the Netherlands and Belgium at that time. Fresh lettuce was even sent by special fast ships across the North Sea from Dutch ports to London for Henry VIII and his first queen, Catherine of Aragon, to enjoy.

Growing new varieties and refining the taste and texture of vegetables is a skill that many farmers and horticulturists have developed over the years; one has only to remember Brussels sprouts and Belgian endive, both of which were unknown elsewhere until the Belgians made them famous.

POTATOES

The most important vegetable in the whole of Belgium and the Netherlands is undoubtedly the potato. It is almost inconceivable to envisage how Dutch and Belgians managed to cook a filling meal before this wonderful tuber arrived

Right: Dutch and Belgian cooks are careful to use the correct type of potato for a specific dish.

from South America in the 16th century. Since that time, main meals have focused on a good amount of meat, some side vegetables and a portion of potatoes in various forms – fried, plain boiled, and mashed on their own or with other vegetables.

The new potato season is especially welcome after the cold winter months, although they are eaten all year round. The quantity of produce required is so great that seed potatoes are sometimes exported to Malta to be grown in the warmer climate there before being re-imported when ripe, thus hastening and increasing the yield.

The Dutch and Belgians are very keen to buy the correct variety of potato for their chosen dish, and there is a wide choice of clearly labelled types on offer everywhere so cooks can pick the right type. Alpha, Santé and Opperdoezer Ronde are widely used in the Netherlands, while in Belgium three-quarters of the potatoes grown

are Bintjes, thought to be the best for making the nation's beloved fries. These tasty deep-fried snacks are sold everywhere, particularly in Belgium, where they can be bought from a street stall in a paper cone with a dollop of mayonnaise on top, and they are even served on a silver plate in Michelin-starred restaurants.

Potatoes are not just used to make mouthwatering side dishes, however; they are also an integral part of many main courses, lending bulk and nutritional qualities to pancakes as part of the base mixture, and to pies in the pastry crust. The tubers are also a major ingredient in many stews, where their flavour and texture adds softness and absorbs all the delicious flavours of the gravy. And if the cook is making a soup that is not quite thick enough, what could be better than whisking in some mashed potato to bring it to the correct thickness. Again, the correct potato for the job must be used and every supermarket or greengrocer will list the cooking qualities of each variety.

It is clear, then, that this humble vegetable is integral to the Dutch and Belgian diet. Indeed, to this day it is common for Dutch people to take a supply of potatoes with them when travelling through other European countries, where the main meal may be accompanied only by bread, and potatoes are not always on the menu.

Left: Potatoes are still harvested in the traditional way on some farms, such as this one in Brabant, the Netherlands.

ENDIVES

Belgian endives (also known as white chicory, or *witloof*) are a particular variety of vegetable that for many years was found only in Belgium. The crisp white leaves grow from the chicory root when it is kept in the dark. The story goes that a Belgian farmer, Jan Lammers, returned from war in 1830 to find his crop of endives, which he had grown to make a coffee substitute, sprouting white leaves where he had left them in the soil. He discovered that these leaves were delicious to eat and continued growing endives in this way. Endives are now grown all year round, but those farmers who follow the traditional method and leave them to mature in the ground in the winter claim their crops have the best flavour.

Left: Belgian endives are an iconic national vegetable, and are used in a number of celebrated recipes.

Every Belgian and Dutch person is brought up on this slightly bitter-tasting vegetable, acquiring the taste in early life. Endives can be eaten in many different ways: raw in salads, where their crunchy texture complements softer salad leaves and cucumber; simmered to make a creamy soup; simply boiled briefly and mashed with butter; or baked as a gratin with cream and cheese.

OTHER ROOT VEGETABLES

Most of the basic dishes of the Dutch and Belgian cuisines are packed with root vegetables. Onions and shallots lend their strong flavour to nearly every recipe for stew and soup, but are also eaten raw in salads, especially with ripe red tomatoes, or as the traditional accompaniment to new-season herring. Turnips have a blander flavour and dense texture that complements the richness of a game or poultry stew perfectly; celeriac is almost essence of celery in a solid, chunky form; and the sweeter taste of carrots is ideal for a side dish, served plain or with a creamy, buttery dressing.

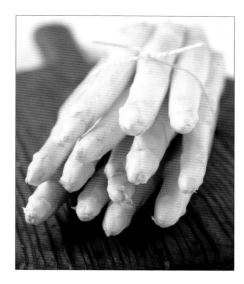

Above: Although the green type is widely enjoyed, it is white asparagus that evokes the most excitement in Belgium and the Netherlands.

In the Netherlands and Belgium, cooks tend to know as much about the cooking qualities of these other root vegetables as they do about their potatoes. The solid, thick carrots sold in winter even have a different name in Dutch (*winterpeen* – winter roots) from the thin, delicate varieties of spring and summer (*wortelen*). The chunky winter ones are an integral part of a warming split pea soup that is a real favourite in the Netherlands.

ASPARAGUS AND HOP SHOOTS

Another speciality of Belgium and the Netherlands, asparagus is a seasonal treat whose arrival in May is eagerly awaited. It is often served simply as an appetizer or side dish, sometimes garnished with hard-boiled eggs. White asparagus is forced in the darkness and has a blander taste than the green variety. Mechelen in northern Belgium and Limburg and Brabant in the Netherlands are especially renowned for growing it, and there is even an Asparagus Society, which organizes peeling competitions and asparagus feasts.

Above: Spring onions, red and white onions and shallots are staple flavouring ingredients in many dishes.

Left: Savoy, green and white cabbage are packed with goodness and flavour.

Hop shoots, picked as tender young sprigs in spring, are another delicacy that is only available for a short time each year, and they can be very expensive. They are usually served simply with melted butter and perhaps topped with a poached egg and a creamy sauce, which complements their delicate flavour superbly well.

CABBAGE, SPINACH AND KALE

Some of the most nutritious vegetables, which are part of the staple diet in Belgium and the Netherlands, are cabbage, spinach and kale. Dieticians

Below: Brussels sprouts have been grown around the city from which they derive their name for over 400 years.

encourage us all to eat more strongly coloured vegetables, and particularly those with dark green leaves, as they are full of iron and vitamins.

The Dutch and Belgians have no trouble eating their full ration of these vegetables as there are so many different ways to cook them. They are often found grated and raw in salads as a crunchy contrast to lettuce and cucumber with a vinegary dressing. Braised red cabbage is a great favourite and goes well as a side dish with sausages, as does the Dutch potato and cabbage mixture known as *stoemp* – mashed floury potatoes and lightly cooked green cabbage stirred together with a good lump of butter. Cabbage can easily be added to a rich game soup to add yet more vitamins and iron. And finally, the individual taste of sauerkraut (known as *zuurkool* in the Netherlands and Belgium) is as well known here as in most other northern European countries. The taste for sauerkraut, like the taste for endives, probably has to be acquired at a young age!

OTHER FRESH VEGETABLES

There is a whole range of vegetables that the Dutch and Belgians love to pile on their plates to accompany a standard dish of meat and potatoes. Brussels sprouts are a regional favourite. Actually tiny

cabbages growing on a long stalk, they have been grown in Belgium for at least 400 years, and probably much longer than that. They are ideally suited to the cool, damp climate of the area, but also need some winter frost to develop their full flavour. The same applies to kohlrabi, a form of cabbage that develops a turnip-like fleshy root and has a flavour similar to turnips.

Cauliflower is a Dutch staple, although it is also enjoyed in Belgium. It is served both cooked and raw in salads, where its crunchy texture can be fully appreciated, while leeks are mainly used like onions, as a basic flavouring for a soup or stew.

Samphire, with its bright green stalks, is a good example of the Dutch and Belgian habit of enjoying free food from the countryside, or in this case the seaside, as it grows wild in the sandy dunes all along the coast. It is best served only when it is really fresh, cooked briefly in boiling water or butter.

Broad (fava) beans, garden peas and green beans are a summer treat, but they are also sold out of season in brine, and the shelves of the greengrocer and supermarket are covered with chunky jars (rather than cans) of these ready-cooked beans and peas, as well as carrots, corn kernels and other vegetables.

Below: Broad beans, runner beans and green beans are served as an accompaniment to main dishes.

DRIED VEGETABLES AND LEGUMES

The thrifty Dutch and Belgians long ago discovered methods of preserving food for times of want, particularly during the chilly winter when the need for calories is greatest and the supply is shortest. Brown and white beans are classic dried ingredients to be found in all sorts of recipes, but they go particularly well with a hearty stew flavoured with bacon, sausage or game. This rib-sticking kind of casserole would certainly help to keep out the cold winds of winter after a hard day working in the turnip field or out hunting rabbits. These days, they can be bought both dried, in which case they must first be reconstituted by soaking and boiling, and ready-cooked in jars and tins.

Dried marrowfat peas are a real Dutch speciality. These are floury, sustaining, greenish-grey legumes that add bulk and flavour to a plate of minced (ground) meat with bacon. They are known as *kapucijners* in the Netherlands, a reference to the colour of Capuchin monks' habits. Split peas form the basis for pea soup, another Dutch classic dish that is prepared fresh or bought ready made by almost

Below: Dried peas, beans and lentils provide a valuable source of sustenance during the cold winter months.

Below: A wide range of lettuces are grown and enjoyed as salads and side dishes, providing colour and texture to dishes.

all Dutch families and eaten at least once a week. The stock really needs some pork meat or bacon for the best flavour – this used to be in the form of a pig's trotter boiled up with the stock – but a vegetarian version can be made quite successfully with well-flavoured vegetable stock.

SALAD VEGETABLES

All kinds of salads feature on menus in Belgium and the Netherlands, both as appetizers and as accompaniments to a main course. Many different varieties of lettuce, including those with pretty red leaves, usually form the basis of a salad. Cucumber is often eaten on its own as a separate vegetable, dressed with vinegar, salt and pepper. Salads can also feature any cold cooked vegetables, such as potatoes or green beans, with a topping of crunchy bacon bits and seasoned with wine vinegar. Small salad vegetables such as radishes are used for garnishes to a lunchtime plateful of bread, cheese and ham, where their spicy, peppery flavour beautifully complements the blander taste of young, fresh Gouda cheese.

The lack of predictable summer sunshine in these northern European countries means that some salad vegetables have to be grown under glass – tomatoes and sweet (bell) peppers, for example, would fail to ripen in the prevailing summer weather. A far better crop of leafy salads such as lettuce can also be grown under glass, preserving the quality of the leaves from summer rain storms, and the Dutch and Belgians make the most of their investment in glasshouses by exporting much of their salad crop to other European countries through a very organized system of auction cooperatives, benefiting both the growers and the buyers.

Below: Tomatoes are often grown under glass in order to produce the best crop.

FRUIT

In both Belgium and the Netherlands fruit is a major part of the daily diet. Greengrocers and supermarkets have counters piled high with all sorts of delicious seasonal specimens, many of which are grown locally. The glasshouses and polytunnels that dot the fields and farms provide much-needed shelter for this precious crop, especially for soft summer fruit such as strawberries, which are easily ruined by heavy rain in August and the unpredictable summer temperatures. However, between the glasshouses there are still plenty of traditional orchards where superb old varieties of apple, cherry and other tree fruits are grown in the open air.

ORCHARD FRUIT

The main fruit-growing region of Belgium, Hageland and Haspengouw, lies in the central part of the country near Brussels, away from the coast, where the land begins to rise gently and the climate is reasonably benign. Both here and in the more exposed flat lands of the Netherlands, apples are grown in large commercial orchards. These are well maintained, with irrigation channels from nearby rivers and streams. These days modern farmers are experimenting with more elaborate methods of cultivation to protect the crop from the

variable weather, especially in the early spring when the blossom is just forming. These techniques, including draping the trees with hail nets, give the orchard its own micro-climate – a cross between growing in the open air and growing under glass.

Every Dutch and Belgian cook is brought up to be well aware of which apples suit which dish – rather as potato varieties are used carefully and discriminately, rather than adopting a 'one size fits all' approach. Some apples will keep their shape when cooked,

Left: Elstar apples are a sweet eating variety enjoyed by the Dutch.

Below: The delicate flesh of pears is best eaten raw or gently poached in wine or a sugar syrup.

Above: Large commercial apple orchards produce vast numbers of apples for sale at home and abroad.

whereas others dissolve into a delicious mousse. The best apple for cooking, used in many Dutch and Belgian recipes and developed from a medieval variety, is the Goudrenet, also known as Belle de Boskoop. This apple's softish texture and tart flavour make a delicious apple sauce to go with savoury dishes, or apple cake (*appelgebak*), a favourite treat for coffee time or dessert. The filling needs plenty of sugar to temper its sharpness. Belgian cooks love to add these apples to savoury dishes for a piquant sweet-and-sour flavour, especially when the main ingredient has its own strong taste, such as sausages and game.

Dutch cooks ask for 'mousse apples' in the shops, which are the softer varieties that children love cooked and made into a sweet purée, maybe topped with yogurt or *vla*. Sweeter eating apples such as Alkmene, Elstar, the new Kanzi and many others are grown and sold both locally and in the export market and make a great snack on their own, or pressed into different varieties of apple juice.

The pear orchards of Belgium and the Netherlands may not be quite so widespread as the apple orchards, but the pear still has its place in the national diet. This delicate fruit should be eaten raw at the point of tender perfection, but even harder pears still taste delicious when simmered gently in syrup or red wine to make a traditional warming dessert or snack dish.

Reliable summer weather is required to grow large numbers of ripe apricots and peaches. Sadly, warm temperatures and plenty of sunshine are not really a feature of Dutch and Belgian summers. However, many gardeners still grow the fruits against a warm brick wall as they do in the UK and elsewhere, and get a reasonable crop. Plums are more hardy, like apples and pears and, providing that the blossom survives the cold winds of early spring, many farmers can rely on a good plum crop to sell fresh or bottled, or dried in the form of prunes. These blend particularly well with bland desserts such as rice pudding.

CHERRIES AND CURRANTS

Both sweet and sour cherries are grown in commercial orchards and private gardens in Belgium and the Netherlands. However, the commercial operation is diminishing, as this is an intensive hand-picked crop that must be harvested at exactly the right point of

Below: Delicious cherries are enjoyed fresh and bottled, and are also used to flavour drinks such as kriek *beer.*

Above: Strawberries are enjoyed raw or are transformed into light desserts such as mousses.

ripeness. The waterways that criss-cross the Netherlands are ideal for transporting this delicate fruit to market. Fresh sweet cherries have a short season in the summer, but the sour varieties can be picked over a longer period and bottled for use in both sweet and savoury recipes. The Belgians love to add their tart flavour to rabbit stew or a tasty sauce for meatballs.

Sour cherries or blackcurrants with plenty of sugar added also make a beautiful dark red sauce to add to vanilla ice cream, or work well as a topping for a cheesecake. They also lend their distinctive, strong flavours to alcoholic and soft drinks. Belgian brewers make a special beer with an infusion of cherries, known as *kriek* beer, and a concentrated distillation of blackcurrants that can be added to white wine or champagne.

BERRIES

The climate in Belgium and the Netherlands is not suitable for outdoor strawberry cultivation on a commercial scale; however, these small plants are easily adapted to growing under glass, and the strawberry crop grown in Belgium is now so extensive that much of it is exported. The fruits are of top quality, suitable for eating on their own at the height of the summer season, or for making into sauce, or dessert recipes such as mousse or strawberry tart.

Cranberries are sharper and harder fruits, with a particular affinity for game or sausage stew, where their tart flavour adds piquancy to the rich gravy.

Above: Blackcurrants can be incorporated into stews or combined with eau de vie and sugar to make a liqueur.

OTHER FRUITS

As in much of the rest of Europe, Belgium and the Netherlands do not have the right climate for growing oranges, lemons or melons outdoors, so these are usually imported from warmer climes or grown on a small scale under glass. However, the astringent flavours of citrus fruit have been used in these countries since the first recipes were recorded in medieval times, both as an addition to blander fruit flavours in apple pie or poached pears, and in their own right in sweet and savoury dishes.

Rhubarb is better suited to the climate and also features in plenty of recipes, although it is mainly made into a sharp compote and served as an accompaniment to savoury dishes such as roast pork or chicken.

Below: Piquant cranberries are artfully used to cut through rich dishes, especially those made with game.

FLAVOURINGS <u>AND</u> CONDIMENTS

First impressions of Dutch and Belgian food are of good, wholesome ingredients made into nourishing dishes cooked in a simple style, where the question of flavourings may seem to be less important than the nutritional qualities of the food. However, nothing could be further from the truth. When basic foodstuffs are used with care and dedication to detail, the subtlest of flavourings makes all the difference to the finished dish.

The cooks of the 16th century left their legacy in the form of spicy sauces and marinades for poultry and game. Nowadays immigrants from warmer countries, especially from former colonies such as parts of Indonesia and Africa, have brought their own spicy ingredients to add colour and warmth to the Dutch and Belgian cuisine in dishes such as fries with satay sauce, *rijsttafel* (savoury rice with spicy side dishes) and *bami goreng* (noodles with stir-fried vegetables).

SAVOURY SPICES

When the spice trade was at its peak during the 16th century, Belgian and Dutch cooks integrated many spices into their cuisine. Antwerp was one of the biggest trading centres in Europe,

Below: Artisan mustards, such as these ones made by Tierenteyn, are sold in specialist condiment shops.

Above: Spices have been used in Dutch and Belgian dishes since the 16th century.

and through this busy city spices such as peppercorns, cinnamon and saffron flowed in from the East and out again to all parts of the world. The legacy of the spice trade can be seen in delicious savoury mixtures such as meatballs or croquettes, where peppercorns and paprika form the basic seasoning alongside local herbs. The Belgian pantry will always include nutmeg to add to potato dishes, as well as sauces and soups. Exotic spices are added to cheese to make a surprising concoction

Above: Fresh herbs are widely grown and used throughout the region.

known as *nagelkaas* (clove cheese) or *komijnkaas* (cumin cheese), where the mild cheese contains little flecks of spice in every bite.

Local spices such as juniper berries, mustard and horseradish, which can be grown in the mild, rainy climate, are often added to stews. Juniper berries, with their tart and distinctive flavour, have a particular affinity with game dishes such as braised partridge or venison, and are also found as an infusion in the grain alcohol, *jenever*.

Grated horseradish is often added to mayonnaise served with cold smoked fish. Mustard is another local flavouring whose use has been recorded since medieval times, and there is a whole mustard industry based on the area around Groningen in the Netherlands and Ghent in Belgium. Hot mustard can be eaten (sparingly) as a separate condiment, mixed with mayonnaise, or added to a creamy sauce for pork chops or plain white fish.

HERBS

Growing herbs is easy in the Dutch and Belgian climate. Chervil is perhaps the favourite, especially when made into a green sauce for fish dishes such as stewed eel. It has an aromatic, mild flavour that blends perfectly with a delicate fish dish. All the well-known garden herbs can also be found in Belgium and the Netherlands, such as parsley, tarragon, chives, bay leaves, sage and thyme, and these all have their place in the local cuisine, particularly in stock and salads.

PICKLES

Most countries have their own traditional ways of preserving fresh produce for the winter months. For centuries the Dutch have made Amsterdam onions, which are available in jars in every food shop. These strong-tasting pickles consist of pearl onions marinated in vinegar with sugar and mustard seeds and as many as 12 other spices. Another Dutch favourite with a long history is *zure bommen*, gherkins pickled in a sweet-and-sour mixture that are traditionally served with herring and have their origin in Jewish cuisine. Belgian pickles consist of a mixture of vegetables preserved in vinegar and spices, with turmeric to give them an attractive bright yellow colour. These are often served with bread, cheese and ham for a cold lunch or supper.

SWEET SPICES

Cinnamon, vanilla and ginger are the flavours that dominate in sweet dishes. Straightforward spicy cakes such as *peperkoek* (pepper cake) and *speculaas* (spice cookies) are eaten on a daily basis with a cup of tea or coffee.

Below: Belgian pickles are given their distinctive colour by turmeric.

Above: Cinnamon lends a warm, spicy note to pancakes and apple dishes.

Festival foods such as *pepernoten*, the delicious little biscuits brought by St Nicholas on 6 December, have a higher spice content. And no apple cake or sweet pancake would be complete without cinnamon and cloves to bring out the taste of the apples.

CHOCOLATE

Belgium has one of the finest chocolate traditions in the world. No preservatives, colourings or artificial flavours are added to Belgian chocolate, which is renowned for its exceptional quality. Belgians take full advantage of this tradition and consume large amounts of chocolate in many forms, including pralines, chocolate bars, countless desserts and sauces, and as chocolate spread served on bread.

Below: Top-quality chocolate is revered in Belgium and used in many forms.

Belgian chocolate spread

Sweet and flavoursome, chocolate spread is a favourite breakfast food spread on freshly baked white bread rolls, delicious with a banana on the side and a glass of milk. Use chocolate with a cocoa solids content of at least 70 per cent. Callebaut is ideal. Makes 800g/1¾lbs

200g/7oz dark (bittersweet) chocolate, broken into pieces
200g/7oz/scant 1 cup unsalted butter, cubed
1 x 400g/14oz can sweetened condensed milk
finely chopped toasted hazelnuts (optional)

1 Put the chocolate in a heatproof bowl. Bring a small pan of water to the boil. Remove it from the heat and fit the bowl on top, making sure it does not touch the water beneath. Alternatively, use a double boiler.

2 Add the butter to the bowl. Stir often to ensure the chocolate melts evenly. When both have melted completely, stir in the sweetened condensed milk.

3 Add the finely chopped hazelnuts, if using, and stir until evenly distributed. Spoon into clean glass jars, cover and leave to cool. Keep in a cool place for up to 2 weeks.

BREAD AND BAKING

Bread is the basic ingredient around which most breakfasts and lunches are based in Belgium and the Netherlands. Many Flemish expressions express the food's importance in the diet, such as *'zijn broodje is gebakken'* (his bread is baked), meaning 'he has made his fortune'. It is not just the aroma of fresh bread that wafts from Dutch and Belgian bakeries, however: cakes and biscuits (or cookies, from the Dutch word *koekje*) are another popular feature of the diet. These are often deliciously spiced with ginger, cinnamon or almonds.

BREAD

Belgian and Dutch cooks tend not to bake bread at home very often; instead they buy it fresh daily from the many wonderful bakeries that exist in every town and village. There is usually a slicing machine so that you can decide on the spot whether you would like your bread evenly sliced or if you would rather cut it yourself at home. Wholemeal (whole-wheat) bread is now popular, especially in the Netherlands, but plain white bread is still made in great quantities in Belgium and each region has its own kind of favourite white bread roll, both sweet and savoury.

Below: Abbey Bread is made with rye, white and wholemeal flours.

Above: Traditional mills, such as this one in the Netherlands, produce a range of different flours for bread-making.

Rye bread (*roggebrood*) is a favourite for both breakfast and lunch, with its dense texture and strong flavour, especially combined with savoury toppings. There are two main types of rye bread: people in the northern parts of the Netherlands like the very dark, sweet and moist type, which resembles

Below: Dark rye bread makes the ideal accompaniment for herrings or cheese.

German rye bread; those in the southern areas and Belgium prefer a lighter texture, with a paler brown colour and a dryish crumb. The dark variety is ideal for serving with new-season herring or cheese, while the lighter kind goes well with stronger flavours such as sausage or smoked ham.

A typical breakfast for any Dutch or Belgian dashing off to work or school might consist of a few slices of bread of any variety, with butter. This will be topped with cheese and ham or maybe an egg, or something sweet such as syrup, peanut butter or *hagelslag* (literally 'hailstones', sugar sprinkles in different colours). Lunch is a similar bread-based meal, but with the addition of different kinds of fish or meat and pickles. A popular variation on bread for lunch or breakfast is *beschuit*, a twice-baked rusk similar to Melba toast or crispbread, with a slightly sweet, milky taste.

CAKES AND DESSERTS

Some Dutch cakes are a cross between a sweet loaf and a cake, and are served sliced with butter and sometimes jam for breakfast. One example of this is the Dutch spice cake, *koek*, a sweet yeast-free soda bread often made of rye flour. It has a smooth texture and a fantastic aroma of cinnamon, cloves and nutmeg, which goes very well with a cup of coffee – it really wakes up the

Above: Pepernoten *are traditionally thrown to children on 6 December.*

taste buds in the morning. This cake is sold in countless variations: for example, studded with orange peel, nuts or raisins. Frisian sugar bread is another example of a sweet loaf that is eaten for breakfast; this time it contains broken lumps of sugar coated with cinnamon and stirred into a yeast dough before baking.

The more traditional teatime or dessert treats are apple cake and cheesecake. *Appelgebak* is a traditional apple tart made of soft cakey pastry with a good solid filling of sliced Goudrenet apples, subtly spiced with cinnamon. Cheesecake tends to be a softer mixture that is sometimes topped with fruit, but just as often eaten plain and unadulterated. The province of Limburg has its own speciality, *Limburgse vlaai*, a flat tart made of soft yeast pastry with an egg custard filling and a fruit topping.

The Dutch love freshly baked *stroopwafels*, delicious syrup-filled thin waffles that go very well with a cup of coffee. Other cookies include *speculaas* in all its forms, traditionally a stiff dough spiced with cinnamon and nutmeg and pressed into shaped moulds.

Every Belgian and Dutch town has a pancake house somewhere within easy reach, and these are ideal for a family outing. The pancakes are hearty affairs, made of wholemeal (whole-wheat) or plain (all-purpose) white flour batter, with all sorts of toppings, both savoury and sweet. The sweet-loving people of both nations tend to drizzle sweet and savoury pancakes indiscriminately with syrup.

SNACK FOODS

The travelling fairs that used to circulate around northern Europe brought all sorts of sweet and savoury treats to the population of Belgium and the Netherlands. Tiny round pancakes called *poffertjes*, made with melted butter and sugar, are cooked on a stall in the open air, using a special pan with rounded indentations. Waffles are more of a Belgian speciality, and they are made of a thicker yeast batter, often with beer used as the main liquid, which gives a special flavour. They are usually served topped with fruit and cream, but all sorts of variations can be bought at street bars and stalls.

BAKING FOR SPECIAL OCCASIONS

The major religious festivals throughout the year each have their own specific foods, which are often based on some kind of baked goods such as cake or bread. Anyone who has been in the Netherlands on 6 December will have seen a procession through the streets, with St Nicholas in his cloak and mitre making his stately way, accompanied by *Zwarte Piet* (Black Peter), who throws little spicy biscuits (*pepernoten*) made of *speculaas* dough for the children to catch. Another Christmas tradition,

Below: A wide range of cookies are sold in bakeries such as this one in Brussels.

Above: Tiny round poffertjes *are made in a special pan and eaten with great relish at the many stalls that sell them.*

from Belgium this time, is the delicious Christmas bread made in Wallonia, which comprises a rich mixture containing eggs and raisins, moulded in the shape of the baby Jesus. *Oliebollen* and *appelflappen* are the traditional foods of New Year's Eve. These are little balls of deep-fried yeast dough flavoured with apples, nuts and raisins, and dusted with icing (confectioners') sugar.

DRINKS

The Roman writer Tacitus mentioned in his description of the Low Countries that the people who lived there drank a lot of beer, and they liked it so much that you could conquer them simply by serving it to them. The people of Belgium and the Netherlands may not be so easily manipulated these days, but there is no doubt that beer is still by far the most popular drink in both countries, and is sold by the crate in every supermarket. Other drinks have their place, of course, such as traditionally made gin (*jenever*) and other spirits, which can be fiercely alcoholic but very welcome in the cold winter weather.

BEER

The most famous Dutch beers are Grolsch and Heineken, which are the lighter type of lager beer, usually served chilled. These major brands are now exported all over the world. But while the Dutch may be content with just a few popular varieties of beer, Belgium

Below: Belgium produces a huge number of different speciality beers, some of which are flavoured with fruit.

is justly famous for the quality and variety of its beer, and more than 500 types are produced in about 130 different breweries around the country. These range from the popular light lager-type beers, such as Stella Artois and Jupiler, which go so well with fries or mussels, to Lambic beers brewed using natural wild yeast, to dark ales, and even white wheat beers. Some of these are now becoming popular in other countries, for instance brands such as Hoegaarden, a white beer made of wheat and barley. Back in Belgium, there are many specialist beer cafés and bars where a huge range of different beers are on sale.

Lambic beer is one of the most intriguing drinks made in Belgium. This ancient brewing method involves letting the beer mature without any added yeast, using only the wild yeast that is naturally present in the atmosphere around the Brussels area for its fermentation. This beer can take anywhere between a few months and several years to reach full maturity. Lambic beer is also the basis for several other flavours of beer that use fruit infusions to achieve a really intriguing taste, such as the popular *kriek* beer, made with cherries. In this case the addition of fruit speeds up the fermentation process. At Christmas time,

Above: Wine, once the preserve of the very wealthy as it had to be imported, is now being produced in Belgium.

special beers are brewed with spices added to the basic mixture to make a warming, extra-alcoholic winter drink.

Belgian cooks do not restrict their beer consumption to a glass with a meal, however, as they use it to flavour a range of meat and game dishes too. One of the best-known Flemish dishes is the rich beef stew known as *Vlaamse stoofkarbonaden*, or *carbonnades flamandes*. This delicious stew is made by simmering chunks of stewing beef in beer at a low temperature for several hours until they are meltingly tender. The gravy is then further enhanced by placing slices of bread spread with mustard on top of the stew for the last part of the cooking, so the mustard is absorbed into the sauce and mingles with the beer and meat juices and the bread thickens the sauce. Either dark or light beer can be used for this classic recipe, giving a slightly different result in each case.

Right: Genever *or* jenever *is a distilled form of gin that is regarded as superior to other gins.*

WINE

Drinking wine with a meal used to be the preserve of the privileged few with the money and resources to keep a good wine cellar. Grapevines do not grow very well in either Belgium or the Netherlands, owing to the lack of summer sunshine and low temperatures. However, the wine industry has made a comeback in Belgium in recent years, particularly in Hageland, Haspengauw and Wallonia, where the sun is strong enough to ripen the grapes on the south-facing slopes. Indeed, one of the best and largest Belgian wine producers, based in the beautiful castle at Genoels-Elderen in Haspengauw, has been awarded the coveted VQPRD (*Vin de Qualité Produit dans une Région Déterminée*).

SPIRITS

Dutch and Belgian gin, or *g/jenever*, got its name from the juniper berries that give it its characteristic flavour. This is

Below: Country Lads and Lasses is a strong Dutch speciality.

a top-class gin distilled from barley, rye, and maize (corn). Lesser-quality gins can be made from other ingredients or have various additives; *g/jenever* proudly contains just the pure grain alcohol and juniper berries. The berries are added during the fourth and final phase of distillation, before the gin is matured in oak barrels for at least two years. It is still usually sold in earthenware bottles, just as it would have been in the Middle Ages. *G/jenever* is generally best served straight from the freezer in a small shot glass, referred to as a *borrel* or *witteke*. In the Netherlands it is the favoured accompaniment to the special treat of a new-season herring, while in Belgium it is more often served as an aperitif or nightcap on its own or mixed with coffee.

The Dutch make fine-quality brandy (the word 'brandy' comes from the Dutch word *brandewijn*, or 'burnt wine', referring to the process whereby wine is heated to distil it). One intriguing Dutch recipe is known as *Boerenjongens en meisjes* (country lads and lasses), which consists of dried fruits plumped up in brandy with spices and sugar, served in a glass with a spoon.

Another famous Belgian and Dutch concoction is *advocaat*, a sweet and sticky mixture that varies in thickness from drinkable to spoonable. It contains egg yolks, sugar and condensed milk, with the kick of *g/jenever*, brandy or vodka. This is a real pick-me-up in a glass – something of an acquired taste for other nationalities, but one the Belgians and Dutch have grown up with.

Right: Milk is often combined with coffee and a dash of alcohol to make a special drink.

Above: Sweet, pale advocaat *can be drunk on its own or mixed with coffee and topped with cream.*

SOFT DRINKS

Tea and coffee are the main non-alcoholic drinks served daily in Belgium and the Netherlands. Both are usually drunk without milk, but the trend of drinking milky coffee for breakfast or mid-morning is spreading from other parts of Europe and America. Special coffee mixtures that are halfway between a drink and a dessert might contain a dash of liqueurs or spirits such as *g/jenever* or *advocaat* with a topping of cream and chocolate. Fruit juices are also popular, and there are many varieties available in shops, restaurants and bars. Although most of the more exotic ingredients (such as oranges, lemons and limes) may not be grown locally, most of the processing is done locally in Belgium and the Netherlands.

Finally, mineral water (both still and sparkling) flows from the springs around Spa in the Ardennes and is drunk with relish for its taste and health-giving properties both at home and abroad.

SOUPS

The Dutch and Belgians enjoy eating a wide range of soups as part of a traditional lunch or dinner. Made with seasonal, often local, ingredients, they are carefully chosen so that they complement the courses that follow, and whet the appetite for what is to come. Some, such as Pea Soup or Funfair Soup, are rustic and hearty and can be served as a meal-in-a-bowl with some bread, while others are more refined and light, such as Cream of Asparagus Soup or Chervil Soup.

ONION SOUP FROM AALST

THE REGION OF AALST IN EAST FLANDERS HAS BEEN KNOWN FOR ITS ONIONS EVER SINCE MASS CULTIVATION STARTED IN THE 19TH CENTURY. ITS INHABITANTS ARE ACCORDINGLY NICKNAMED 'AJUINBOEREN' (ONION FARMERS) OR 'AJUINE FRETTERS' (ONION GOBBLERS). ONION SOUP IS OFTEN SERVED AS A HANGOVER CURE AFTER NEW YEAR'S EVE OR MARDI GRAS, BOTH OF WHICH ARE CELEBRATED IN AALST, WHICH HOLDS THE MOST FAMOUS AND OLDEST CARNIVAL CELEBRATION IN FLANDERS.

4 Remove the herbs and purée the mixture with a hand-held blender or in a food processor, until it reaches the desired consistency.

5 Season with salt and ground black pepper, to taste. Reheat if necessary, then ladle the soup into bowls.

6 Top each serving with parsley and add grated cheese, if you like. Serve immediately with bread or croûtons.

VARIATION

To make Onion Soup au Gratin, place some grated Gruyère in each bowl and top with a slice of toasted baguette before pouring in the hot soup. Sprinkle with a little more Gruyère and place under the grill (broiler) for 5–10 minutes, or until bubbly and lightly browned.

SERVES FOUR–SIX

INGREDIENTS
50g/2oz/¼ cup butter
4 medium onions, (total weight about 800g/1¾lb), chopped
4 garlic cloves, finely chopped
1 medium potato (about 200g/7oz), peeled and chopped
45ml/3 tbsp sherry or Calvados (if not using beer, *see* below)
1 litre/1¾ pints/4 cups vegetable, chicken or beef stock, or half stock and half beer (preferably Rodenbach)
1–2 sprigs fresh thyme
1 bay leaf
salt and ground black pepper, to taste
45ml/3 tbsp freshly chopped parsley, to garnish
freshly grated Gruyère cheese (optional)
hearty country bread or croûtons, to serve

1 Melt the butter in a large pan and sauté the onions for about 10 minutes or until lightly caramelized. Add the garlic and sauté for 1 minute more.

2 Add the potato to the onions and stir well. If you are using sherry or Calvados instead of beer, add it to the pan and let the mixture simmer for 3 minutes more.

3 Pour in the stock (or stock and beer) and add the thyme and bay leaf. Bring to the boil, reduce the heat and simmer for 35 minutes.

Per portion Energy 146kcal/608kJ; Protein 2.5g; Carbohydrate 16.3g, of which sugars 8.1g; Fat 7.5g, of which saturates 4.4g; Cholesterol 18mg; Calcium 38mg; Fibre 2.2g; Sodium 339mg.

POTATO AND LEEK SOUP

LEEKS ARE A FAVOURITE BELGIAN VEGETABLE, ENJOYED ON THEIR OWN FOR THEIR PLEASING SUBTLETY AND ALSO INDISPENSABLE AS THE BASIS OF MANY SOUPS. SLIGHTLY TRICKY TO CLEAN, IT IS IMPORTANT THAT YOU WASH LEEKS VERY CAREFULLY BEFORE USING THEM, AS ANY GRIT THAT IS NOT WASHED OFF CAN RUIN A DISH. SMOOTH AND CREAMY, THIS SIMPLE SOUP CAN BE SERVED WARM AS AN APPEALING APPETIZER OR LIGHT MEAL, BUT IS ALSO DELICIOUS COLD, AS VICHYSSOISE.

SERVES FOUR–SIX

INGREDIENTS

25g/1oz/2 tbsp unsalted butter
1 onion, thinly sliced
2–3 leeks (white and pale green parts only), thinly sliced and well rinsed
3 garlic cloves, roughly chopped
120ml/4fl oz/½ cup dry white vermouth or white wine (optional)
3 medium waxy potatoes, peeled and chopped small
1.5 litres/2½ pints/6¼ cups chicken or vegetable stock
bouquet garni, made from 3 sprigs fresh parsley, 3 sprigs fresh thyme and 1 bay leaf, tied together with kitchen string (twine)
200ml/7fl oz/scant 1 cup single (light) cream or milk (optional)
salt and ground white pepper, to taste
30ml/2 tbsp thinly chopped fresh chives or chopped parsley, to garnish

1 Gently heat the butter in a large, heavy pan over a medium heat. Add the onion, leeks and garlic to the pan and sauté gently for about 12 minutes, stirring occasionally, until softened but not browned.

2 Increase the heat and pour in the vermouth or wine, if using. Boil for about 4 minutes, or until the mixture is almost dry. Add the potatoes and stock.

3 Add the bouquet garni to the soup. Bring to the boil, lower the heat and partially cover the pan, leaving the lid slightly ajar to allow steam to escape. Simmer for 20 minutes, until the potatoes are very tender.

4 Lift out and discard the bouquet garni. With a hand-held blender or in a food processor, purée the soup until the desired consistency is reached.

5 If using the milk or cream, whisk it into the soup. Season to taste with salt and pepper and heat through.

6 Divide among warm bowls, garnish with chives or parsley and serve immediately.

Per portion Energy 127kcal/534kJ; Protein 3.4g; Carbohydrate 19.6g, of which sugars 3.9g; Fat 4.4g, of which saturates 2.4g; Cholesterol 9mg; Calcium 40mg; Fibre 3.2g; Sodium 180mg.

CREAM OF BELGIAN ENDIVE SOUP

FROM APPETIZERS AND SOUPS TO ENTRÉES AND SIDE DISHES, ENDIVES (OR CHICORY, AS THE VEGETABLE IS KNOWN IN THE UK) ARE EXTREMELY POPULAR IN BELGIUM. THIS SOUP, WITLOOF ROOMSOEP/SOUPE DE CRÈME D'ENDIVE, AS IT IS KNOWN IN FLEMISH AND FRENCH, IS A CLASSIC DISH FROM THE REGION. IT FEATURES ON THE MENU OF ALMOST EVERY FESTIVE MEAL AND BANQUET, ESPECIALLY DURING THE WINTER, SINCE THIS IS THE TRADITIONAL SEASON FOR ENDIVES.

SERVES FOUR

INGREDIENTS
   25g/1oz/2 tbsp unsalted butter
   1 white onion, chopped
   3 garlic cloves, chopped
   8 Belgian endives (chicory), cored
     and chopped
   2 medium potatoes, peeled
     and chopped
   1 litre/1¾ pints/4 cups chicken,
     veal or vegetable stock
   500ml/17fl oz/generous 2 cups
     single (light) cream or milk
   pinch of nutmeg
   salt and white pepper, to taste
For the garnish
   30ml/2 tbsp chopped fresh chives
     or dill sprigs
   small endive leaves

1 Melt the butter in a pan and sauté the onion over medium heat for 5 minutes, until it has softened but not browned.

2 Add the garlic and endives and sauté for 5 minutes more. Add the potatoes and stock, bring to the boil, reduce the heat and simmer for about 30 minutes or until the potatoes are soft.

3 Pour in the cream or milk and heat through. With a hand-held blender or in a food processor, blend until the desired consistency is reached.

4 Add nutmeg, salt and white pepper, to taste. Reheat the soup if necessary. Ladle into bowls and garnish with the herbs and small endive leaves.

VARIATIONS
• Cream of Endive Soup can also be served chilled in ice-cold shot glasses for an elegant *amuse bouche*, served before the hors d'œuvre or first course of a meal.
• To make Cream of Endive Soup en Croute, have ready 4 sheets of puff pastry, cut to rounds slightly larger than your heatproof bowls, and 1 beaten egg. Ladle the soup into the bowls. Brush the pastry rounds with egg. Fit a round over each bowl and crimp the edges. Place the bowls in a preheated oven at 180°C/350°F/ Gas 4 for about 10 minutes or until the pastry is golden. Serve immediately.

Per portion Energy 185kcal/778kJ; Protein 6.4g; Carbohydrate 24.6g, of which sugars 8.4g; Fat 7.9g, of which saturates 4.8g; Cholesterol 21mg; Calcium 172mg; Fibre 1.7g; Sodium 104mg.

CREAM OF ASPARAGUS SOUP

BELGIANS CALL WHITE ASPARAGUS THE 'QUEEN OF THE VEGETABLES' AND AWAIT THE ANNUAL CROP WITH KEEN ANTICIPATION. THE SEASON STARTS ABOUT MID APRIL AND LASTS UNTIL THE LAST WEEK OF JUNE. WHITE ASPARAGUS HAS A MILDER FLAVOUR THAN GREEN AND IS MORE TENDER, BUT BECAUSE SALES ARE LIMITED OUTSIDE EUROPE, THESE LUXURY VEGETABLES ARE EXPENSIVE. CREAM OF ASPARAGUS SOUP IS A DELICACY IN BELGIUM, TRADITIONALLY SERVED FOR SPECIAL OCCASIONS.

SERVES FOUR

INGREDIENTS
500g/1¼lb white asparagus spears
500ml/17fl oz/generous 2 cups
   chicken stock
500ml/17fl oz/generous 2 cups
   vegetable stock
50g/2oz/¼ cup butter
15g/½oz/2 tbsp plain
   (all-purpose) flour
pinch of ground nutmeg
1 egg yolk
150ml/¼ pint/⅔ cup double
   (heavy) cream
salt and ground white pepper, to taste
handful of fresh herbs, such as
   chives, chervil or parsley, chopped,
   to garnish

1 Trim the asparagus spears or snap them so that the tender stalk separates from the tougher base. Cut off the tips and set them aside. Peel the remaining stalks with a vegetable peeler if necessary, then cut them into 2.5cm/½in pieces.

2 Mix the chicken and vegetable stock in a pan, add the asparagus tips and cook for about 3 minutes or until just tender. Lift out the tips with a slotted spoon and immediately refresh them in iced water to prevent them from cooking any further.

3 Add the sections of asparagus stalk to the stock and simmer, covered, for 15–20 minutes or until tender.

4 Using a hand-held blender or a food processor, purée the soup until smooth. For a very fine consistency, pass it through a food mill or sieve (strainer).

5 Melt the butter in a pan and stir in the flour. Cook over low heat for about 4 minutes, making sure the butter does not brown. Pour in the soup, stirring all the time, then simmer, still stirring, for 6 minutes more, until thickened. Season with nutmeg, salt and pepper to taste, and remove from the heat.

VARIATION
Green asparagus can be used instead of the white type, but will result in a different texture, colour and taste.

6 In a bowl, whisk the egg yolk with the cream. Add to the warm soup. Reheat gently if necessary but do not let it boil.

7 Ladle into bowls, add the asparagus tips and garnish each serving with herbs. Serve immediately.

Per portion Energy 338kcal/1394kJ; Protein 5.4g; Carbohydrate 6.1g, of which sugars 3.2g; Fat 32.6g, of which saturates 19.6g; Cholesterol 128mg; Calcium 66mg; Fibre 2.3g; Sodium 88mg.

WATERCRESS SOUP

Watercress (Nasturtium officinale) and garden cress (Lepidium sativum) are nutritious aquatic leaf vegetables that grow wild alongside Flanders' cold river streams. Nowadays they are commercially produced to accommodate year-round demand. The peppery flavour of watercress makes it ideal for garnishes, sauces, salads and soups.

2 Pour in the stock and add the bay leaf. Bring to the boil, reduce the heat, cover and simmer for 20–30 minutes, until the potatoes are tender.

3 Stir in the watercress and garden cress. Simmer uncovered for exactly 3 minutes, to cook the cress lightly.

4 Remove the bay leaf. With a hand-held blender or in a food processor, purée the soup until smooth. Season to taste with salt and pepper.

5 Reheat if necessary, ladle into warm bowls and serve, garnished with fresh watercress leaves.

VARIATION
To make Cream of Watercress Soup, add 120–200ml/4–7fl oz/½–scant 1 cup single (light) cream or milk with the watercress during the final 3 minutes' cooking.

SERVES FOUR

INGREDIENTS
  25g/1oz/2 tbsp unsalted butter or vegetable oil
  1 large onion, chopped
  1 leek, white part only, chopped
  1 garlic clove, roughly chopped
  2 large potatoes, peeled and cubed
  1.5 litres/2½ pints/6¼ cups hot chicken or vegetable stock
  1 bay leaf
  1 large bunch of watercress, well rinsed, large stems removed, roughly chopped
  1 large bunch of garden cress, well rinsed, large stems removed (*see* Cook's tip)
  salt and ground black pepper, to taste
  60ml/4 tbsp watercress leaves, to garnish

1 Heat the butter or oil in a large pan over medium-high heat. Stir in the onion, then sauté for 2–3 minutes. Add the leek, garlic and potatoes. Sauté for 5 minutes more, stirring until the mixture becomes fragrant.

COOK'S TIP
If you cannot locate garden cress, use two bunches of watercress.

Per portion Energy 598kcal/2515kJ; Protein 19.9g; Carbohydrate 76.3g, of which sugars 14.3g; Fat 25.9g, of which saturates 14.5g; Cholesterol 53mg; Calcium 602mg; Fibre 13.7g; Sodium 348mg.

CHERVIL SOUP

CHERVIL IS A SUPERSTAR IN THE BELGIAN KITCHEN REPERTOIRE. THIS VERSATILE HERB FEATURES IN SAUCES, DIPS, COMPOUND BUTTERS, OMELETTES AND GARNISHES, AND IS ONE OF THE FIVE ESSENTIAL COMPONENTS IN THE CLASSIC FINES HERBES COMBINATION. IT GIVES A SUBTLE ANISEED FLAVOUR TO THIS DELICATE SOUP, WHICH IS AN IDEAL INTRODUCTION TO AN ELEGANT DINNER.

SERVES FOUR

INGREDIENTS
  25g/1oz/2 tbsp butter
  1 onion, finely chopped
  1 leek, white part only,
    finely chopped
  1 large potato, peeled and chopped
  1 litre/1¾ pints/4 cups hot chicken
    or vegetable stock
  stems and leaves from 1 bunch
    fresh chervil (about 150g/5oz),
    chopped and kept separate, plus
    a few chervil sprigs for the garnish
  50g/2oz/½ cup cooked white long
    grain rice
  salt and ground white pepper,
    to taste

1 Melt the butter in a large pan over medium to high heat. Add the onion and sauté for about 5 minutes, until fragrant and translucent.

2 Add the leek and potato and sauté, stirring constantly, for 5 minutes more.

COOK'S TIP
Although chervil stems can be cooked, the leaves are much more delicate. Avoid reheating the soup after adding them, if you can. If you must reheat the soup, use gentle heat and do not let it approach boiling point.

3 Pour in the chicken or vegetable stock. Add the chopped chervil stems, bring to the boil, reduce the heat and simmer for 20 minutes or until the potatoes are tender. Add salt and pepper to taste.

4 Using a hand-held blender or food processor, purée the soup until smooth.

5 Stir in the chopped chervil leaves and cooked rice. Ladle into warm soup bowls and serve garnished with the chervil sprigs.

VARIATIONS
• Tiny meatballs can be added to the soup instead of the rice for a more substantial dish. In this case, add the chervil only when the meatballs are completely cooked through.
• For a creamier texture, mix the chervil leaves with 60ml/4 tbsp crème fraîche before adding them to the soup.

Per portion Energy 137kcal/573kJ; Protein 3.5g; Carbohydrate 17.6g, of which sugars 3.7g; Fat 6.3g, of which saturates 3.4g; Cholesterol 13mg; Calcium 98mg; Fibre 3.8g; Sodium 59mg.

ALKMAAR CHEESE SOUP

Cheese tarts were made in the Netherlands as early as 1514, but cheese soups came much later, about the time of the Great Depression in the 1930s. During this period, four top Dutch chefs published a book of inexpensive recipes featuring dairy products to cater for their hungry compatriots. This soup was created by F. A. Lamers, a chef from The Hague, and it is named after the Alkmaar, the oldest cheese market in the country.

SERVES FOUR

INGREDIENTS
40g/1½oz/3 tbsp butter
1 onion, chopped
50g/2oz/½ cup plain
 (all-purpose) flour
1.2 litres/2 pints/5 cups milk
150g/5oz/1¼ cups grated mature
 (sharp) Gouda cheese
1 small celeriac
salt, to taste
chopped fresh chives, to garnish
toast, to serve

1 Melt the butter in a large pan over medium to high heat. Add the onion and sauté for about 5 minutes, until fragrant and translucent.

2 Stir in the flour and cook, stirring constantly, for 2 minutes, then gradually stir in the milk.

3 Continue to cook, stirring, until slightly thickened. Add 50g/2oz/½ cup of the grated Gouda and cook, stirring occasionally, for about 15 minutes.

4 Meanwhile, peel and finely dice the celeriac, then cook in a pan of boiling water for about 10 minutes, until softened. Drain the celeriac and add to the soup with the remaining cheese.

5 Season to taste with salt, ladle into warm soup bowls and garnish with chives. Serve immediately with toast.

VARIATION
This version, created by a cheese-maker from the Alblasserwaard, in South Holland, uses a farmhouse Gouda:
   Colour the Alkmaar Cheese Soup at Step 2 with a little powdered saffron, and add some puréed potatoes to thicken it, and then flavour it with 2.5ml/½ tsp crushed caraway seeds. Top the soup with a cheese crust made from a mixture of 3 crushed rusks, 200g/7oz/1¾ cups grated Gouda and a pinch of mild paprika sprinkled over. Place the pan under a preheated grill (broiler) and cook until the crust is a golden brown.

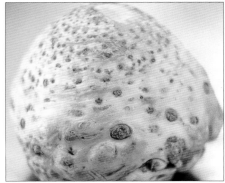

Per portion Energy 407kcal/1703kJ; Protein 21.5g; Carbohydrate 25.7g, of which sugars 15.9g; Fat 25.2g, of which saturates 16.1g; Cholesterol 71mg; Calcium 704mg; Fibre 1.4g; Sodium 582mg.

ZEELAND MUSSEL SOUP

THE DUTCH LOVE AFFAIR WITH MUSSELS GOES BACK MANY HUNDREDS OF YEARS. IN THE 17TH CENTURY, ORDINARY DUTCH PEOPLE LIKED TO EAT THEIR MUSSELS RAW WITH BEER FOR BREAKFAST, BUT THEY WERE ALSO SERVED ON THE HEAVILY LOADED TABLES OF THE RICH, SO TEMPTINGLY DEPICTED IN PAINTINGS BY THE FAMOUS DUTCH PAINTERS OF THAT PERIOD, SUCH AS CORNELIS DE HEEM AND FLORIS VAN SCHOOTEN. HERE, THEY ARE USED TO MAKE A FRAGRANT, NOURISHING SOUP.

SERVES FOUR

INGREDIENTS
  1 bottle (750ml/1¼ pints/3 cups)
    dry white wine
  1 chicken leg
  1 large carrot, thinly sliced
  pinch of powdered saffron
  4kg/8¾lb live mussels
  4 onions, sliced into rings
  2 bay leaves
  2 celery sticks
  6 black peppercorns, lightly crushed
  2 leeks, thinly sliced
  75g/3oz cornflour (cornstarch)
  200ml/7fl oz/scant 1 cup
    whipping cream
  salt and ground black pepper, to taste
  celery leaves, to garnish
  buttered soft rolls (kadetjes) filled
    with watercress, to serve

1 Pour the wine into a large pan, add 1 litre/1¾ pints/4 cups water, the chicken leg, carrot and saffron and season to taste. Bring to the boil, lower the heat, cover and simmer for 1 hour.

2 Scrub the mussels under cold water and pull off the 'beards'. Discard any with broken shells or those that do not shut immediately when tapped.

3 Put the mussels, onions, bay leaves, celery, peppercorns and 150ml/¼ pint/ ⅔ cup water into a pan, cover and cook shaking the pan a few times, for 5 minutes, until the shells have opened.

4 Strain the mussels through a sieve (strainer) lined with kitchen paper, keeping the liquid. Discard any that remain closed. Remove the rest from their shells.

5 Strain 500ml/17fl oz/generous 2 cups of the liquid again. Add to the soup.

6 Using a slotted spoon, remove the chicken leg from the pan and transfer to a chopping board. Cut off the meat and chop finely. Add the leeks to the pan and cook for 2 minutes.

7 Mix the cornflour with 150ml/¼ pint/ ⅔ cup water to a paste in a small bowl and stir into the soup, cooking for a short time over a medium heat, stirring, to thicken.

8 Remove the pan from the heat and stir in the cream, mussels and chicken meat. Ladle into warmed soup bowls, sprinkle with celery leaves and serve immediately with buttered soft rolls filled with watercress.

Per portion Energy 692kcal/2910kJ; Protein 62g; Carbohydrate 32.9g, of which sugars 12.1g; Fat 22.6g, of which saturates 14.5g; Cholesterol 150mg; Calcium 712mg; Fibre 4.2g; Sodium 713mg.

GRONINGEN PRAWN SOUP

DELICIOUS SMALL BROWN PRAWNS ARE A SPECIALITY OF THE NORTH COAST OF GRONINGEN AS WELL AS ZEELAND. AT DAWN, THE PRAWN BOATS STEAM INTO THE HARBOUR OF LAUWERSOOG, WHERE THEIR CATCH IS BOILED IN SEAWATER ABOARD THE VESSELS. THIS RECIPE, BASED ON A DISH CREATED BY LUKTJE LANDMAN, A FISHERMAN'S WIFE FROM TERMUNTENERZIJL, IS THE PERFECT WAY TO ENJOY THEM.

SERVES TWO

INGREDIENTS

1 small haddock
50g/2oz/½ cup cooked peeled
  brown prawns (shrimp)
½ rusk, crumbled
1 egg, lightly beaten
40g/1½ oz/3 tbsp butter
a small piece of leek, cut
  into rings
15ml/1 tbsp cornflour (cornstarch)
5ml/1 tsp Groningen or
  Dijon mustard
15ml/1 tbsp chopped celery leaves
salt and ground black pepper,
  to taste
50–100g/2–3½ oz/½–scant 1 cup
  cooked peeled brown prawns
  (shrimp), to garnish
For the stock
  ½ leek
  2 carrots
  2 potatoes
  8 celery leaves
  1 bay leaf
  pinch of salt

1 Fillet the haddock, reserving the head and bones. Alternatively, ask your fishmonger to do this for you. Using a small, sharp knife, cut out the gills from the fish head; discard.

2 To make the stock, pour 750ml/ 1¼ pints/3 cups water into a pan. Add the fish head and bones, leek, carrots, potatoes, celery leaves, bay leaf and a pinch of salt. Simmer for 30 minutes.

3 Skin and chop the haddock fillets, then process in a food processor. Scrape into a bowl, add the prawns and rusk and season to taste with salt and pepper.

4 Knead the mixture together, adding enough egg to make a firm mixture. Form into balls and leave to rest in the refrigerator for about 30 minutes.

5 Melt the butter in a non-stick frying pan. Add the fish balls and leek rings and cook over a medium-low heat, stirring occasionally, for about 10 minutes, until the balls are evenly browned on all sides and the leeks are soft but not brown. Remove and set aside.

6 Meanwhile, using a slotted spoon, remove the fish head and bones, leek, carrots, potatoes, celery leaves and bay leaf from the stock.

7 Add the remaining egg to the frying pan, season with salt and cook until set. Remove and cut into strips.

8 Dice the carrots and potatoes and return them to the soup. Discard the remaining flavourings.

9 Mix the cornflour with 30ml/2 tbsp water to a paste in a small bowl and stir into the soup, cooking for a short time over a medium heat, stirring, to thicken. Add the mustard, celery leaves, fish balls, leek rings and egg strips. Garnish with the peeled prawns and serve.

VARIATION
For a simpler recipe with more fish, use 500g/1¼ lb small flounders and dabs to make the stock. Place them upright with water to cover, in a covered pan with sliced leek, a bay leaf and salt. Simmer for about 20 minutes until they are so tender that they fillet themselves when shaken by the tails. Strain the stock, then add fish balls made in the same way as in the recipe, but replace the cooked prawns with 250g/9oz fried prawns.

Per portion Energy 496kcal/2082kJ; Protein 43.8g; Carbohydrate 29.7g, of which sugars 9.2g; Fat 23.8g, of which saturates 11.5g; Cholesterol 289mg; Calcium 230mg; Fibre 1.1g; Sodium 373mg.

QUEEN'S SOUP

This is a variation of a French recipe, originally named after the wife of Henry IV, La Reine Marguérite. It was popular in the Netherlands during the 1940s, when the occupying Germans banned the French language during World War II. The Dutch responded by ordering this soup as a mark of patriotism to the Dutch Queen Wilhelmina, who was exiled in Britain.

2 Remove the boiling fowl from the pan with a slotted spoon and leave to cool.

3 Pass the stock through a sieve (strainer) lined with dampened muslin (cheesecloth) into a clean pan. Add the rice to the pan and return to the heat. Bring to the boil and cook for 30 minutes, until the rice is tender.

4 Ladle the soup into a food processor, in batches if necessary, and process. Return the soup to the pan.

5 Remove the meat from the bones and dice neatly. Add the chicken to the pan and bring the soup to the boil again.

6 Remove the pan from the heat. Beat the egg yolk with a ladleful of the soup, then stir it into the pan with the cream.

7 Warm through gently, but do not let it boil. Sprinkle with tarragon and serve.

SERVES FOUR

INGREDIENTS
  1 boiling fowl (stewing chicken)
  7.5ml/1½ tsp salt
  1 small leek
  1 tarragon sprig, plus extra to garnish
  1 chervil sprig
  1 thyme sprig
  1 mace blade
  65g/2½oz/⅓ cup rice
  50ml/2fl oz/¼ cup egg yolk
  50ml/2fl oz/¼ cup whipping cream

COOK'S TIP
Using tarragon is a homage to Queen Wilhelmina, who was fond of this herb.

1 Put the boiling fowl, salt, leek, tarragon, chervil, thyme and mace in a large pan and add 1.5 litres/2½ pints/6¼ cups water. Bring to the boil, then lower the heat, cover and simmer for 2 hours.

Per portion Energy 369kcal/1547kJ; Protein 48.8g; Carbohydrate 14g, of which sugars 0.9g; Fat 13g, of which saturates 5.4g; Cholesterol 328mg; Calcium 45mg; Fibre 0.6g; Sodium 160mg.

SPLIT PEA AND SAUSAGE SOUP

WHEN THE CANALS AND LAKES FREEZE OVER IN THE WINTER IN THE NETHERLANDS, EVERYBODY GOES SKATING AND STALLS APPEAR, OFFERING SKATERS THE CHANCE TO WARM UP WITH A CUP OF PEA SOUP. THERE ARE MANY VARIATIONS OF THIS DISH. MOST DUTCH FOLLOW THE PROVINCE OF GELDERLAND IN USING SMOKED SAUSAGE, BUT THE FRISIANS IN THE NORTH PREFER FRESH SAUSAGES.

SERVES FOUR

INGREDIENTS
  800g/1¾ lb/3½ cups green
    split peas
  500g/1¼ lb uncured gammon
    (fresh ham)
  250g/9oz pork spare ribs
  1 split pig's trotter (foot)
  250g/9oz lean bacon in a
    single piece
  pinch of salt
  1 bunch of celery leaves
  1 small celeriac, peeled and sliced
  500g/1¼ lb leeks, thickly sliced
  1 carrot, sliced
  1 smoked (Gelders) sausage,
    about 250g/9oz
  rye bread spread with mustard,
    to serve

1 Rinse the peas under cold running water and place in a large pan. Add 2.5 litres/4¼ pints/10⅔ cups water, bring to the boil and skim off any scum that rises to the surface.

2 Add the gammon, spare ribs, pig's trotter and bacon to the pan, season with a pinch of salt and simmer over a low heat for about 3 hours, until the meat is tender.

3 Remove the bacon from the pan and set aside to cool.

4 Chop half the celery leaves and reserve the remainder for garnish. Add the celeriac, chopped celery leaves, leeks and carrot to the soup and simmer for 30 minutes, until tender.

5 Put the smoked sausage in a pan, add enough water to cover and poach over a low heat for about 20 minutes.

6 Using a slotted spoon, remove the meat from the soup. Cut the meat from the bones and dice it. Return the meat to the soup and add the sausage.

7 Ladle the soup into bowls and garnish with the reserved celery leaves. Slice the bacon and serve on rye bread spread with mustard, as an accompaniment.

Per portion Energy 914kcal/3843kJ; Protein 68.5g; Carbohydrate 87g, of which sugars 8.4g; Fat 34.8g, of which saturates 12.5g; Cholesterol 75mg; Calcium 222mg; Fibre 18.1g; Sodium 2216mg.

BROAD BEAN SOUP

Long before Columbus discovered the green beans that the Dutch love, the broad bean was thriving in the vegetable gardens of Europe. These beans are not favourites with everybody — traditional nicknames include 'woollen mittens', 'farmers' toes', 'thick thumbs', 'poop beans' and 'horse beans'. However, don't let this put you off — most simply, broad beans can be enjoyed with bacon, parsley and savory or in a white sauce. A more adventurous approach is this regional soup from De Achterhoek, which is best served with the summer savory cake shown here.

SERVES FOUR

INGREDIENTS
2 onions
800g/1¾lb gammon (smoked or
  cured ham), rind removed
pinch of salt
1.2–1.6kg/2½–3½lb shelled
  broad (fava) beans
15g/½oz/1 tbsp butter
1 bunch of spring onions
  (scallions), diced
30ml/2 tbsp cornflour (cornstarch)
1 bunch of parsley, chopped
single (light) cream, to serve
For the summer savory cake
(*Bonenkruidkoek*)
500g/1¼lb potatoes, peeled
2 eggs, lightly beaten
pinch of freshly grated nutmeg
30ml/2 tbsp finely chopped fresh
  summer savory
25g/1oz/2 tbsp butter
salt and ground black pepper, to taste

1 Chop one of the onions and place in a pan with the gammon and a pinch of salt. Pour in 1.5 litres/2½ pints/6¼ cups water and bring to the boil, then lower the heat and simmer for 1 hour.

VARIATION
Core and quarter a red (bell) pepper, then place under a grill (broiler) until the skin blackens. Peel, dice and add to the soup.

2 To make the summer savory cake, rinse the potatoes and pat dry on kitchen paper. Coarsely grate them and put into a bowl, then stir in the eggs, nutmeg and savory and season.

3 Melt half the butter in a 20cm/8in diameter non-stick frying pan. Scoop the potato mixture into the pan, pressing it out evenly with a fish slice or metal spatula, and cook over low heat until the top is dry. Loosen the edges with a knife, and turn out on to a plate.

4 Melt the remaining butter in the pan, slide the cake back into it, the cooked side uppermost, and cook until browned on the underside. Keep warm over very low heat.

5 Remove the meat from the pan and reserve the stock. Add the beans to the pan and cook for 15–20 minutes, until tender. Slice the remaining onion.

6 Melt the butter in a small frying pan. Add the meat and sliced onion and cook over low heat, stirring occasionally, for about 10 minutes, until lightly browned. Keep warm.

7 Remove half the beans and process in a food processor or blender. Stir the bean purée into the soup with the spring onions and cook for 2 minutes.

8 Mix the cornflour to a paste with 60ml/4 tbsp water in a small bowl and stir into the soup, cooking for a short time to thicken.

9 Season to taste with salt, sprinkle with parsley and serve with the summer savory cake, the meat (sliced at the table), onion mixture and some cream.

Soup per portion Energy 428kcal/1793kJ; Protein 46g; Carbohydrate 26.2g, of which sugars 5.1g; Fat 16g, of which saturates 5.2g; Cholesterol 46mg; Calcium 108mg; Fibre 9.2g; Sodium 1777mg.
Savory cake per portion Energy 173kcal/727kJ; Protein 5.5g; Carbohydrate 20.4g, of which sugars 1.8g; Fat 8.4g, of which saturates 4.2g; Cholesterol 108mg; Calcium 38mg; Fibre 1.6g; Sodium 89mg.

RUNNER BEAN SOUP

THE DUTCH NAME FOR THIS DISH, HUMKESSOEP, USES THE DIALECT FROM THE EASTERN PART OF THE COUNTRY. THE SOUP ITSELF IS A DIRECT LEGACY OF THE TRADITION OF COOKING MEALS OVER AN OPEN FIRE. THE WHITE BEANS WERE IN SEASON AT HARVEST TIME, SO THE SOUP WAS OFTEN MADE AS A FESTIVE DISH. IT SHOULD BE SERVED WITH BUTTERED WHITE BREAD AND TOPPED WITH A THIN SLICE OF NAEGELHOLT, A DRIED PIECE OF SILVERSIDE SPICED WITH NUTMEG OR CLOVES.

6 Add the runner beans, potatoes, leeks and celeriac to the soup and simmer for 20 minutes, until tender.

7 Taste, adjust the seasoning and garnish with chopped herbs.

8 Carve the meat into slices and serve with the buttered bread and soup.

VARIATIONS
• The stock can also be made from pork. You will need 500g/1¼lb pork spare ribs, 300g/11oz fresh sausage and 100g/3¾oz lean smoked bacon.
• You can also use other kinds of green beans, if you prefer.

SERVES FOUR

INGREDIENTS
  250g/9oz/1⅓ cups dried white
    beans, soaked in cold water for
    12 hours
  800g/1¾lb rib of beef
  pinch of salt
  800g/1¾lb celeriac
  800g/1¾lb runner (green) beans,
    cut into short lengths
  250g/9oz potatoes, thickly diced
  2 leeks, thickly diced
  chopped fresh parsley or celery
    leaves, to garnish
  buttered white bread, to serve

1 After soaking for at least 12 hours, drain the white beans and rinse thoroughly under cold running water.

2 Put the rib of beef in a large pan, add 2 litres/3½ pints/8¾ cups water and a pinch of salt and bring to the boil.

3 Skim off any scum that rises to the surface, then lower the heat and simmer for about 1 hour.

4 Add the white beans to the pan, re-cover and simmer for 1 hour more.

5 Peel and thickly dice the celeriac.

Per portion Energy 462kcal/1952kJ; Protein 43.2g; Carbohydrate 48.4g, of which sugars 11.7g; Fat 12g, of which saturates 4.3g; Cholesterol 58mg; Calcium 240mg; Fibre 18.6g; Sodium 204mg.

TURNIP SOUP

Even in a small country such as the Netherlands, tastes differ significantly from region to region. In the northern provinces turnips are regarded as food for deer and wild boar, or as fodder for livestock. But in the southern provinces of Brabant and Limburg, turnips are eaten frequently, especially in spring when their taste is milder. This soup originates in Limburg where it is made with the tender Geuldal lamb that live on the moors.

SERVES FOUR

INGREDIENTS
 300g/11oz boneless shin (shank)
  of lamb, diced
 1 rosemary sprig
 4 bay leaves
 salt and ground black pepper,
  to taste
 500g/1¼lb young turnips,
  diced
 100g/3¾oz carrots, diced
 100g/3¾oz potatoes, diced
To garnish
 8 thin slices smoked streaky
  (fatty) bacon
 chopped fresh chervil

4 Dry-fry the smoked streaky bacon in a heavy frying pan until crisp. Remove the bacon from the pan and drain on kitchen paper.

5 Ladle the soup into warm soup bowls, garnish with the chervil and bacon and serve immediately.

1 Put the lamb, rosemary and bay leaves in a large pan, add 1.5 litres/2½ pints/6¼ cups water, season and bring to the boil. Lower the heat, cover and simmer for 3 hours.

2 Remove the rosemary sprig and bay leaves from the stock with a slotted spoon and discard.

3 Add the turnips, carrots and potatoes to the pan, re-cover and simmer for a further 15 minutes, until the vegetables are tender but retain some 'bite'.

COOK'S TIP
For a more sustaining meal, serve this soup with *soldaatjes* (little soldiers), strips of stale bread browned in a frying pan with a little butter.

Per portion Energy 345kcal/1437kJ; Protein 25.3g; Carbohydrate 11.9g, of which sugars 7.8g; Fat 22.2g, of which saturates 8.6g; Cholesterol 94mg; Calcium 77mg; Fibre 3.9g; Sodium 801mg.

TOMATO SOUP <u>WITH</u> MEATBALLS

*ONCE REGARDED AS PEASANT FARE — A WAY OF TRANSFORMING LEFTOVERS INTO A FILLING MEAL —
SOUPS ARE NOW IN A CULINARY CATEGORY OF THEIR OWN. THIS FLAVOURSOME TOMATO SOUP WITH
MEATBALLS AND VERMICELLI IS THE BEST-LOVED ONE BY FAR IN BELGIUM, WHETHER MADE WITH THE
UTMOST SIMPLICITY OR DRESSED UP WITH BRANDY AND CREAM FOR A SPECIAL TREAT.*

SERVES FOUR–SIX

INGREDIENTS
  30ml/2 tbsp vegetable oil
  1 large onion, finely chopped
  2 garlic cloves, crushed
  2 carrots, finely chopped
  2 celery sticks, finely chopped
  1–2 potatoes, peeled and chopped
  800g/1¾lb ripe tomatoes, peeled, or
    2 x 400g/14oz cans chopped tomatoes
  30ml/2 tbsp tomato purée (paste)
  pinch of paprika
  1 litre/1¾ pints/4 cups chicken stock
  20g/¾oz vermicelli (optional)
  salt and ground black pepper
  chopped fresh parsley, to garnish
For the meatballs
  250g/8oz/1 cup minced (ground)
    beef, pork or veal
  1 egg
  pinch of ground nutmeg
  50g/2oz/1 cup soft white breadcrumbs
  salt and ground black pepper, to taste

1 Heat the oil in a large, heavy pan over medium heat. Add the onion and sauté for 5 minutes, until softened but not browned. Stir in the garlic, carrots, celery and potatoes and cook over low heat for 10 minutes, until the vegetables soften.

2 Add the tomatoes and tomato purée, with a pinch of paprika. Stir until the tomato purée has dissolved, then pour in the stock and bring to the boil. Reduce the heat, partially cover the pan and simmer for 30–40 minutes.

3 Meanwhile, make the meatballs. Put the meat in a bowl, then add the egg, nutmeg, breadcrumbs, salt and pepper. Mix with clean hands until the mixture holds together.

4 With damp hands, roll the meat mixture into tiny balls – less than 1cm/½in across – and set aside.

5 Purée the soup, using a hand-held blender or a food processor. Return to the pan, if necessary, and reheat. Season to taste.

6 Add the meatballs, with the vermicelli, if using, and cook for 10 minutes on medium high, until the meatballs are cooked through.

7 Ladle into warm bowls and garnish with parsley. Serve immediately.

VARIATION
Stir in 200ml/7fl oz/scant 1 cup single (light) cream towards the end of cooking, and heat through for 3 minutes. Do not let it boil.

Per portion Energy 251kcal/1051kJ; Protein 13g; Carbohydrate 23.5g, of which sugars 10.9g; Fat 12.4g, of which saturates 3.8g; Cholesterol 57mg; Calcium 58mg; Fibre 3.6g; Sodium 320mg.

WESTLAND TOMATO SOUP

IN HIS CRUYDT-BOECK OF 1554, REMBERT DODOENS DESCRIBED THE TOMATO AS A 'LOVE APPLE' AND REGARDED IT AS AN APHRODISIAC. THE TOMATO WAS DIFFICULT TO CULTIVATE IN THE DUTCH CLIMATE AND REMAINED VERY EXPENSIVE UNTIL THE TECHNIQUE OF GROWING THEM UNDER GLASS WAS DEVELOPED IN THE WESTLAND. EVER SINCE THAT TIME, THIS SOUP HAS BEEN A SATURDAY TRADITION IN THE REGION.

SERVES FOUR

INGREDIENTS
    2kg/4½lb ripe tomatoes, halved
    25g/1oz/2 tbsp butter
    1 onion, finely chopped
    1 leek, finely chopped
    25g/1oz/¼ cup plain (all-purpose) flour
    500ml/17fl oz/generous 2 cups
      hot beef stock
    150ml/¼ pint/⅔ cup milk
    30ml/2 tbsp tomato purée (paste)
    1 bay leaf
    200g/7oz minced (ground) steak
    15ml/1 tbsp soft brown sugar
    50ml/2fl oz/¼ cup whipping cream
    salt and ground black pepper
    chopped fresh basil, chives, parsley
      and celery leaves, to garnish

1 Put the tomatoes in a heavy pan and cook over medium low heat, stirring occasionally, for 10 minutes, until the tomatoes are pulpy.

2 Pass the tomatoes through a food mill or a sieve (strainer) into a clean pan and heat gently, stirring occasionally, until reduced to 1 litre/1¾ pints/4 cups. Remove the tomatoes from the heat and set aside.

COOK'S TIP
This soup is best made in the summer months, when tomatoes are at their most flavoursome and abundant. In other seasons you could substitute fresh tomatoes for two 400g/14oz cans of chopped tomatoes.

3 Melt the butter in a large, heavy pan. Add the onion and leek and cook gently over a low heat, stirring occasionally, for 5 minutes, until the vegetables have softened.

4 Stir the flour into the onion and leek mixture and cook, stirring constantly, for about 2 minutes until just coloured. Gradually stir in the hot beef stock, mixing to combine the flour and liquid thoroughly with each addition.

5 Pour in the milk and add the tomato purée and the bay leaf. Bring to the boil, stirring constantly, and lower to a simmer.

6 Season the minced steak and form into small balls. Simmer for 10 minutes in the pan.

7 Stir in the sugar and cream, then season to taste with salt and pepper. Ladle into soup bowls, sprinkle with chopped herbs and serve.

Per portion Energy 306kcal/1290kJ; Protein 17.2g; Carbohydrate 29g, of which sugars 23.5g; Fat 14.4g, of which saturates 8.9g; Cholesterol 47mg; Calcium 118mg; Fibre 6.4g; Sodium 130mg.

SUNDAY SOUP

THE DUTCH HAVE ALWAYS HAD A STRONG CHRISTIAN CULTURE, AND CHURCH ON SUNDAYS WAS AN ESSENTIAL PART OF THE WEEKLY ROUTINE. WHATEVER YOUR DENOMINATION, THIS SUBSTANTIAL SOUP WAS ALWAYS SERVED FOR DINNER AFTERWARDS, A LUXURY THAT YOU COULD NOT EXPECT ON A WEEKDAY. WHEN COMING HOME FROM SCHOOL ON SATURDAY, CHILDREN WOULD KNOW THAT THE WEEKEND HAD STARTED BECAUSE A POT OF BROTH WAS SIMMERING ON THE STOVE.

3 Remove the beef from the pan, cut the meat off the bone and dice it. Reserve.

4 Strain the stock through a sieve (strainer) lined with dampened muslin (cheesecloth) into a clean pan.

5 Mix together the veal, breadcrumbs and nutmeg in a bowl and season with a generous pinch of salt. Form the mixture into small meatballs.

6 Bring the stock to the boil again, add the meatballs, diced vegetables and vermicelli and cook for 15 minutes, until the vegetables are tender.

7 Add the reserved sliced beef to the pan and warm through. Season to taste with salt and pepper.

8 Ladle into soup bowls, garnish with chopped parsley and serve immediately.

SERVES FOUR

INGREDIENTS
  1 onion
  2 cloves
  400g/14oz shin (shank) of beef
    with bone
  1 bunch of parsley
  bay leaf
  150g/5oz minced (ground) veal
  15ml/1 tbsp breadcrumbs or
    rusk crumbs
  pinch of freshly grated nutmeg
  400g/14oz mixed diced vegetables,
    such as carrots, leeks, green
    beans and cauliflower, or winter
    vegetables such as celeriac and
    Brussels sprouts
  40g/1½oz broken vermicelli
  salt and ground black pepper, to taste
  chopped fresh parsley, to garnish

1 Stud the unpeeled onion with the cloves. Put the beef in a pan, add 1.5 litres/2½ pints/ 6¼ cups water and bring to the boil.

2 Skim off any scum that rises to the surface of the pan. Add the onion, parsley and bay leaf and season with salt and pepper. Lower the heat, cover and simmer for 3 hours.

Per portion Energy 318kcal/1330kJ; Protein 32.4g; Carbohydrate 19.8g, of which sugars 8.4g; Fat 12.4g, of which saturates 5g; Cholesterol 81mg; Calcium 44mg; Fibre 2.7g; Sodium 150mg.

FUNFAIR SOUP

THIS SUBSTANTIAL SOUP USED ALWAYS TO BE SERVED ON SPECIAL OCCASIONS, SUCH AS THE ANNUAL FUNFAIRS THAT WERE SO POPULAR IN THE SOUTHERN PROVINCES OF THE NETHERLANDS. TRADITIONALLY, A HUGE SHIN OF BEEF WOULD BE SERVED ALONGSIDE ROLLED MEAT AND MEATBALLS. FAT YELLOW VERMICELLI AND COARSELY CHOPPED CELERY LEAVES WERE ALSO INCLUDED. SORREL, SPINACH, SALAD, PARSLEY ROOT AND EVEN ASPARAGUS ARE ALL IDEAS FOR FLAVOURING THE SOUP.

SERVES FOUR

INGREDIENTS
1kg/2¼lb boned and rolled meat
250g/9oz lean minced (ground) beef
1 rusk, crushed
2.5ml/½ tsp ground mace
salt
2 onions
1 bouquet garni, consisting of
 1 parsley sprig, 1 sage sprig
 and 1 bay leaf
500g/1¼lb white asparagus
100g/3¾oz vermicelli
1 bunch of celery leaves
To serve
lamb's lettuce (corn salad)
cocktail onions
gherkins
lemon segments
mustard
buttered wholemeal
 (whole-wheat) bread
Dutch brandy (optional)

3 Remove the rolled meat from the pan and leave to cool. Strain the stock through a sieve (strainer) lined with dampened muslin (cheesecloth) into a clean pan. Rinse the meatballs and return them to the stock.

4 Peel the asparagus, then cut into 5cm/2in pieces. Add to the stock and cook for 10 minutes, then add the vermicelli and cook for a further 10 minutes. Finally, add the celery leaves and season to taste with salt.

5 Make a bed of lamb's lettuce on a plate. Cut the cold rolled meat into neat slices and arrange them in the middle of the plate. Put the cocktail onions and gherkins around the rim and garnish with lemon segments.

6 Serve the soup with buttered slices of bread topped with slices of rolled meat, mustard and pickles. Squeeze a drop of lemon juice into the soup and sip brandy between spoonfuls of soup, if you like.

1 Put the rolled meat in a large pan, pour in 2.5 litres/4½ pints/11¼ cups water and bring to the boil. Mix together the minced beef, crushed rusk, mace and 5ml/1 tsp salt and form the mixture into small balls.

2 When the water in the pan comes to the boil, add the meatballs, onions (washed but unpeeled) and bouquet garni and skim off any scum that rises to the surface. Lower the heat and simmer for 2 hours.

Per portion Energy 331kcal/1368kJ; Protein 6.1g; Carbohydrate 18g, of which sugars 3.6g; Fat 26.5g, of which saturates 16.2g; Cholesterol 66mg; Calcium 80mg; Fibre 2.7g; Sodium 108mg.

APPETIZERS

Appetizers in Belgium and the Netherlands are usually quite simple, allowing the flavours of seasonal ingredients such as asparagus or hop shoots to shine through, often accompanied by an egg. Fish and shellfish are the predominant theme, from smoked fish salads and terrines to a range of classics made with the local brown shimps, as well as raw mussels and oysters. Chicken appears in the form of a spiced terrine called Stone Pudding, which is served with pickles and gherkins.

FLEMISH-STYLE ASPARAGUS

MECHELEN IN NORTHERN BELGIUM IS RENOWNED FOR ITS WHITE ASPARAGUS. WITH A UNIQUE, DELICIOUS FLAVOUR, THE VEGETABLE HERALDS THE ARRIVAL OF SPRING AND ITS SHORT SEASON IS CELEBRATED WITH A RANGE OF DELECTABLE SOUPS, APPETIZERS AND OTHER DISHES. WHEN IT IS NOT IN SEASON, GREEN ASPARAGUS CAN BE USED INSTEAD, AS HERE.

SERVES FOUR

INGREDIENTS
16 white or green asparagus spears
115g/4oz/½ cup clarified butter
4 hard-boiled eggs, finely chopped
grated rind and juice of ½ lemon
salt and ground black or white pepper
a handful of fresh parsley, chopped,
    to garnish

COOK'S TIP
Green asparagus seldom needs peeling but white asparagus has a tougher, woodier stem, so removing the tougher skin towards the base improves the texture and lets the stalks cook evenly.

VARIATION
Some cooks prefer to garnish the asparagus with alternate bands of chopped hard-boiled egg yolks – pressed through a sieve (strainer) – and finely chopped whites.

1 Trim the asparagus spears with a knife or snap them so that the tender stalk separates from the tougher base. Soak the spears in a bowl of cold water, refreshing the water a couple of times; this makes the stalks more juicy and easier to peel.

2 Bring a large pan of lightly salted water to the boil. Peel the asparagus if necessary (*see* Cook's tip), and add the spears to the pan.

3 Blanch the asparagus spears for about 5 minutes (depending on the thickness of the stalks) or until they are crisp-tender.

4 Drain the asparagus and pat dry with kitchen paper. Arrange on individual plates or on a serving platter and cover to keep warm.

5 Heat the clarified butter in a frying pan for about 3 minutes, until pale brown. Add the chopped hard-boiled eggs, and season with salt and pepper.

6 Cook the egg mixture for 45 seconds, stirring constantly, to warm through, then add the lemon juice. Pour the mixture over the warm asparagus, sprinkle with the lemon rind and freshly chopped parsley and serve immediately.

Per portion Energy 313kcal/1289kJ; Protein 9.3g; Carbohydrate 2.2g, of which sugars 2.1g; Fat 29.8g, of which saturates 16.6g; Cholesterol 252mg; Calcium 61mg; Fibre 1.7g; Sodium 245mg.

POACHED EGGS ON HOP SHOOTS

Hops are usually associated with beer or beer-making, but in Belgium hop shoots are also a unique regional delicacy. Each year, for just four weeks in March/April, young hop shoots are harvested in the Poperinge area of south-western Flanders. This classic combination of poached egg and hop shoots on toast is a classic, best enjoyed with a Belgian white beer.

SERVES FOUR

INGREDIENTS
   450g/1lb hop shoots or soy
     beansprouts
   20ml/4 tsp salt
   5ml/1 tsp lemon juice
   15ml/1 tbsp white vinegar
   4 eggs
   4 slices wholemeal
     (whole-wheat) bread
   chervil sprigs, to garnish
For the mousseline sauce
   3 egg yolks
   pinch each of salt and ground
     white pepper
   pinch of paprika
   30ml/2 tbsp lemon juice
   100g/3¾oz/scant ½ cup
     unsalted butter
   50ml/2fl oz/¼ cup whipping cream

1 Rinse the hop shoots or soy beansprouts and put them in a deep frying pan with boiling water to cover. Add 15ml/1 tbsp salt and lemon juice and bring to the boil. Blanch for about 5 minutes, until crisp-tender.

2 Drain the hop shoots or beansprouts and prevent them from cooking further by either rinsing them briefly under cold running water or by dunking them in iced water. Drain again and set aside.

COOK'S TIP
Poaching eggs can be intimidating. For best results, use a 25cm/10in frying pan with a lid and fill with water to a depth of about 7.5cm/3in. Put the pan over high heat. Crack each egg into a small cup. When the water boils, add vinegar and salt. Lower each cup in turn so that the lip is level with the water and let the egg glide into the water. Immediately cover the pan with the lid and turn off the heat. Cook for 3 minutes for medium-firm yolks. Carefully lift each poached egg out of the water with a slotted spoon.

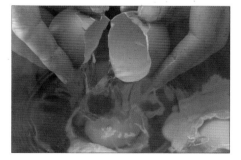

3 To make the sauce, beat the egg yolks, 5ml/1 tsp salt, white pepper and paprika in the top pan of a double boiler. Gradually add the lemon juice, stirring constantly.

4 Add about a third of the butter and cook over simmering water, stirring constantly, until it melts. Repeat with half the remaining butter. As the sauce starts to thicken, stir in the remaining butter and cook until the sauce is smooth and thick. Remove from the heat and leave to cool to room temperature.

5 Fill a wide, deep frying pan with water and bring to the boil. Stir in the vinegar and salt. Poach the eggs (*see* Cook's Tip) for about 3 minutes, until the yolks are just firm.

6 Beat the whipping cream until soft peaks form. Fold it gently into the sauce. Toast the bread and place on warm plates. Divide the hop shoots or beansprouts among the slices of toast and top each portion with a poached egg. Drizzle with mousseline sauce, garnish with the chervil and serve.

Per portion Energy 452kcal/1873kJ; Protein 14.4g; Carbohydrate 15.5g, of which sugars 3.5g; Fat 37.5g, of which saturates 19.7g; Cholesterol 411mg; Calcium 98mg; Fibre 3.2g; Sodium 373mg.

KAMPEN STURGEON

THIS FAMOUS DISH IS FROM KAMPEN, A CITY IN THE EASTERN NETHERLANDS ON THE RIVER IJSSEL. THE STORY GOES THAT THE CITY COUNCIL, PREPARING FOR A VISIT FROM THE PRINCE OF LIÈGE, ORDERED A LOCAL FISHERMAN TO CATCH A FINE STURGEON. WHEN THE PRINCE DID NOT SHOW UP, THEY RELEASED THE FISH BACK INTO THE RIVER WITH A LITTLE BELL AROUND ITS NECK SO THEY COULD TRACE IT WHEN IT WAS NEEDED. NATURALLY WHEN THE PRINCE DID ARRIVE, THE RUSE FAILED AND SO THE CITIZENS OF KAMPEN CREATED THIS IMPROVISED 'STURGEON' RECIPE — WITH NO STURGEON.

3 Using a slotted spoon, remove the eggs from the pan and immediately plunge into cold water. Leave for a few minutes, then remove from the water and shell them with your fingers. Cut each egg in half lengthways.

4 Remove the sauce from the heat, whisk in the mustard and pour it on to a warm, flat serving plate.

5 Arrange the eggs, cut side up, on the sauce, garnish with celery leaves and serve immediately with warm toast and butter.

COOK'S TIP
Don't allow the hard-boiled eggs to stay in the cold water for too long or they may be hard to peel. They should be just warm so the shells come away easily.

SERVES FOUR

INGREDIENTS
  8 eggs
  65g/2½oz/5 tbsp butter
  65g/2½oz/9 tbsp plain
    (all-purpose) flour
  30ml/2 tbsp ready-made brown
    mustard, such as Dijon
  salt and ground black pepper, to taste
  celery leaves, to garnish
  toast and butter, to serve

VARIATION
Finely chop the boiled eggs, keeping the whites and yolks apart. Arrange in rows, alternating chopped yolk and chopped white with a row of finely chopped celery leaves. Cover with a fried fillet of fish. Ladle the sauce over it.

1 Boil the eggs in a small pan of boiling water for 10 minutes.

2 Meanwhile, melt the butter in another small pan over low heat. Stir in the flour and cook, stirring, for 2 minutes, then gradually stir in 600ml/1 pint/2½ cups water. Season with salt and pepper and simmer, stirring frequently, for 5 minutes.

Per portion Energy 325kcal/1350kJ; Protein 14.7g; Carbohydrate 13.5g, of which sugars 0.9g; Fat 24.3g, of which saturates 11g; Cholesterol 412mg; Calcium 88mg; Fibre 0.5g; Sodium 453mg.

MARINATED HERRING

HERRINGS HAVE BEEN A STAPLE FOOD IN THE LOW COUNTRIES FOR CENTURIES. ABUNDANT, VERSATILE AND CHEAP, THEY CAN BE PREPARED AND SERVED RAW, CURED, PICKLED OR COOKED. THE TERM 'ROLLMOP' DESCRIBES A HERRING FILLET THAT HAS BEEN ROLLED AROUND A PIECE OF PICKLED CUCUMBER, FASTENED WITH A SMALL WOODEN STICK AND MARINATED WITH ONIONS AND OTHER FLAVOURINGS IN A VINEGARED BRINE. PARTNERED WITH A RYE BREAD, MAYONNAISE AND A REFRESHING COLD BEER, ROLLMOPS MAKE AN EXCELLENT LIGHT SNACK OR APPETIZER.

SERVES FOUR

INGREDIENTS

    4 unsalted herring fillets, cleaned
      and tails removed
    400ml/14fl oz/1⅔ cups white
      distilled vinegar or white wine vinegar
    15ml/1 tbsp coarse sea salt
      (kosher salt)
    5ml/1 tsp sugar
    2 bay leaves
    4 black peppercorns
    4 cornichons (small pickled gherkins)
    1 onion, thinly sliced rings
    1 lemon, thinly sliced
    rye or wholegrain bread, Mayonnaise
      (*see* page 33) and lemon slices

1 Rinse the herrings under cold water, pat them dry with kitchen paper and set them aside.

2 Bring the vinegar to the boil in a medium non-reactive pan. Add the coarse sea salt, sugar, bay leaves and peppercorns, lower the heat and simmer for 5 minutes. Remove from the heat and leave to cool completely.

COOK'S TIP
If using salted herrings, soak the fish overnight in a bowl of milk to remove the excess salt, rinse and pat dry. If you do not have time to do this, use the salted herrings without soaking them but omit the salt from the vinegar mixture.

3 Place a cornichon widthways on each herring fillet and roll up, using a cocktail stick (toothpick) to hold each rollmop together.

4 Place the rollmops in a clean glass jar, large enough to hold them snugly. Tuck the onion and lemon slices between the herrings.

5 Pour enough of the cooled vinegar mixture over the herrings in the jar to cover them completely.

6 Cover the top of the jar with clear film (plastic wrap) to prevent the vinegar from corroding the lid, then close the jar tightly.

7 Place the jar in the refrigerator and leave for 4 to 5 days for the flavours to develop, shaking the jar gently every day to redistribute the ingredients. Rollmops will keep for about 10 days in the refrigerator.

8 When ready to eat, serve the rollmops with slices of rye bread or wholegrain bread, home-made mayonnaise and lemon slices.

Per portion Energy 94kcal/393kJ; Protein 7.7g; Carbohydrate 3.4g, of which sugars 3.2g; Fat 5.6g, of which saturates 1.4g; Cholesterol 21mg; Calcium 29mg; Fibre 0.2g; Sodium 52mg.

HERRING SALAD

The Dutch love matjes herring, a special type that is produced by gutting and salting the fish at sea immediately after they have been caught. According to legend, the process was invented in the 14th century, but ancient documents prove that the technique was used much earlier. Here they are served with a sweet-and-sour salad.

SERVES FOUR

INGREDIENTS
- 1 lettuce, finely shredded
- 1 shallot, finely chopped
- 15ml/1 tbsp chopped fresh dill
- 15ml/1 tbsp vegetable oil
- 15ml/1 tbsp white wine vinegar
- 2 apples
- 2 cooked beetroots (beet)
- 2 boiled potatoes (optional)
- 15ml/1 tbsp cocktail onions
- 15ml/1 tbsp coarsely chopped
  gherkins, plus 30ml/2 tbsp of the
  vinegar from the jar
- 2–4 hard-boiled eggs, mashed
- 4 matjes herrings, with skin and
  backbones removed
- salt and ground black pepper, to taste
- chopped fresh chives, to garnish

1 Mix together the shredded lettuce, finely chopped shallot, dill, vegetable oil and white wine vinegar in a small bowl and season to taste with salt and pepper. Spread out on a flat platter.

2 Peel, core and dice the apples, then peel and dice the beetroots and potatoes, if using.

3 Mix together the apples, beetroots, potatoes, if using, onions, gherkins and vinegar from the jar in a bowl. Spoon into the middle of a platter. Make a border of mashed egg and garnish with the chives.

4 Cut off and discard the tails of the herrings and halve the fish. Curl the fish over the middle of the dish and serve.

Per portion Energy 315kcal/1323kJ; Protein 21.4g; Carbohydrate 19.5g, of which sugars 18.8g; Fat 17g, of which saturates 1.2g; Cholesterol 137mg; Calcium 58mg; Fibre 2.3g; Sodium 901mg.

SMOKED FISH AND HORSERADISH SAUCE

THIS COMBINATION OF COLD HORSERADISH SAUCE AND SMOKED FISH HAS BEEN A DUTCH CLASSIC SINCE 1795. SMOKED EEL HAS ALWAYS BEEN THE MOST POPULAR CHOICE FOR THIS DISH, BUT IT IS NOW LESS EASILY AVAILABLE BECAUSE IT IS ENDANGERED, SO YOU CAN SUBSTITUTE THE EEL WITH ANY OTHER SMOKED FISH, INCLUDING SMOKED TROUT, AS HERE, OR SALMON.

SERVES FOUR

INGREDIENTS
   300g/11oz smoked trout or other
     smoked fish, cut into strips
   150g/5oz lamb's lettuce (corn salad)
   60ml/4 tbsp cress
   2 radishes, sliced
   30ml/2 tbsp very finely chopped
     fresh parsley
   50g/2oz/½ cup cooked brown
     prawns (shrimp) or other
     small prawns
   8 canned anchovy fillets, drained
   lemon wedges, to garnish
   15ml/1 tbsp grated horseradish
   30ml/2 tbsp mayonnaise
   salt and ground black pepper,
     to taste
   toasted white bread and butter,
     to serve

1 Place the fish in a small dish, add water to cover and soak for 30 minutes. Drain and pat dry with kitchen paper.

2 Divide the lamb's lettuce among four plates. Arrange the cress around the edges of the plates and add the radishes. Place the trout strips in the lamb's lettuce and surround with a ring of parsley and a ring of prawns.

3 Top each plate with two anchovy fillets and garnish with lemon wedges.

4 Mix together the horseradish and mayonnaise in a bowl and season to taste with salt and pepper. Serve with the salad and toast and butter.

Per portion Energy 134kcal/561kJ; Protein 19.5g; Carbohydrate 3.1g, of which sugars 2.7g; Fat 4.9g, of which saturates 0.3g; Cholesterol 30mg; Calcium 89mg; Fibre 1.4g; Sodium 413mg.

TERRINE OF SMOKED LIMBURG TROUT

LIMBURG IS A NARROW STRIP OF LAND ALONG THE RIVER MEUSE AT A CROSSROADS BETWEEN FRANCE, GERMANY, THE NETHERLANDS AND BELGIUM. FAR REMOVED FROM THE INFLUENCE OF THE CAPITAL'S POLITICIANS, THE CITY OF MAASTRICHT WAS AN IDEAL PLACE TO ESTABLISH A POWERFUL BISHOPRIC AND IT WAS THE CATHOLIC CLERGY THAT DETERMINED THE QUALITY OF LIMBURG'S CUISINE. THIS RECIPE, WHICH EVOLVED FROM THIS TRADITION, IS A SPECIAL GIFT FROM REMY MOOREN, THE CHEF AT CASTLE VAALSBROEK IN VAALS, EAST OF MAASTRICHT, WHO CALLS IT 'A PARISH PRIEST'S DELIGHT'.

MAKES NINE SLICES

INGREDIENTS
1 large carrot, thinly sliced
15g/½oz gelatine leaves
500ml/17fl oz/generous 2 cups
  double (heavy) cream
30ml/2 tbsp finely chopped fresh dill
5 smoked trout fillets
salt and ground white pepper, to taste
oakleaf or frisée lettuce, toasted
  white bread and tomato slices,
  to serve

1 Cook the sliced carrot in a pan of boiling water for 10 minutes, until softened. Drain and refresh under cold running water.

COOK'S TIP
A Müller-Thurgau wine from Maastricht's well-known vineyard Apostelhoeve is a good accompaniment to this dish.

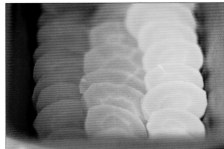

2 Line a non-stick, 6cm/2½in-deep rectangular cake tin (pan) with the slices of carrot.

3 Place the gelatine in a bowl of cold water and leave to soak for 5 minutes, until softened. Meanwhile, bring the cream just to the boil in a small pan, then remove from the heat. Squeeze out the gelatine and dissolve it in the cream. Stir in the dill and season generously with salt and pepper.

4 Pour a layer of cream into the cake tin, place a trout fillet on top and cover with another layer of cream. Continue until all the cream and fish have been used up. Chill for 8 hours or overnight.

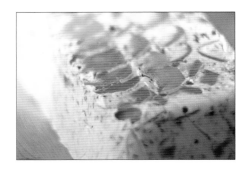

5 About 30 minutes before you are ready to serve, turn out the terrine and cut it into slices. Arrange on a plate and allow to come to room temperature. Garnish with lettuce and tomato slices and serve with toast.

Per portion Energy 348kcal/1437kJ; Protein 13.2g; Carbohydrate 1.9g, of which sugars 1.8g; Fat 32g, of which saturates 18.6g; Cholesterol 76mg; Calcium 38mg; Fibre 0.3g; Sodium 47mg.

SAMPHIRE WITH BROWN SHRIMP

SALICORNIA EUROPEA OR MARSH SAMPHIRE, ALSO KNOWN AS GLASSWORT, GROWS NATURALLY ON THE SALT MARSHES OF THE PROVINCE OF ZEELAND IN THE SOUTH-WEST OF THE NETHERLANDS. BEFORE THE 20TH CENTURY IT WAS REGARDED AS FOOD FIT ONLY FOR POOR PEOPLE AND SHEEP, BUT IT IS NOW A COMMON SIGHT IN FASHIONABLE RESTAURANTS. THE LITTLE STEMS, WHICH LOOK A BIT LIKE A CACTUS, TASTE BEST FRIED IN BUTTER, GIVING THEM A CRUNCHY BITE. THE SALTY TASTE COMBINES SUPERBLY WITH THE SMALL BROWN SHRIMP OR 'CRANGON CRANGON' FROM THE NORTH SEA.

SERVES TWO

INGREDIENTS
- 250g/9oz marsh samphire
- 40g/1½oz/3 tbsp butter
- 2 spring onions (scallions), coarsely chopped
- 100g/3¾oz/scant 1 cup cooked peeled brown prawns (shrimp) or other small prawns
- 15ml/1 tbsp white wine
- white bread slices, to serve

COOK'S TIP
In Zeeland, where this dish originates, a local white wine would be used in the recipe, because early-ripening grape varieties now thrive well there. A good alternative is a Pinot Blanc. Serve the dish with a glass of the same wine.

1 Wash the samphire thoroughly in cold running water, then carefully remove any woody parts, along with pieces of shell and seaweed.

2 Melt the butter in a large frying pan. Add the spring onions and cook them over a low heat, stirring occasionally, for 3–5 minutes, until softened.

3 Add the samphire to the pan and cook, stirring constantly, for 1–2 minutes, until it is just beginning to wilt.

4 Add the prawns (shrimp), increase the heat to medium, and cook quickly until just warmed through. Pour in the white wine, toss lightly and serve immediately with slices of bread.

Per portion Energy 190kcal/785kJ; Protein 2.2g; Carbohydrate 6.7g, of which sugars 6.6g; Fat 16.8g, of which saturates 10.5g; Cholesterol 44mg; Calcium 70mg; Fibre 2.8g; Sodium 132mg.

TOMATOES STUFFED <u>WITH</u> GREY SHRIMP

THIS ELEGANT BELGIAN CLASSIC IS SERVED AT MANY RESTAURANTS AND BRASSERIES IN SUMMER, WHEN TOMATOES ARE ABUNDANT AND AT THEIR PEAK. IT ALSO FEATURES TOP-QUALITY PURUS GREY SHRIMP, WHICH NORTH SEA FISHERMEN HAVE FOR CENTURIES CAUGHT AND COOKED AT SEA. SERVE THIS AS A FIRST COURSE TO WHET THE APPETITE OR AS A SATISFYING LUNCH WITH CRISPY FRIES. AN ICE-COLD LOCAL BLOND ALE WILL BALANCE THE SALTINESS OF THE SHRIMP.

SERVES FOUR

INGREDIENTS

    4 medium unblemished tomatoes
    grated rind of 1 lemon
    15ml/1 tbsp chopped fresh parsley
      or chopped chives
    60ml/4 tbsp Mayonnaise, preferably
      home-made (*see* page 33)
    200g/7oz peeled cooked grey shrimp
      or pink salad shrimp
    salt and ground black pepper, to taste

To garnish
    2 slices of lemon, halved
    4 small sprigs of parsley

To serve
    lettuce leaves or mixed greens
    baby green peas (optional)
    raw or cooked radishes (optional)
    alfalfa sprouts (optional)
    grated carrots (optional)

1 Slice the top off each tomato and set aside as lids. Using a spoon or melon baller, scoop out the flesh and save it for making a soup or sauce. Season the inside of each tomato with salt. Stand upside-down on paper towels to drain.

2 Mix the lemon rind and herbs with the mayonnaise and season to taste. Fold in the shrimp carefully.

3 Carefully spoon the shrimp mixture into each hollowed-out tomato and replace the caps, setting them slightly askew to reveal the filling.

4 Line a platter or individual plates with lettuce, watercress or mixed greens. Arrange the stuffed tomatoes on top and garnish each one with a twist of lemon and a sprig of parsley.

5 Surround the tomatoes with the remaining vegetables, if you like, and serve immediately.

COOK'S TIP
For the best flavour, use vine-ripened tomatoes and ensure they are red all over. They should not be too soft, or they will not hold their shape when stuffed with the shrimp mixture.

Per portion Energy 186kcal/776kJ; Protein 13.2g; Carbohydrate 4.2g, of which sugars 4.2g; Fat 13.1g, of which saturates 2.1g; Cholesterol 76mg; Calcium 182mg; Fibre 1.5g; Sodium 1998mg.

BELGIAN SHRIMP COCKTAIL

THIS FAMILIAR APPETIZER BECOMES A SPECIAL TREAT WHEN MADE BELGIAN-STYLE WITH FRESH GREY PRAWNS FROM THE NORTH SEA AND GARDEN-FRESH TOMATOES AND LETTUCE. LAYERING THE INGREDIENTS WITH THE DECADENT SAUCE IGNITES AN EXPLOSION OF FLAVOURS WHEN A SPOON IS DIPPED INTO THE COCKTAIL. ALTHOUGH TRADITIONALLY SERVED IN A WINE OR COCKTAIL GLASS FOR FESTIVE OCCASIONS, THE SAME COMBINATION OF INGREDIENTS IS OFTEN SERVED ON TOAST AS A LUNCH OR SNACK IN BRASSERIES.

SERVES FOUR

INGREDIENTS
    200g/7oz grey North Sea prawns
        (shrimp) or pink salad prawns,
        cooked and peeled
    2 hard-boiled eggs
    2 small ripe tomatoes
    1 small romaine or cos lettuce
    4 lemon slices and 4 parsley sprigs,
        to garnish
For the sauce
    200ml/7fl oz Mayonnaise
        (*see* page 33)
    30ml/2 tbsp tomato purée (paste)
        or 45ml/3 tbsp tomato ketchup
    15ml/1 tbsp brandy
    15ml/1 tbsp sherry
    pinch of paprika
    5ml/1 tsp Worcestershire sauce
        (optional)
    5ml/1 tsp lemon juice
    45–60ml/3–4 tbsp lightly whipped
        cream (unsweetened)

1 To make the sauce, put the mayonnaise, tomato purée or ketchup, brandy, sherry, paprika, Worcestershire sauce and lemon juice in a small bowl. Whisk gently until smooth. Fold in the cream, cover and chill in the refrigerator until needed.

2 Shell the hard-boiled eggs and cut each in eighths. Peel the tomatoes, if you like. Cut each in eighths. Stack the lettuce leaves, roll them up and shred them thinly.

3 Chill four cocktail glasses. Spoon a little of the cocktail sauce into each glass to cover the base. Add a layer of shredded lettuce and then a few pieces of tomato and egg. Top with prawns and spoon more sauce over to cover. Repeat the layers, finishing with cocktail sauce.

VARIATIONS
• Use scampi (jumbo shrimp) if you prefer. You will need about 20 scampi for the cocktail and 4 scampi, with tails intact, for the garnish. For elegant presentation, place one on the rim of each filled glass, with the tails on the inside.
• If shrimp or scampi are not available, substitute canned salmon or lobster or smoked salmon.

4 Dust each cocktail with some extra paprika. Slit each lemon slice from the rind to the centre so that they can be fitted on the rim of the glasses. Add a parsley sprig to complete the garnish. Serve immediately or put in the refrigerator until ready to use.

Per portion Energy 511kcal/2112kJ; Protein 16.8g; Carbohydrate 5.8g, of which sugars 5.5g; Fat 45.6g, of which saturates 9.8g; Cholesterol 199mg; Calcium 206mg; Fibre 1g; Sodium 2315mg.

MARINATED MUSSELS

LARGE, ULTRA-FRESH CULTIVATED MUSSELS, SERVED RAW ON THE HALF SHELL IN A FLAVOURSOME VINAIGRETTE, ARE A SPECIALITY OF BRUSSELS. THEY ARE PARTICULARLY POPULAR AROUND THE TIME OF BRUSSEL'S KERMIS – ZUIDFOOR, AN ANNUAL SUMMER FAIR IN THE CAPITAL THAT LASTS FOR ONE MONTH, WHEN LOCALS AND VISITORS ARE INVITED TO SAMPLE MUSSELS AND ESCARGOTS AT SEVERAL SPOTS IN THE CITY, TO CELEBRATE THE START OF THE NEW MUSSEL SEASON.

SERVES FOUR–SIX

INGREDIENTS

24 large live mussels, scrubbed
  and bearded
7.5ml/1½ tsp red wine vinegar or
  lemon juice
30ml/2 tbsp vegetable or olive oil
1 shallot, finely chopped
1 spring onion (scallion), finely chopped
1 medium ripe but firm tomato,
  finely chopped
salt and ground white pepper, to taste
30ml/2 tbsp freshly chopped parsley
  and 4–6 lemon wedges, to garnish
crusty bread, to serve

COOK'S TIPS

• Mussels for serving raw must be
bought from a reputable fishmonger
so they are guaranteed to be fresh.
• Marinated mussels can be kept in the
refrigerator for 4 days.

1 Discard any mussels that are not tightly closed, or which do not snap shut when tapped. Holding a mussel between the thumb and index finger of one hand, carefully lever it open from the side with a sharp, short-bladed knife.

2 Carefully insert the knife blade in the cavity of the shell and cut the muscle to which the mussel meat is attached. Work the knife blade around the shell to free the mussel.

3 Put the mussel in a non-reactive bowl. Repeat the process with the remaining mussels. Wash and dry the mussel shells and save them.

4 In a separate bowl, whisk the vinegar or lemon juice with the oil. Season to taste with salt and pepper, then drizzle over the mussels.

5 Add the shallot, spring onion and tomato to the dressing and mussel mixture. Stir gently to combine, then cover with clear film (plastic wrap) and leave to marinate in the refrigerator for at least 1 hour.

6 To serve, arrange half the mussel shells on a large platter and place a marinated mussel on each. Garnish with parsley and lemon wedges and serve with crusty bread.

VARIATION

To make Marinated Cooked Mussels, steam 24 prepared mussels until the shells open. Discard any that remain shut. Remove the flesh from the remaining mussels. Mix together 100ml/3½ fl oz/scant ½ cup white wine, 5ml/1 tsp Tierenteyn or Dijon mustard, 1 chopped shallot, 2 crushed garlic cloves and 15ml/1 tbsp each of chopped fresh parsley and chives. Season, then add the mussels, cover and marinate for at least 1 hour, stirring several times. Spear on cocktail sticks (toothpicks), or put back on to the half shells. Serve with lemon wedges.

Per portion Energy 59kcal/246kJ; Protein 3.5g; Carbohydrate 1.8g, of which sugars 1.1g; Fat 4.3g, of which saturates 0.6g; Cholesterol 11mg; Calcium 14mg; Fibre 0.4g; Sodium 81mg.

OYSTERS GRATIN

OYSTERS ARE A DELICACY IN BELGIUM, EAGERLY DEVOURED BY SEAFOOD CONNOISSEURS ON SPECIAL OCCASIONS, EITHER RAW OR, AS IN THIS RECIPE, AU GRATIN. ALTHOUGH BELGIUM CULTIVATES ITS OWN OYSTERS IN OSTEND, MOST ARE BROUGHT IN FROM FRANCE OR THE NETHERLANDS. THE FRENCH WORD FOR OYSTERS, HUÎTRE, DERIVES FROM THE CONCEPT THAT OYSTERS SHOULD ONLY BE EATEN DURING THE EIGHT MONTHS WITH AN 'R' IN THE NAME: THE WORD 'HUITRE' LITERALLY TRANSLATES AS EIGHT 'RS'.

SERVES FOUR

INGREDIENTS
    24 live oysters
    1 shallot, finely chopped
    1 garlic clove, finely chopped
    15ml/1 tbsp each finely chopped
      parsley, tarragon and chives
    75g/3oz/6 tbsp unsalted
      butter, softened
    5ml/1 tsp brandy
    5ml/1 tsp lemon juice
    salt and ground black pepper, to taste
    lemon slices, to garnish
    triangles of buttered white toast,
      to serve

1 Scrub the oysters under running water to remove loose grit or barnacles. Pull off the beards, if present. Protecting your hand with a towel or heavy glove, hold an oyster firmly, cupped side down, in your palm. Push the tip of an oyster knife into the small gap in the hinge and twist until the hinge breaks and the top shell can be levered off.

2 Slide the knife blade back and forth to cut the abductor muscle and release the oyster from the shell. Try not to puncture the oyster meat. Lift off the top shell, leaving the oyster in its juices in the bottom shell. Repeat with the remaining oysters. Arrange the oysters on a baking sheet. Preheat the grill (broiler) to the highest setting.

3 In a bowl, mix the shallot and garlic with the chopped herbs. Mix in the softened butter, season well, then stir in the brandy and lemon juice.

4 Spread herb butter over each oyster, covering it completely. Place the baking sheet under the grill, at a distance of about 10cm/4in, for 3–4 minutes, until the butter bubbles and the oysters are hot. Serve with buttered white toast.

COOK'S TIPS
• Do not wash the oysters once you have opened them, as flavour would be lost, and the taste would become insipid.
• If you prefer to bake the oysters in the oven, preheat it to 200°C/400°F/Gas 6 and cook for 10 minutes.

Per portion Energy 215kcal/887kJ; Protein 6.8g; Carbohydrate 3g, of which sugars 1g; Fat 19.3g, of which saturates 11.9g; Cholesterol 82mg; Calcium 92mg; Fibre 0.2g; Sodium 443mg.

STONE PUDDING

THE TYPICALLY DUTCH FLAVOUR OF THIS DISH COMES FROM AN INGREDIENT CALLED ROMMELKRUID, *MEANING 'JUMBLE HERBS'. THIS USED TO BE MADE WITH A RATHER UNHEALTHY MIXTURE OF SPICES AND 'SPANISH RED', AN IRON RESIDUE USED TO ENHANCE THE COLOUR. TODAY IT GETS A NATURAL RED COLOUR FROM WOOD EXTRACTS. THIS KIND OF* ROMMELKRUID *IS STILL USED FOR DUTCH GINGERBREAD AS WELL AS FOR MAKING SAUSAGES. MILD PAPRIKA IS A SATISFACTORY SUBSTITUTE.*

SERVES EIGHT

INGREDIENTS

butter, for greasing
500g/1¼lb skinless chicken
  breast fillets
500g1¼lb minced (ground)
  chicken
30ml/2 tbsp breadcrumbs
50g/2oz onion, very finely chopped
15ml/1 tbsp finely chopped
  fresh parsley
15ml/1 tsp mild paprika
salt and ground white pepper,
  to taste
lemon slices, to garnish
gherkins and pickled onions,
  to serve

1 Grease a 1.2-litre/2-pint/5-cup charlotte mould with butter.

2 Thinly slice the chicken fillets horizontally with a sharp knife. Season with salt and pepper and divide the slices into four portions.

COOK'S TIP
Traditionally, the weight used to compress the mould is a foil-wrapped stone, weighing about 1.6kg/3½lb. Ideally the shape of the stone should approximate that of the charlotte mould to evenly distribute its pressure.

VARIATION
You could use minced (ground) veal instead of chicken.

3 Mix together the minced chicken, breadcrumbs, onion and parsley in a large bowl and stir in 5ml/1 tsp salt and pepper. Divide into three portions.

4 Make a layer of one portion of chicken slices in the prepared charlotte mould and top with a layer of one portion of the minced chicken mixture.

5 Carefully sprinkle with 5ml/1 tsp of the paprika, without letting it stick to the sides of the mould.

6 Continue in this way, building layers until all the chicken has been used, ending with a layer of chicken slices.

7 Cover the final layer of chicken slices with a round of baking parchment, one that reaches 2cm/¾in below the rim of the mould, and a layer of foil, and tie it in place with kitchen string.

8 Press down firmly on the mould and place a saucer on top. Place a weight on top of the saucer.

9 Place the mould in a wide pan and add boiling water to reach about three-quarters of the way up the side.

10 Cover and simmer gently for 3 hours. Remove the mould from the pan and leave to cool for 12 hours.

11 Briefly dip the base of the mould in hot water, then invert on to a plate. Garnish with lemon slices and serve with pickles.

Per portion Energy 154kcal/653kJ; Protein 30.9g; Carbohydrate 4.1g, of which sugars 0.5g; Fat 1.7g, of which saturates 0.4g; Cholesterol 88mg; Calcium 20mg; Fibre 0.3g; Sodium 105mg.

SNACKS AND STREET FOOD

Whether bought from a street vendor or eaten in a café with friends, snacks are an integral part of the daily routine in Belgium and the Netherlands. There is a great range of savoury and sweet treats on offer, from open sandwiches, pastries, pancakes, dumplings and the iconic waffles to more substantial meals, such as Vol-au-Vents with Assorted Fillings, Meat Croquettes or Brabant Brawn.

SOUTH HOLLAND CHEESE DIP

THIS DISH IS A PERFECT ONE FOR CHILDREN, AS THE TRADITIONAL WAY TO EAT IT IS SIMPLY TO PICK UP A POTATO FROM THE PAN AND DIP IT INTO THE DELICIOUS SAUCE. TO ACHIEVE AN AUTHENTIC FLAVOUR, YOU NEED TO USE A YOUNG FARMHOUSE GOUDA CHEESE MADE FROM RAW MILK.

SERVES FOUR

INGREDIENTS
　　mixed salad leaves
　　60ml/4 tbsp olive oil
　　30ml/2 tbsp white wine vinegar
　　pinch of sugar
　　500ml/17fl oz/generous 2 cups milk
　　400g/14oz/3¼ cups grated young
　　　Gouda cheese
　　45ml/3 tbsp potato flour
　　75ml/5 tbsp of Dutch brandy
　　pinch of freshly grated nutmeg
　　salt and ground black pepper, to taste
　　500g/1¼lb new potatoes, boiled
　　　and drained to serve

1 Place the salad leaves in a serving bowl. Whisk together the oil, vinegar and sugar in a small bowl and season to taste with salt and pepper. Set aside until ready to serve.

2 Bring the milk just to the boil in a heavy pan and gradually stir in the cheese. Continue to stir over a very low heat until the cheese has melted.

3 Mix the potato flour to a smooth paste with the brandy in a small bowl and stir into the cheese sauce.

4 Cook the sauce on low heat, stirring constantly, for about 5 minutes or until it has thickened. Be careful not to let it stick on the bottom or it will burn.

5 Stir in the nutmeg to the sauce and season to taste with pepper. Transfer the pan to a stand set over a spirit burner (like a fondue).

6 Pour the dressing over the salad and toss lightly. Put the hot potatoes in a bowl. To eat, spear a potato with a fork and dip it into the cheese sauce. Serve with the salad and more brandy, if you like.

VARIATION
Gouda has an especially good texture for this dip, but you could also use Emmenthal, Cheddar, Gruyère or any other melting cheese, although they will all give a different end taste.

Per portion Energy 701kcal/2920kJ; Protein 33.2g; Carbohydrate 36.7g, of which sugars 9.2g; Fat 44.7g, of which saturates 23.5g; Cholesterol 92mg; Calcium 961mg; Fibre 2.4g; Sodium 996mg.

CHERVIL PIE

CHERVIL PIE IS A LONG-ESTABLISHED RECIPE. A SAVOURY PIE SUCH AS THIS TENDS TO BE ASSOCIATED WITH THE FRENCH, AND IS SOMETIMES KNOWN AS QUICHE, BUT THIS RECIPE IS AN UPDATED VERSION OF ONE FROM A DUTCH COOKBOOK WRITTEN IN THE 16TH CENTURY.

SERVES FOUR

INGREDIENTS

40g/1½oz/3 tbsp butter, softened,
   plus extra for greasing
100g/3¾oz/scant 1 cup plain
   (all-purpose) flour, plus extra
   for dusting
100g/3¾oz/scant 1 cup self-raising
   (self-rising) flour
2.5ml/½ tsp salt
100ml/3½fl oz/scant ½ cup
   white wine
beaten egg, for brushing
For the filling
300g/11oz/1⅓ cups fresh
   cream cheese
2.5ml/½ tsp salt
4 large (US extra large) eggs
90g/3½oz/scant 2 cups chopped
   fresh chervil
15ml/1 tbsp chopped fresh chives
15ml/1 tbsp chopped fresh tarragon

1 Preheat the oven to 200°C/400°F/ Gas 6. Grease a 28cm/11in loose-based fluted flan tin (pan) with butter.

2 Sift both types of flour and the salt into a bowl. Stir in the butter and wine with a knife and knead quickly to form a smooth and elastic dough. (You may need to add a little more wine or flour.)

3 Roll out the dough on a lightly floured surface to a 33cm/13in round.

COOK'S TIP
This pastry dough can be used to make many other vegetarian pies.

4 Line the tin with the dough and trim the edge, so that the pastry case (pie shell) is no deeper than 3cm/1¼in. Brush with beaten egg. Place the flan tin on a baking sheet.

5 Beat the cream cheese until smooth, then beat in the salt and eggs, one at a time. Stir in the herbs and spoon the filling into the pastry case. Bake for about 45 minutes, until golden and the filling has set.

VARIATION
To make Fennel and Smoked Cheese Pie, halve 500g/1¼lb fennel bulbs, place them in a pan, add enough water to cover and cook for 30 minutes. Drain well. Leave to cool and then slice. Make the pastry as per the recipe for Chervil Pie, line the flan tin (pan) with the pastry and preheat the oven to 200°C/400°F/Gas 6. Melt 40g/1½oz/ 3 tbsp butter in a frying pan, add 2 sliced leeks and cook over low heat, stirring occasionally, for 5 minutes, until softened. Cover the base of the pastry case (pie shell) with 150g/5oz sliced smoked cheese, and top with the leek and the fennel. Beat 3 eggs with 150ml/¼ pint/⅔ cup whipping cream and 150g/5oz/1¼ cups grated mature (sharp) Gouda cheese in a bowl and pour the mixture into the pastry case. Bake for about 45 minutes, until golden and the filling has set.

Per portion Energy 672kcal/2793kJ; Protein 14.1g; Carbohydrate 39.4g, of which sugars 1.6g; Fat 50.4g, of which saturates 29.1g; Cholesterol 283mg; Calcium 289mg; Fibre 3.1g; Sodium 703mg.

CHEESE PUFFS

To give your guests a special surprise at a dinner party, or simply for a light snack, try making these elegant Dutch cheese puffs as a delicious savoury titbit — these were highly popular in the 1960s and still have an enthusiastic following in The Netherlands.

4 Transfer the dough to a large bowl and beat in the eggs, one at a time, with a hand-held mixer fitted with dough hooks. Continue beating until the dough is smooth and glossy. Add 50g/2oz/½ cup of the cheese and season with nutmeg, salt and pepper to taste. Stir to mix.

5 Using two teaspoons, place 25 walnut-size mounds of the mixture on the prepared baking sheets, spacing them about 5cm/2in apart. Bake for about 20 minutes, until puffed up and light golden brown.

6 Remove from the oven and leave to cool. Cut the puffs open with scissors and fill with the remaining cheese using a teaspoon.

7 Just before serving, heat through in a hot oven for a few minutes. Cheese puffs also freeze well. Reheat from frozen in a preheated oven at 220°C/425°F/Gas 7 for 10 minutes.

MAKES 50

INGREDIENTS
    100g/3¾oz/3 tbsp butter
    250ml/8fl oz/1 cup water
    150g/5oz/1¼ cups plain
       (all-purpose) flour
    4 eggs
    150g/5oz/1¼ cups grated extra-
       mature (sharp) Gouda cheese
    freshly grated nutmeg
    salt and ground black pepper, to taste

1 Preheat the oven to 220°C/425°F/Gas 7. Line two baking sheets with baking parchment if they aren't non-stick.

COOK'S TIP
These are made from choux pastry, which can be temperamental. For best results, ensure you add all the flour at once.

2 Heat the butter, water and salt to taste in a small covered pan over low heat until the butter has melted. Bring to the boil, remove from the heat and tip in all the flour immediately.

3 Return the pan to the heat and cook, stirring constantly, until the mixture comes away from side of the pan and forms a ball. This may take a few minutes.

Per portion Energy 43kcal/181kJ; Protein 1.6g; Carbohydrate 2.3g, of which sugars 0.1g; Fat 3.1g, of which saturates 1.8g; Cholesterol 22mg; Calcium 29mg; Fibre 0.1g; Sodium 40mg.

TOAST FROM PAJOTTENLAND

THE AREA OF PAJOTTENLAND IN BELGIUM IS FAMOUS FOR ITS 'POTTEKEIS', A MIXTURE OF PLATTE KAAS (QUARK OR SOUR CREAM) AND 'BRUSSELSE STINKKEIS' (MEANING 'STINKY CHEESE FROM BRUSSELS'). HERE, THE PLATTE KAAS IS SPREAD ON DARK RYE TOAST, AND SERVED WITH RADISHES AND CHIVES.

SERVES FOUR

INGREDIENTS

4 thick slices dark rye bread
15g/½oz/1 tbsp unsalted
    butter, softened
200g/7oz/scant 1 cup Quark or
    sour cream
45ml/3 tbsp fresh chives,
    finely chopped
1–2 shallots, finely chopped
salt and ground black pepper,
    to taste
8–10 red radishes, to serve

3 Season to taste with salt and ground black pepper, then stir in the finely chopped shallots.

4 Spread a thick layer of the cheese or sour cream mixture on each slice of toasted rye bread. Cover the top with plenty of radish slices, to cover the cheese completely.

5 Season again with salt and pepper to taste. Sprinkle with the remaining chives and serve.

1 Toast the rye bread and spread with the softened butter. Cut the radishes into paper-thin slices.

2 In a bowl, mix the Quark or sour cream with 15ml/1 tbsp of the chopped fresh chives.

COOK'S TIP
Miniature versions of these snacks can be made by cutting the toast into small squares; they make great finger food for serving with drinks. Gueuze or Lambic beers would be especially appropriate.

Per portion Energy 203kcal/845kJ; Protein 4.2g; Carbohydrate 17.3g, of which sugars 5.2g; Fat 13.6g, of which saturates 8.3g; Cholesterol 38mg; Calcium 80mg; Fibre 1.8g; Sodium 190mg.

BOUNCER

This open sandwich made with eggs and beef is a traditional Dutch bar food. The derivation of its name could be because the eggs need to be removed from the pan very quickly, or because it was the last dish any guests could have before they were 'bounced', or asked to leave the bar at closing time. It is seen as a typically Dutch dish, a meal that has been described as good 'blotting paper' to soak up large amounts of beer and Dutch gin. It is certainly a favourite among social drinkers wanting a solid, filling meal.

VARIATIONS
• Cooked veal slices, minced (ground) veal and prawns (shrimp) may be substituted for the boiled ham or roast beef.
• The slices of bread may be fried in butter on both sides until golden before they are topped with the meat. Serve with mustard.
• If you prefer your eggs with crispy brown edges, cook them over a slightly higher heat.
• For a vegetarian bouncer, use slices of young or old Gouda cheese.

SERVES ONE

INGREDIENTS
    25g/1oz/2 tbsp butter, plus extra
      for spreading
    2 slices white bread
    4 slices boiled ham or roast beef
    2–3 lettuce leaves
    1–2 gherkins
    1 tomato, quartered
    2 eggs
    15ml/1 tbsp chopped fresh parsley
    salt and ground black pepper, to taste

1 Spread butter on one side of each slice of bread, then place the bread on a serving plate and cover with the meat of your choice.

2 Arrange the lettuce leaves beside the bread. Cut the gherkin(s) lengthways into several slices, leaving it attached at the top, and then spread out into a fan and place on top of the lettuce with the tomato quarters.

3 Melt the butter in a frying pan until foamy. Slide the eggs into the pan, keeping the yolks intact. Cook over low heat until the whites are just set but the yolks are still runny. This is the classic way to cook *spiegelei*, or fried eggs.

4 Using a slotted fish slice or metal spatula, carefully transfer the fried eggs to the prepared bread, without breaking the yolk. Sprinkle the top with the parsley, season with salt and pepper to taste and serve immediately.

Per portion Energy 593kcal/2481kJ; Protein 37g; Carbohydrate 31.8g, of which sugars 6.5g; Fat 36.6g, of which saturates 17.4g; Cholesterol 492mg; Calcium 173mg; Fibre 2.8g; Sodium 1787mg.

STEAK TARTARE ᴼᴺ TOAST

STEAK TARTARE, AS THIS DISH IS KNOWN ELSEWHERE, IS CALLED FILET AMÉRICAIN IN BELGIUM. IT HAS ALSO BEEN DUBBED 'TOAST KANNIBAAL' OR 'CANNIBALE', A REFERENCE TO THE FACT THAT THE MEAT USED IS RAW. EVERY BUTCHER'S SHOP IN THE COUNTRY PREPARES AND SELLS THIS MIXTURE, WHICH IS USED TO TOP TOAST, AS A SANDWICH FILLING OR SPREAD ON A BAGUETTE FOR THE SNACK LOCALS CALL A MARTINO. THE KEY TO A SUCCESSFUL AND, ABOVE ALL, SAFE STEAK TARTARE IS TO USE ONLY ULTRA-FRESH BEEF OF SUPERIOR QUALITY, AND TO CHOP IT ONLY AT THE VERY LAST MINUTE.

SERVES FOUR

INGREDIENTS
 2 fresh egg yolks
 15ml/1 tbsp Dijon mustard
 15ml/1 tbsp tomato ketchup
 10ml/2 tsp Worcestershire sauce
 Tabasco sauce, to taste
 75ml/5 tbsp vegetable oil
 2 shallots, finely chopped
 30ml/2 tbsp capers, rinsed
 6 cornichons (small pickled
   gherkins), finely chopped
 30ml/2 tbsp finely chopped parsley
 500g/1¼ lb fresh sirloin steak, finely
   minced (ground) or finely chopped
   (*see* Cook's tip)
 4 slices good quality white bread,
   toasted, crusts removed
 15g/½ oz/1 tbsp unsalted butter
 salt and ground black pepper, to taste
For the garnish
 4 lettuce leaves
 16 tomato slices
 4 cornichons
 4 parsley sprigs

1 Place the egg yolks in a large stainless-steel bowl. Add the mustard. With a wire whisk, mix in the ketchup, Worcestershire sauce and Tabasco, with a little salt and pepper. Slowly whisk in the oil until the mixture is smooth.

2 Fold in the shallots, capers, cornichons and parsley with a wooden spatula.

3 Add the chopped or minced meat to the bowl and mix, using a spoon or clean hands. Shape into four patties by hand or use a small round mould.

4 Spread the toasted bread with butter. Place a patty of steak tartare on each slice and press it down to cover the surface evenly.

5 Using a knife, score diamond shapes into the top of the meat. Garnish four serving plates with lettuce leaves and top with the toast. Place four tomato slices alongside.

6 Slice each cornichon lengthways, keeping one end intact, then fan the slices out. Place one fan on each slice of toast and garnish with a parsley sprig. Serve immediately.

COOK'S TIP
The preferred way of preparing the meat is by chopping it very finely with a sharp knife or cleaver. This gives the ideal texture. Alternatively, mince (grind) the steak with a mincer (grinder) fitted with a mesh blade. Don't use a food processor or it will turn it into meat paste.

Per portion Energy 538kcal/2237kJ; Protein 29.7g; Carbohydrate 20.4g, of which sugars 5.5g; Fat 38.3g, of which saturates 12.7g; Cholesterol 184mg; Calcium 84mg; Fibre 1.5g; Sodium 318mg.

VOL-AU-VENTS WITH ASSORTED FILLINGS

LITTLE PUFF PASTRY BASKETS, ALSO KNOWN AS VOL-AU-VENTS, CAN BE PACKED WITH A RANGE OF DELICIOUS FILLINGS, SUCH AS CREAMY CHICKEN FRICASSÉE, TINY MEATBALLS OR PAN-FRIED MUSHROOMS. THEY ARE SERVED AT ALL SORTS OF FESTIVE OCCASIONS IN BELGIUM, FROM SUNDAY LUNCH AND ANNIVERSARIES TO BIRTHDAY PARTIES AND CHRISTENINGS. THEY ARE ALSO STANDARD OFFERINGS ON BRASSERIE MENUS, OFTEN ENJOYED WITH FRIES AND A COLD BEER.

SERVES FOUR–SIX

INGREDIENTS
  1 carrot, halved
  1 onion, quartered
  1 leek, thickly sliced
  2 bay leaves
  1 chicken, 1.3–1.8kg/3–4lb
  1.5 litres/2½ pints/6¼ cups water
  50g/2oz/¼ cup butter
  50g/2oz/½ cup plain
    (all purpose) flour
  200ml/7fl oz/scant 1 cup single
    (light) cream or milk
  1 egg yolk
  30ml/2 tbsp Madeira or sherry (optional)
  juice of 1 lemon
  8 bought or home-made vol-au-vent
    cases (*see* Cook's tip)
  salt and ground black pepper
  fresh sprigs of parsley or chervil,
    to garnish
For a meatball filling
  150g/5oz/⅔ cups minced (ground)
    veal, pork or beef or a mixture
  15ml/1 tbsp fresh soft
    white breadcrumbs
  1 egg
For a mushroom filling
  15g/½oz/1 tbsp butter
  1 garlic clove, finely chopped
  250g/9oz/3½ cups mushrooms, such
    as button (white) or morels, sliced

COOK'S TIP
If you prefer to make your own, smaller vol-au-vents, you will need 450g/1lb puff pastry, thawed if frozen. Roll out the pastry to 5mm/¼in thick and stamp out 16 rounds using a floured 10cm/4 inch cutter. Remove and discard the centres from half the pastry rounds, using a 7.5cm/3in cutter. Place the complete rounds on a baking sheet and brush around the edges with beaten egg, then place a pastry ring on top of each. Chill for ½ hour, then brush with beaten egg and bake at 220°C/425°F/Gas 7 for 15–18 minutes until golden.

1 Put the carrot, onion, leek and bay leaves in a large pan. Place the chicken on top, pour over the water and bring to a gentle boil.

2 Reduce the heat and simmer for about 1 hour or until the chicken is cooked. Lift the chicken out of the stock with a slotted spoon and leave to cool. Save the pan of stock.

3 When the chicken is cool enough to handle, remove and discard the skin and shred the meat from the bones in bitesize pieces. Set this aside to make a chicken filling.

4 To make the meatball filling, mix the minced meat with the breadcrumbs, egg and seasoning. Form into balls 1cm/½in across.

5 Reheat the chicken stock, add the meatballs and cook for 2–3 minutes, until they rise to the surface. Remove from the heat, transfer the meatballs to a bowl, cover and keep hot.

6 To make the mushroom filling, melt the butter in a frying pan over medium-high heat. Add the garlic and cook for 1 minute, until softened but not browned. Add the mushrooms to the pan and cook for 5 minutes more. Season to taste with salt and pepper, cover and keep warm.

7 Preheat the oven to the temperature given on the packet of vol-au-vents or to 220°C/425°F/Gas 7 if using home-made ones.

8 Melt the butter in a heavy pan. Add the flour and cook, stirring, for 1 minute. Gradually add the chicken stock, stirring all the time, then add the cream. Continue to stir for about 8 minutes to make a thick and creamy sauce.

9 Remove the sauce from the heat and stir in the egg yolk. Add the meatballs, mushrooms or shredded chicken with the Madeira or sherry, and lemon juice and heat through. Adjust the seasonings. Remove from the heat, cover and keep warm.

10 Cook the vol-au-vents in the oven for 15–18 minutes or according to the instructions on the packet, until the pastry is golden. Place two vol-au-vents on each plate and spoon in a filling of your choice. Garnish with parsley or chervil sprigs and serve immediately, or the pastry will become soggy.

Per portion Energy 648kcal/2695kJ; Protein 37.8g; Carbohydrate 22.6g, of which sugars 2.3g; Fat46.1g, of which saturates 14.7g; Cholesterol 244mg; Calcium 100mg; Fibre 0.8g; Sodium 345mg.

MEAT CROQUETTES

DUTCH RESTAURANTS AND PUBS SERVE CROQUETTES WITH TWO SLICES OF BREAD AND A SPRIG OF DEEP-FRIED PARSLEY. MOST MEAT CROQUETTES ARE NOW READY-MADE, THE BEST USING GELATINOUS VEAL. FOR A TYPICAL AMSTERDAM CROQUETTE, A GOOD-QUALITY, LIGHT MARGARINE SHOULD BE USED INSTEAD OF BUTTER. THIS IS TO CATER FOR JEWS, WHO CANNOT MIX MEAT AND DAIRY.

MAKES EIGHT

INGREDIENTS

200g/7oz lean veal, cut into pieces
2.5ml/½ tsp salt
40g/1½oz/3 tbsp margarine
1 onion, cut into wedges
1 carrot, halved
1 fresh parsley sprig
1 fresh thyme sprig
1 bay leaf
1 mace blade
6 black peppercorns
250ml/8fl oz/1 cup hot water
25g/1oz/¼ cup plain
   (all-purpose) flour
1 egg yolk
5ml/1 tsp very finely chopped
   fresh parsley
few drops of lemon juice
vegetable oil for deep-frying
salt and ground black pepper, to taste
For the coating
   115g/4oz/2 cups fine breadcrumbs
   2 eggs
   10ml/2 tsp olive oil
For the garnish
   ready-made mustard
   deep-fried parsley sprigs

VARIATIONS
Form the chilled meat mixture into walnut-size balls to make *bitterballen*, or 'bitter balls'. These are part of the *bittergarnituur*, or canapés, served with drinks, mostly iced Dutch gin, around 5 p.m. These include cubes of cheese, sliced sausage and gherkins.

1 Season the veal with the salt. Melt 10g/¼oz/1½ tsp of the margarine, add the veal and cook over medium heat for about 5 minutes, until evenly browned.

2 Add the onion, carrot, parsley, thyme, bay leaf, mace, peppercorns and hot water, bring to the boil, then lower the heat, cover and simmer for 1–2 hours, until the meat is tender.

3 Remove the veal with a slotted spoon, leave it to cool slightly, then dice it finely. Strain the stock into a bowl and reserve 200ml/7fl oz/scant 1 cup.

4 Melt the remaining margarine in a pan over low heat, without allowing it to colour. Stir in the flour and cook for 2 minutes, then stir in the reserved stock. Cook until thickened.

5 Beat the egg yolk with a small ladleful of the sauce in a bowl, then stir the mixture into the pan. Stir constantly for a few seconds until thickened, not allowing the mixture to boil. Remove from the heat.

6 Stir the meat into the sauce, season to taste and stir in the parsley and lemon juice. Spread evenly over a plate, leave to cool and chill for at least 2 hours.

7 Divide the meat mixture into eight portions and shape into cylindrical croquettes with two spoons. Spread out the breadcrumbs in a shallow dish. Beat the eggs with the olive oil in another shallow dish and season.

8 Roll the meat croquettes in the breadcrumbs, dip them in the beaten egg mixture and roll them in the breadcrumbs again. Flatten the ends. Put the croquettes on a plate and chill in the refrigerator until you are ready to cook them.

9 Heat the vegetable oil in a deep-fryer or pan to 180°C/350°F or until a cube of day-old bread browns in 30 seconds. Deep-fry the croquettes in two batches for 5–6 minutes, until chestnut brown. Remove with a slotted spoon and drain on kitchen paper. Serve with mustard and deep-fried parsley.

Per portion Energy 247kcal/1028kJ; Protein 9.3g; Carbohydrate 14.3g, of which sugars 1g; Fat 17.4g, of which saturates 1.7g; Cholesterol 94mg; Calcium 41mg; Fibre 0.6g; Sodium 344mg.

BRABANT BRAWN

IN THE NETHERLANDS, BRAWN (HEAD CHEESE) IS A TERRINE MADE WITH MEAT FROM A PIG'S HEAD, AND IS TRADITIONALLY COMBINED WITH OTHER LEFTOVER PIECES OF FRESH PORK, SUCH AS THE GELATINOUS TROTTERS. NOWADAYS, THE DUTCH WORD FOR THIS RECIPE, KIP-KAP, MEANS 'MINCED MEAT' AND CAN BE ANY SORT OF MEAT. THIS RECIPE USES OXTAIL TO PREPARE THE STOCK THAT BECOMES THE CRYSTAL CLEAR BRAWN THAT IS TYPICAL OF BRABANT, IN THE SOUTH.

SERVES NINE

INGREDIENTS
  1.2kg/2½lb oxtail, cut into pieces
    (ask your butcher to do this, or use
    a meat cleaver)
  2 carrots, scraped
  1 onion, halved
  2 cloves
  bouquet garni, made from thyme,
    rosemary, parsley and bay leaves
  200ml/7fl oz/scant 1 cup red wine
  30ml/2 tbsp red wine vinegar
  10g/¼oz gelatine leaves
  vegetable oil, for greasing
  15ml/1 tbsp chopped fresh parsley
  15ml/1 tbsp chopped fresh chives
  salt and ground black pepper,
    to taste

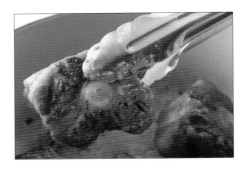

1 Cook the oxtail, in batches, in an open pressure cooker or large pan, without any added fat. Cook over low heat for 5–10 minutes on each side until evenly browned, turning with tongs as required.

2 Add the carrots, onion, cloves, bouquet garni, wine, vinegar and 2.5ml/½ tsp salt and pour in 100ml/3½fl oz/scant ½ cup water.

3 Cover and bring to high pressure, then cook for 2 hours. If using a standard pan, you will need to cook the meat for 4 hours. It should be meltingly tender and falling apart when it is ready.

4 Remove the meat from the pan with a slotted spoon and reserve the stock. Place the cooked oxtail in a sieve (strainer) and rinse under cold water, then drain and leave to cool.

5 Remove the meat from the bones and cut into neat pieces, discarding any sinews. Chill the meat for several hours in the refrigerator.

6 Ladle the stock through a sieve lined with dampened muslin (cheesecloth) into a large bowl positioned underneath. Add enough water to make up the volume to 500ml/17fl oz/generous 2 cups, if necessary.

7 Place the gelatine in a bowl of cold water and soak for 5 minutes.

8 Bring 50ml/2fl oz/¼ cup of stock to the boil, then remove from the heat. Squeeze out the gelatine and dissolve it in the stock. Stir into the rest of the stock, then taste and season if necessary. Chill until set.

9 Brush a 1-litre/1¾-pint/4-cup mould with oil and ladle a thin layer of half-set stock into it. Sprinkle the stock with half the parsley and chives and chill until fully set.

10 Reserve 150ml/¼ pint/⅔ cup of the stock and mix the rest with the chilled meat. Ladle the mixture into the mould and sprinkle the top with the remaining chopped herbs.

11 Stand the reserved stock in hot water for a few seconds until it is liquid, then gently ladle the liquid stock over the herbs. Cover with clear film (plastic wrap) and place in the refrigerator for about 12 hours or overnight, until set.

12 Briefly dip the base of the mould in hot water, then invert on to a plate or board. Cut into thick slices with a sharp knife and serve.

Per portion Energy 163kcal/683kJ; Protein 16.68g; Carbohydrate 2.36g, of which sugars 2.1g; Fat 8.12g, of which saturates 0.1g; Cholesterol 0mg; Calcium 18.7mg; Fibre 0.7g; Sodium 104mg.

HERBED TANSY PANCAKES FROM DIEST

THE MAIN INGREDIENT IN THESE PANCAKES — TANSY — IS A PERENNIAL FLOWERING PLANT. NATIVE TO EUROPE AND ASIA, IT ENLIVENS ANYTHING FROM POTATO DISHES TO PANCAKES, PUDDINGS AND OMELETTES. A SPECIALITY OF DIEST IN THE PROVINCE OF FLEMISH BRABANT, HERBED TANSY PANCAKES ARE MADE IN SPRING, WHEN THE TANSY LEAVES ARE TENDER, AND ARE DELICIOUS SERVED WITH CHEESE.

3 Set a large non-stick frying pan over medium-high heat. When it is hot, grease the inside with butter. Off the heat, pour in enough batter to coat the pan generously.

4 Immediately tilt the pan and swirl the batter to coat the base. Tiny bubbles will form on the surface. Set the pan back over the heat and cook for 1–3 minutes, until the surface looks dry and the edges are lightly browned.

5 Run a wide spatula under the pancake to loosen it. Turn it over and cook for 30 seconds more, until cooked through. Keep warm while cooking four more pancakes in the same way. Serve with slices of cheese.

COOK'S TIP
Stack the cooked pancakes with baking parchment between each to prevent them from sticking. Wrap the package in foil and keep warm until ready to serve.

MAKES ABOUT FIVE

INGREDIENTS
  250g/9oz/2¼ cups plain
    (all-purpose) flour
  2 eggs
  500ml/17fl oz/generous 2 cups
    full-fat (whole) milk
  50g/2oz/¼ cup butter, melted,
    plus extra for greasing
  25g/1oz/½ cup finely chopped
    freshly-picked tansy leaves
    (not larger than 2.5cm/1in)
    or a mixture of dandelions,
    tarragon, parsley and dill,
    finely chopped
  pinch of salt
  a variety of aged cheeses,
    to serve

1 In a large bowl, whisk the flour, eggs, milk, melted butter and a pinch of salt to make a smooth batter. Fold in the chopped herbs.

2 Pour the batter into a jug (pitcher), cover and leave to stand for 1 hour so the flour absorbs more of the liquids.

Per portion Energy 319kcal/1341kJ; Protein 9.6g; Carbohydrate 43.9g, of which sugars 5.7g; Fat 12.9g, of which saturates 7g; Cholesterol 108mg; Calcium 221mg; Fibre 2.1g; Sodium 112mg.

OLD-FASHIONED PANCAKES

PANCAKES, IN DUTCH PANNENKOEKEN, APPEAL TO ADULTS AND CHILDREN ALIKE, AND EVERY PART OF THE WORLD HAS ITS OWN VARIATIONS. THIS EASY-TO-MAKE PANCAKE WAS, AND IS STILL USED AS, AN IDEAL MAIN DISH FOR INFORMAL PARTIES, SERVED WITH A RANGE OF TOPPINGS. IT IS ONE OF THE FIRST RECIPES THAT DUTCH CHILDREN LEARN TO MAKE FOR THEMSELVES.

MAKES EIGHT

INGREDIENTS
    125g/4¼oz/generous 1 cup plain
      (all-purpose) flour
    125g/4¼oz/generous 1 cup
      buckwheat flour
    1 sachet easy-blend (rapid-rise)
      dried yeast
    500ml/17fl oz/generous 2 cups
      lukewarm milk
    1 egg
    15ml/1 tbsp sugar
    5ml/1 tsp salt
    25–40g/1–1½oz/2–3 tbsp butter
    melted butter, golden (light corn)
      syrup, jam or sugar, to serve

2 Melt a little butter in a 20cm/8in pan. Stir the batter and pour a ladleful (about 100ml/3½fl oz/scant ½ cup) into the pan, tilting and turning the pan until the base is evenly covered.

3 Cook the batter until the surface of the pancake is dry and covered with small holes.

4 Run a wide spatula under the pancake to loosen it. Turn it over and cook for 30 seconds more, until cooked through.

5 Slide the pancake out of the pan and keep warm. Cook the other pancakes in the same way, adding more butter to the pan as required.

6 Serve the pancakes with a topping of your choice, such as melted butter, golden syrup, jam or sugar.

1 Sift both types of flour into a bowl, stir in the yeast and make a well in the centre. Gradually pour the milk in, stirring all the time. Beat the mixture to form a smooth batter. Beat in the egg, then stir in the sugar and salt. Cover and leave to rise for 1 hour.

Per portion Energy 179kcal/752kJ; Protein 5.7g; Carbohydrate 30.3g, of which sugars 5.2g; Fat 4.8g, of which saturates 2.5g; Cholesterol 34mg; Calcium 104mg; Fibre 0.8g; Sodium 301mg.

POFFERTJES

THESE SOFT LITTLE PUFFS WERE A TRADITIONAL NEW YEAR'S TREAT IN NORTH HOLLAND, AND ARE KNOWN TO HAVE BEEN EATEN AS FAR BACK AS THE 17TH CENTURY. THEY USED TO BE POPULAR WITH CHILDREN, AND A PAINTING IN THE FRANS HALS MUSEUM IN HAARLEM SHOWS A BOY STEALING ONE. MANY HOUSEHOLDS STILL OWN A POFFERTJESPLAAT, A HOTPLATE WITH ROUND CAVITIES FOR MAKING THEM. THESE ARE TRADITIONALLY ACCOMPANIED BY A CHOCOLATE DRINK.

MAKES 72

INGREDIENTS
200g/7oz/1¾ cups plain
  (all-purpose) flour
50g/2oz/½ cup buckwheat flour
½ sachet easy-blend (rapid-rise)
  dried yeast
300ml/½ pint/1¼ cups
  lukewarm milk
2 eggs
pinch of salt
25g/1oz/2 tbsp butter, melted
To decorate
butter
icing (confectioners') sugar

1 Sift both types of flour into a bowl and make a central well. Pour in the yeast and mix with 15ml/1 tbsp of the milk Cover with a dampened dish towel and leave to stand for 10 minutes.

2 Whisk in half the remaining milk and the eggs using a hand-held mixer fitted with dough hooks. Continue mixing until the batter starts to come away from the bowl. Whisk in the remaining milk and then the salt. Cover the bowl with a dampened dish towel and leave the batter to rise for 1 hour.

3 Heat a *poffertjesplaat*, flat cast-iron griddle or heavy frying pan over medium heat. Brush with melted butter and fill each cavity. Otherwise, dot the mixture on the griddle or pan, spaced well apart. Cook until the top is dry, turn over and cook until no longer sticky.

4 Keep warm while you cook the remaining puffs in the same way, brushing with more butter as necessary. Serve on warm plates with plenty of butter, sprinkled with icing sugar.

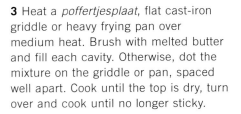

COLD CHOCOLATE DRINK (*FOSCO*)

Mix 50g/2oz/½ cup unsweetened cocoa powder, 150g/5oz/¾ cup sugar, a pinch of ground cinnamon and a pinch of ground cloves to a smooth paste with 5ml/1tsp water. Bring 200ml/7fl oz/ scant 1 cup water to the boil, stir it into the paste and return the mixture to the pan. Cook, stirring occasionally, for about 20 minutes, until reduced to a light syrup. Strain, leave to cool, then chill in the refrigerator. To serve, pour 50ml/2fl oz/ ¼ cup of the syrup into six glasses and stir in 200ml/7fl oz/scant 1 cup milk to each. Sprinkle with cinnamon.

Chocolate drink per portion Energy 217kcal/ 919kJ; Protein 8.5g; Carbohydrate 36.5g, of which sugars 35.5g; Fat 5.2g, of which saturates 3.2g; Cholesterol 12mg; Calcium 264mg; Fibre 1g; Sodium 167mg.
Poffertjes per portion Energy 19kcal/78kJ; Protein 0.6g; Carbohydrate 2.9g, of which sugars 0.2g; Fat 0.6g, of which saturates 0.3g; Cholesterol 6mg; Calcium 10mg; Fibre 0.1g; Sodium 6mg.

THREE-IN-ONE-PAN

COOKING PANCAKES IN A FLAT PAN IS DEPICTED IN MANY DUTCH PAINTINGS, FROM THE 16TH CENTURY ONWARDS. SUCH WORKS USUALLY SHOW A WOMAN COOKING THE PANCAKES, WEARING A SCARF TO PROTECT HER HAIR FROM THE SMOKE. THIS SUBJECT BECAME SO POPULAR THAT IT WAS EVEN IMITATED BY REMBRANDT. PANCAKES USUALLY FILL THE ENTIRE BASE OF THE PAN, BUT IN HIS ETCHING THREE OR FOUR SMALLER PANCAKES ARE BAKED AT THE SAME TIME — AS THEY ARE HERE.

MAKES ABOUT 12

INGREDIENTS
200g/7oz/1¾ cups self-raising
  (self-rising) flour
pinch of salt
250ml/8fl oz/1 cup milk
1 large (US extra large) egg
50g/2oz/scant ½ cup raisins
50g/2oz/¼ cup currants
butter, for frying
caster (superfine) sugar or jam, to serve

1 Sift the flour and salt into a bowl and make a well in the centre. Add the egg and 150ml/¼ pint/⅔ cup of the milk and beat to a smooth batter with a hand-held mixer fitted with dough hooks.

2 Stir in the remaining milk. Stir in the raisins and currants and leave the batter to rest for 30 minutes.

3 Melt a knob (pat) of butter in a 20cm/8in non-stick frying pan over low heat. Drop three heaps of batter into the pan and flatten into rounds.

4 Cook the pancakes for about 3 minutes, until the round tops are dry, puffed and full of bubbles.

5 Turn over the pancakes with a fish slice or metal spatula and cook the other sides for about 1 minute, until they are browned.

6 Remove the pancakes from the pan and keep warm while you cook the remaining batter in the same way, adding more butter as required. Serve hot with sugar or jam.

VARIATION
For an extra fruity texture, add 30ml/2 tbsp finely chopped apple to the batter.

Per portion Energy 208kcal/878kJ; Protein 9.5g; Carbohydrate 28.6g, of which sugars 15.9g; Fat 7.1g, of which saturates 4.2g; Cholesterol 35mg; Calcium 286mg; Fibre 0.7g; Sodium 121mg.

EGG PANCAKES

A QUICKER, MODERN AND MORE LUXURIOUS WAY OF MAKING PANCAKES THAN THAT USED FOR OLD-FASHIONED PANCAKES IS TO USE EGGS AS A RAISING AGENT. WHEN ADDING MORE MILK, THESE CAN BE BAKED THINLY TO SERVE AS A DESSERT CALLED FLENSJES, EATEN WITH SUGAR, JAM OR ICE CREAM.

VARIATIONS
• Cook some thin slices of bacon in a dry frying pan until crisp. Remove from the pan, pour in the batter and return the bacon. Serve with treacle (molasses) or a salad.
• Add apple slices to the batter and serve the pancakes with brown sugar and ground cinnamon.
• Add slices of cheese to the batter and serve with salad.

MAKES 25

INGREDIENTS
400g/14oz/3¼ cups plain
   (all-purpose) flour
5 eggs
1 egg yolk
5ml/1 tsp salt
750ml/1¼ pints/3 cups full-fat
   (whole) milk
25g/1oz/2 tbsp butter

1 Sift the flour into a bowl and make a well in the centre. Add the eggs, egg yolk and salt, mix the eggs and stir, gradually incorporating the flour.

2 Gradually add half the milk and beat to make a smooth thick batter. Gradually stir in the remaining milk. Cover and leave to rest in the refrigerator for 30 minutes.

3 Melt the butter in a 20cm/8in non-stick frying pan, and stir it into the batter. Re-heat the pan and and pour a ladleful into the pan, tilting and turning the pan until the base is evenly covered.

4 Cook the batter until the surface of the pancake is dry and covered with small holes.

5 Run a wide spatula under the pancake to loosen it. Turn it over and cook for 30 seconds more, until cooked through.

6 Slide the pancake out of the pan and keep warm. Cook the other pancakes in the same way. Do not add any extra butter to the pan. Serve the pancakes with a topping of your choice.

Per portion Energy 93kcal/392kJ; Protein 3.9g; Carbohydrate 13.8g, of which sugars 1.7g; Fat 2.9g, of which saturates 1.2g; Cholesterol 50mg; Calcium 65mg; Fibre 0.5g; Sodium 112mg.

APPLE DUMPLINGS FROM ANTWERP

WHOLE APPLES STUFFED WITH BROWN CINNAMON SUGAR AND BAKED IN PASTRY ARE A SPECIALITY OF THE PROVINCE OF ANTWERP. ALONG WITH SAUSAGE BREADS, THEY ARE TRADITIONALLY SERVED ON 'LOST MONDAY', WHICH TAKES PLACE ON THE FIRST MONDAY AFTER THREE KINGS' DAY ON 6 JANUARY.

SERVES FOUR

INGREDIENTS
  500g/1¼lb pack puff pastry,
    thawed if frozen
  50g/2oz/¼ cup sugar
  5ml/1 tsp ground cinnamon
  4 crisp eating apples, such as
    Boskoop, Jonagold, Pippin or
    Granny Smith, peeled and cored
  1 egg mixed with 15ml/1 tbsp water
  icing (confectioners') sugar for dusting
For the filling
  100g/3½oz/½ cup soft light
    brown sugar
  ground cinnamon, to taste
  25ml/1½ tsp cold butter, cut into
    small pieces

1 Roll out the pastry on a floured surface and cut it into four squares, each large enough to wrap an apple easily.

2 Mix the sugar and cinnamon in a bowl and roll each apple in it, to coat.

3 Preheat the oven to 200–220°C/ 400–425°F/Gas 6–7. Place an apple in the centre of each square of pastry.

4 Mix together all the ingredients for the filling and use to stuff the cavities of the apples.

COOK'S TIPS
• The dumplings can be made in advance and baked shortly before serving.
• Cut out leaves or other shapes from the pastry and use egg wash to fix them in place on the dumplings before baking.

5 Brush the edges of the pastry with water, then lift the corners and bring them together in the centre. Pinch the edges of the pastry together with wet fingers, to seal the seams.

6 Place on a baking sheet, spacing them at least 2.5cm/1in apart, and brush with the egg mixture. Bake for 20–30 minutes until the pastry is crisp and golden.

7 Remove from the oven, and leave to cool for 5 minutes. Transfer to individual plates, sift icing sugar over and around the dumplings and serve.

Per portion Energy 659kcal/2768kJ; Protein 9.1g; Carbohydrate 92.1g, of which sugars 47.5g; Fat 32.1g, of which saturates 0.4g; Cholesterol 48mg; Calcium 103mg; Fibre 1.2g; Sodium 409mg.

BRUSSELS WAFFLES

THESE WAFFLES ARE FAMOUS THROUGHOUT THE WORLD, ALTHOUGH THE BREAKFAST FOOD WHICH MANY KNOW AS THE 'BELGIAN WAFFLE' BEARS LITTLE RESEMBLANCE TO THE GENUINE ARTICLE. WHETHER ENJOYED AT ONE OF THE MANY COFFEE OR TEA HOUSES OR SERVED AT HOME AFTER AN AFTERNOON OF 'WAFELEN BAK' (WAFFLE BAKING), THESE LIGHT TREATS ARE ALWAYS SAVOURED. RECIPES VARY, BUT THE BASIC INGREDIENTS REMAIN SIMPLE: FLOUR, YEAST AND EGGS MIXED WITH MILK, BEER OR SPARKLING WATER. YOU WILL NEED A SPECIAL BELGIAN WAFFLE IRON TO MAKE THESE.

4 Beat the egg whites in a clean bowl until stiff peaks form and carefully fold them into the batter.

5 Cover the bowl with clear film (plastic wrap) and leave the mixture in a warm place for 45–60 minutes or until it has doubled in bulk.

6 Preheat a 17 x 9cm/6½ x 3½in waffle iron. Pour in batter to the level recommended in the instruction book (generally about three quarters full) and bake for 4–5 minutes until golden brown. The waffle should be crisp on the outside. Do not open the waffle iron during the first few minutes.

MAKES SEVEN–NINE

INGREDIENTS
  500g/1¼lb/5 cups plain
    (all-purpose) flour, sifted
  pinch of salt
  15ml/1 tbsp easy-blend (rapid-rise)
    dried yeast
  30ml/2 tbsp soft light brown sugar
    or golden caster (superfine) sugar
  5ml/1 tsp pure vanilla extract or
    1 x 8g/⅓oz sachet vanilla sugar
  4 eggs, at room temperature,
    separated, plus 2 egg whites
  500ml/17fl oz/generous 2 cups
    sparkling water, full-fat (whole)
    milk or beer, at room temperature
  200g/7oz/scant 1 cup unsalted
    butter, melted and cooled
  icing (confectioners') sugar, for dusting
  butter or whipped cream and/or
    chopped fruit, to serve

1 Sift the flour and salt into a bowl. Add the yeast, sugar and vanilla sugar, if using.

2 In a separate bowl, beat the egg yolks with the milk or other liquid. Stir in the vanilla extract, if using.

3 Make a well in the dry ingredients and add the egg mixture. Beat, gradually incorporating the dry ingredients to make a smooth batter. Stir in the melted butter.

7 Carefully remove the waffles with a wooden spatula and keep warm while you make more in the same way. Transfer to dessert plates and dust with icing sugar. Serve with butter or whipped cream and/or chopped fruits so guests can add their own topping.

Per portion Energy 444kcal/1856kJ; Protein 8.6g; Carbohydrate 46.8g, of which sugars 4.5g; Fat 26g, of which saturates 15.3g; Cholesterol 149mg; Calcium 96mg; Fibre 1.7g; Sodium 215mg.

LIÈGE WAFFLES

ON A COLD AFTERNOON — OR AT ANY OTHER TIME — THERE'S NOTHING LIKE THE TASTE OF A CRISP, BUTTERY LIÈGE WAFFLE. THESE DELICIOUS SWEET SNACKS ARE SOLD THROUGHOUT BELGIUM. THEIR TEMPTING AROMA WAFTS THROUGH TOWNS AND CITIES AND THERE ARE INEVITABLY QUEUES AT THE MANY STREET STALLS THAT BAKE AND SELL THE DISTINCTIVE ROUND WAFFLES, WRAPPING THEM IN PAPER FOR IMMEDIATE CONSUMPTION. YOU WILL NEED A WAFFLE IRON FOR THESE AND SHOULD START PREPARATION A DAY AHEAD. DUST WITH GROUND CINNAMON, IF YOU LIKE.

MAKES ABOUT TEN

INGREDIENTS
500g/1¼lb/5 cups plain
(all-purpose) flour
pinch of salt
pinch of ground cinnamon
5ml/1 tsp easy-blend (rapid-rise)
dried yeast
½ sachet vanilla sugar or 5ml/1 tsp
vanilla extract
2 eggs, at room temperature
120ml/4fl oz/½ cup lukewarm milk
5ml/1 tsp clear honey
250g/9oz/generous 1 cup unsalted
butter, softened
250–300g/9–11oz/1–1½ cups pearl
sugar (polished sugar crystals)
or loaf sugar crushed into tiny
chunks with a rolling pin

1 Mix the flour, salt, cinnamon and yeast in a large mixing bowl. Add the vanilla sugar, if using.

2 Beat the eggs, milk, honey and vanilla extract, if using, in a bowl or jug (pitcher). Make a well in the centre of the dry ingredients and pour in the liquid. Beat, gradually incorporating the flour mixture to make a stiff batter. Cover and leave to stand for 30 minutes.

3 Beat the butter into the dough, adding a little at a time until all of it has been incorporated.

4 Add the pearl sugar and mix until evenly distributed, then continue to work the dough until it forms a soft, sticky ball. Put it in an oiled bowl, cover and leave overnight in the refrigerator to cold rise.

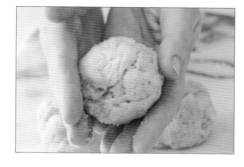

5 Next day, pinch off 100g/3½oz pieces of dough and form these into balls. Heat a waffle iron and brush the grid lightly with butter or oil.

6 Put several dough balls on to the iron, leaving room for them to spread. Cook for about 3 minutes or for the time recommended for your machine. The waffles should be dark brown. Keep each batch hot while cooking the next.

COOK'S TIP
Take care when handling and eating the waffles as the sugar melts and caramelizes, and can easily cause burns.

Per portion Energy 477kcal/2001kJ; Protein 6.6g; Carbohydrate 66.1g, of which sugars 28g; Fat 22.5g, of which saturates 13.6g; Cholesterol 92mg; Calcium 108mg; Fibre 1.6g; Sodium 174mg.

FISH AND SHELLFISH DISHES

An iconic emblem of Belgium, and to a lesser extent the Netherlands, mussels and other shellfish play a key role in the nations' cuisines. Both freshwater and salt water fish are consumed with great gusto, often served fairly simply with plenty of seasonal vegetables. Among the favourites are trout, cod, eel and monkfish, depending on what the fishermen have caught and whether you are on the coast or inland. Preserved herring is enjoyed everywhere in the Netherlands as a snack.

SALMON <u>WITH</u> ORANGE

THIS DISH COULD EASILY HAVE BEEN CREATED IN THE LAST DECADE OF THE 20TH CENTURY, WHEN EVERYONE WAS INSPIRED BY MEDITERRANEAN CUISINE. IN FACT, THE IDEA OF ORANGE JUICE COMBINED WITH FISH WAS INTRODUCED BY A DOCTOR CALLED CAREL BATEN AS EARLY AS 1593. THE IDEA PROBABLY CAME TO HIM VIA SICILY, FROM WHERE THE THEN BITTER ORANGES WERE IMPORTED INTO THE NETHERLANDS. HERE, THE FISH IS POACHED IN WINE AND ORANGE JUICE TO PRODUCE A MOIST, FRAGRANT DISH.

SERVES FOUR

INGREDIENTS
    300ml/½ pint/1¼ cups Rhine wine
    300ml/½ pint/1¼ cups freshly
      squeezed orange juice
    30ml/2 tbsp finely chopped onion
    10ml/2 tsp grated orange rind
    pinch of ground cinnamon,
      plus extra to garnish
    pinch of ground ginger
    pinch of salt
    4 salmon fillets, each about 175g/6oz
    25g/1oz/2 tbsp butter
    2 oranges, thinly sliced, to garnish
    boiled rice, to serve

1 Pour the wine and orange juice into a pan, add the onion, orange rind, cinnamon and ginger and season with salt. Bring to the boil, then lower the heat, cover and simmer for 10 minutes.

2 Add the salmon to the pan, cover and poach gently for 10 minutes, until cooked through.

3 Using a fish slice or metal slotted spatula, transfer the fish to a heatproof dish and keep warm.

4 Bring the cooking liquid back to the boil and cook for a few minutes, until thickened and reduced.

5 Season the sauce with salt to taste, stir in the butter and ladle the sauce over the salmon.

6 Garnish the salmon with thin unpeeled orange slices, and sprinkle with cinnamon. Serve the salmon dish immediately with boiled rice.

Per portion Energy 347kcal/1445kJ; Protein 21.5g; Carbohydrate 12.8g, of which sugars 12.6g; Fat 18.4g, of which saturates 6.5g; Cholesterol 69mg; Calcium 67mg; Fibre 1.2g; Sodium 112mg.

TROUT WITH ALMONDS

THE ARDENNES REGION IN THE SOUTH OF BELGIUM (WALLONIA) IS FAMOUS FOR ITS PICTURESQUE MOUNTAIN SCENERY, DEEP VALLEYS AND COOL, CLEAR, FOREST STREAMS. THIS IS A POPULAR DESTINATION FOR RECREATIONAL FISHING, ESPECIALLY DURING THE TROUT SEASON FROM MID-MARCH TO THE END OF SEPTEMBER. FRESH TROUT IS BEST COOKED SIMPLY, TO BRING OUT ITS SWEET FLAVOUR, AND THIS CLASSIC METHOD OF PREPARATION REMAINS ONE OF THE BEST.

SERVES FOUR

INGREDIENTS

    4 whole trout, cleaned
    8 lemon slices
    30ml/2 tbsp finely chopped fresh
      flat leaf parsley
    30ml/2 tbsp vegetable oil
    100ml/3½fl oz/scant ½ cup
      dry white wine
    115g/4oz/½ cup unsalted butter
    75g/3oz/1 cup flaked (sliced)
      almonds, lightly toasted
    juice of 1 small lemon
    salt and ground black pepper, to taste
    lemon wedges, to garnish

1 Rinse the trout under running water. Pat dry with kitchen paper. With scissors, cut away the fins.

2 Turn each fish in turn on its back and ease open the cavity. Season inside and out and place two lemon slices and a quarter of the parsley in each cavity. Close with cocktail sticks (toothpicks).

3 Heat two 30cm/12in non-stick pans or oval fish pans over medium-high heat and add 15ml/1 tbsp oil to each.

4 Place two trout, skin side down, in each pan and sauté for 4 minutes, then turn over and cook for 3 minutes on the other side. As soon as the flesh becomes opaque and flakes when tested with the tip of a sharp knife, transfer to serving plates. Cover with foil.

5 Using one pan over medium–high heat, pour in the wine and heat for 3 minutes, scraping the pan to incorporate the sediment.

6 Add the butter and a pinch of salt to the wine mixture in the pan. When the butter begins to brown, add half the flaked almonds.

7 Shake the pan over the heat for 5 minutes, taking care not to let the butter burn. When the almonds are golden brown, add the parsley and lemon juice.

8 Spoon the foaming butter and almonds over the warm fish and serve with extra lemon wedges and the remaining toasted almonds sprinkled over the top.

COOK'S TIP
If you prefer to use a thermometer to check that the fish is fully cooked, the interior temperature should be 60°C/140°F.

VARIATION
The trout can be dipped in flour before being fried, to give them a light crust, if you like.

Per portion Energy 475kcal/1978kJ; Protein 39.2g; Carbohydrate 7.6g, of which sugars 0.8g; Fat 32.2g, of which saturates 12.4g; Cholesterol 187mg; Calcium 101mg; Fibre 1.2g; Sodium 249mg.

EELS IN GREEN HERB SAUCE

THE EELS FOR THIS DISH COME MAINLY FROM THE RIVERS SCHELDE AND NETE, CLOSE TO ANTWERP, AND RESTAURANTS ALL ALONG THE NORTH SEA COAST FREQUENTLY FEATURE IT. ALTHOUGH RECIPES VARY, THE SIGNATURE BELGIAN HERBS CHERVIL AND SORREL, AS WELL AS SPINACH AND PARSLEY, ARE ALWAYS USED. THESE ARE ADDED TOWARDS THE END OF THE COOKING TIME SO THEIR FULL FLAVOUR COMES THROUGH.

4 Fry the pieces of eel on both sides for about 8 minutes, until golden, then pour over the wine and enough fish stock to cover.

5 Cover the pan and simmer for about 15 minutes, then lift out the pieces of eel with a fish slice or metal spatula and put them on a plate.

6 Remove the pan from the heat. Add the chervil, parsley and spinach, with the remaining herbs. Blend with a hand-held blender or in a food processor to chop the herbs further.

SERVES FOUR–SIX

INGREDIENTS
  1.6kg/3½lb small river eels, skinned and gutted (ask your fishmonger to do this)
  2 egg yolks
  juice of 1 large lemon
  120ml/4fl oz/½ cup water
  25g/1oz/2 tbsp butter, plus extra for thickening sauce if needed
  2–3 shallots, finely chopped
  1 sprig of thyme
  1 bay leaf
  300ml/½ pint/1¼ cups white wine
  200ml/7fl oz/scant 1 cup fish stock
  50g/2oz/1 cup fresh chervil, chopped
  50g/2oz/1 cup fresh parsley, chopped
  200g/7oz spinach, leaves torn and tough stems removed
  15ml/1 tbsp each of chopped fresh sorrel, mint, sage, savory and tarragon
  salt and ground black pepper, to taste
For the garnish
  30ml/2 tbsp freshly chopped parsley
  4 lemon wedges

1 Rinse the eel and pat dry with kitchen paper, then cut into 5cm/2in lengths. Mix together the egg yolks, lemon juice and water. Set the mixture aside.

2 Melt the butter in a large, heavy frying pan and sauté the shallots for 2–3 minutes over low heat until almost softened.

3 Meanwhile, strip the leaves from the thyme and put them into a mortar with the bay leaf. Crush with a pestle. Rub the mixture into the pieces of eel, then add to the pan. Sprinkle with salt and pepper.

7 Blend in the egg yolk mixture and add a little butter if necessary to thicken the sauce. Return to the pan if necessary.

8 Replace the pieces of eel and warm through over gentle heat. Stir until the sauce thickens but do not let it approach boiling point. Adjust the seasoning,

9 Spoon into a serving dish and garnish with lemon wedges and parsley. Serve warm or cold.

Per portion Energy 290kcal/1213kJ; Protein 32.7g; Carbohydrate 1.9g, of which sugars 1.6g; Fat 13.4g, of which saturates 2.8g; Cholesterol 76mg; Calcium 218mg; Fibre 1.2g; Sodium 183mg.

VOLENDAM EEL STEW

EEL FISHING TYPICALLY TAKES PLACE IN THE IJSSELMEER, OR LAKE IJSSEL, A SHALLOW DIKE-ENCLOSED LAKE IN THE NORTH OF THE NETHERLANDS. VOLENDAM, AN OLD FISHING VILLAGE, IS PARTICULARLY KNOWN FOR ITS EEL, WHICH CAN BE BOUGHT FRESHLY CAUGHT, SMOKED OR BAKED. THIS VOLENDAM EEL STEW WAS ORIGINALLY A FISHERMAN'S MEAL, AS IT WAS EASY TO PREPARE IN THE GALLEY OF SHIPS.

SERVES FOUR

INGREDIENTS

   1kg/2¼lb waxy potatoes, cut
     into pieces
   8 eels, skinned, cleaned and cut
     into pieces
For the sauce
   100g/3¾oz /scant ½ cup butter
   100ml/3fl oz/scant ½ cup white wine
     vinegar
   salt and ground black pepper,
     to taste

1 Peel the potatoes, cut into pieces and put into a large pan. Pour in 400ml/ 14fl oz/1⅔ cups water. Put the pieces of eel on top of the potatoes, cover and cook over very low heat for about 20 minutes, until the potatoes are tender.

COOK'S TIP
To eat, spear the potatoes with a fork and dip them in the sauce. For the eel, it is best to use clean hands to dip the eel in the sauce.

2 Meanwhile, make the sauce. Melt the butter with the vinegar over very low heat and season with salt and pepper.

3 Ladle the potatoes and eels on to warm plates, preferably ones with holes, placed on top of other plates.

4 Transfer the sauce to bowls and place one on each plate. Serve immediately.

VARIATION
In Marken, an island opposite Volendam, they use the following preparation: Pack 500g/1¼lb eel, cut into small pieces upright in a small, rinsed-out pan. Season with black pepper and cook over low heat for about 5 minutes, until the fat starts to run. Add 125g/4¼oz/8½ tbsp butter and a small dash of vinegar. Cover and cook until the liquid has evaporated. Sprinkle the eel with two crushed rusks. Serve with the Volendam sauce mixed with half a crumbled cooked potato. Eat this with your fingers, accompanied by rice porridge sprinkled with sugar.

Per portion Energy 613kcal/2560kJ; Protein 29.3g; Carbohydrate 40.4g, of which sugars 3.4g; Fat 38.3g, of which saturates 17.6g; Cholesterol 278mg; Calcium 48mg; Fibre 2.5g; Sodium 313mg.

FISH GRATIN OSTEND-STYLE

OSTEND, A COASTAL TOWN IN THE FLEMISH PROVINCE OF WEST FLANDERS, IS RENOWNED FOR THE QUALITY OF ITS FISH AND SHELLFISH. THE FISH MINE (DE VISMIJN) AND THE FISH MARKET (VISTRAP) OFFER THE FRESHEST CATCH OF THE DAY, WHICH IS PUT TO GOOD USE BY LOCAL RESTAURANTS WHO FEATURE CLASSIC DISHES LIKE THIS GRATIN.

SERVES FOUR

INGREDIENTS
  400g/14oz firm fish fillets,
    such as monkfish, salmon,
    turbot or cod
  200g/7oz cooked grey shrimp
    or/and shelled cooked mussels,
    or peeled uncooked scampi
    (extra large shrimp)
  1 litre/1¾ pints/4 cups fish stock
  100g/3½oz/scant ½ cup butter
  50g/2oz/½ cup plain
    (all-purpose) flour
  100ml/3½fl oz/scant ½ cup dry
    white wine or dry vermouth
  100ml/3½fl oz/scant ½ cup double
    (heavy) cream
  115g/4oz/1 cup grated cheese
  45ml/3 tbsp chopped fresh parsley
  salt and ground white pepper, to
    taste
  crusty bread or potato croquettes,
    to serve

1 Preheat the oven to 200°C/400°F/Gas 6. Grease a 1.2-litre/2-pint/5-cup baking dish or 4 individual dishes. Cut the fish into even cubes, removing any bones.

2 Bring the fish stock to the boil in a pan. Add the fish cubes, reduce the heat and poach for 2 minutes. If using scampi, poach for 1 minute, until pink.

3 As soon as the fish is cooked, lift it out with a slotted spoon and layer in the dish or dishes.

4 Season to taste and cover to keep warm. Pour the fish stock into a measuring jug (cup).

5 Melt the butter in a pan over medium heat. When it foams, whisk in the flour and stir for 2 minutes.

6 Stirring all the time, add 500ml/17fl oz/ generous 2 cups of the reserved stock in a steady stream, saving the rest to thin the sauce later if necessary. Add the wine or vermouth in the same way. Simmer for 3 minutes, stirring, then add the cream. Season and simmer for 1 minute more.

7 Remove from the heat and add the grated cheese, reserving 45ml/3 tbsp for the topping. Stir in the grey shrimp and/or mussels, with 15ml/1 tbsp of the parsley, and spoon evenly over the fish. Sprinkle with the reserved cheese.

8 Bake for 10–15 minutes, until the cheese melts and turns golden. Sprinkle with the remaining parsley and serve with crusty bread or potato croquettes.

Per portion Energy 612kcal/2541kJ; Protein 36g; Carbohydrate 10.5g, of which sugars 1g; Fat 45.3g, of which saturates 27.9g; Cholesterol 190mg; Calcium 358mg; Fibre 0.4g; Sodium 531mg.

FRISIAN PLAICE

THE HOUSEKEEPER OF A WEALTHY FRISIAN FAMILY FIRST RECORDED THIS RECIPE IN 1772, BUT IT HAS APPEARED IN OTHER BOOKS TOO. THE FRISIANS, FROM THE WEST FRISIAN ISLANDS ON THE NORTH EDGE OF THE COUNTRY, ARE REGARDED BY THE DUTCH AS RATHER UNCOMPROMISING CHARACTERS WITH IDIOSYNCRATIC WAYS, AND THEIR OWN LANGUAGE. THIS REMAINS A POPULAR RECIPE TODAY.

SERVES THREE–FOUR

INGREDIENTS

    1 plaice or flounder, 1kg/2¼lb
    1 carrot, chopped
    1 leek, chopped
    1 branch celery, chopped
    1 bay leaf
    5ml/1 tsp fresh parsley
    50g/2oz/¼ cup butter, plus extra
      for greasing
    juice of 1 lemon
    freshly grated nutmeg
    4 thin lemon slices
    4 coarsely cut sage leaves
    4 rusks, crushed
    salt and ground black pepper, to taste
    chives, to garnish
To serve
    dressed green salad
    crusty bread
    sugar, for sprinkling

1 Cut off the tail and head from the fish with a sharp knife and snip off the fins with kitchen scissors. Remove and discard the gills.

2 Put the fish trimmings and the carrot, leek and celery with the bay leaf and parsley in a large pan, season and add water to cover. Bring to the boil, then lower the heat, cover and simmer for 1 hour. Strain the stock into a bowl and leave to cool.

3 Preheat the oven to 200°C/400°F/Gas 6. Grease an ovenproof dish with butter.

4 Cut the fish into six thick strips and push out the guts. Add the lemon juice to a bowl of water, rinse the fish strips, and pat dry with kitchen paper. Sprinkle with nutmeg and season.

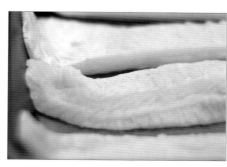

5 Place the strips upright, with the cut sides underneath them, in the dish and tuck the lemon slices in between.

6 Measure 200ml/7fl oz/scant 1 cup of the fish stock and pour it around the fish.

7 Sprinkle with the sage and cover with the crushed rusks. Dot the butter over the top and bake for 20 minutes. Garnish with chopped chives, and sprinkle the salad with sugar, before serving.

Per portion Energy 325kcal/1358kJ; Protein 27.6g; Carbohydrate 21.2g, of which sugars 8.4g; Fat 14.9g, of which saturates 7g; Cholesterol 94mg; Calcium 208mg; Fibre 0.6g; Sodium 259mg.

MONKFISH IN BEER ON A BED OF LEEKS

In Belgium, monkfish is called 'Lotte' or 'Zeeduivel'. The latter means 'devil of the sea' and refers to the ugly appearance of the fish. For a long time, superstitious fishermen believed that this fish brought bad luck and any that were caught were thrown back into the sea. Fortunately, the sweet taste and dense flesh has since gained greater appreciation by Belgian fish lovers. Here it is combined with leeks and beer.

3 Stir in the mustard, if using, and continue to stir while gradually adding the beer or wine to the pan.

4 When the sauce thickens, after about 5 minutes, season it to taste, then scrape it into a baking dish. Level the surface.

5 Arrange the fish fillets on the sauce, and sprinkle over the capers.

6 Cover the dish with foil and bake for about 30 minutes, or until the fish flakes when tested with the tip of a sharp knife.

7 Transfer to serving plates, garnish with the herbs and serve with the potatoes or rye bread, offering the lemon wedges separately for squeezing.

COOK'S TIP
In Belgium, a potato purée is often served with this dish, but boiled or steamed new potatoes or crusty rye bread would also taste delicious.

SERVES FOUR

INGREDIENTS
  4 medium fillets of monkfish
  50g/2oz/¼ cup unsalted butter
  2 leeks, white parts only,
    finely chopped
  25ml/1½ tbsp plain
    (all-purpose) flour
  5ml/1 tsp mustard (optional)
  300ml/½ pint/1¼ cups Belgian
    Abbey beer or dry white wine
  1–2 tbsp capers, rinsed and dried
  salt and ground black pepper,
    to taste
  15ml/1 tbsp chopped fresh chives,
    chervil or parsley, to garnish
  cooked potatoes or rye bread, and
    lemon wedges, to serve

1 Preheat the oven to 180°C/350°F/ Gas 4. Rinse the fish fillets and pat them dry. Season both sides and set aside.

2 Melt the butter in a frying pan over medium heat. Add the leeks and sauté for 3 minutes. Add the flour and stir for 2 minutes until it has been absorbed.

Per portion Energy 268kcal/1125kJ; Protein 33.3g; Carbohydrate 2.6g, of which sugars 2g; Fat 11.6g, of which saturates 6.8g; Cholesterol 55mg; Calcium 65mg; Fibre 2.3g; Sodium 123mg.

FLEMISH-STYLE COD

THIS DISH WAS ONCE AVAILABLE ONLY TO THOSE WHO LIVED NEAR THE SEA. FRIDAY, THE DAY WHEN CATHOLICS EAT FISH, SIGNALLED THE ARRIVAL OF THE FISH MAN IN THE VILLAGES, HIS VAN FILLED WITH THE CATCH OF THE DAY. COD IS ONE OF BELGIUM'S FAVOURITE TYPES OF FISH, AS IT HAS A MILD FLAVOUR AND PLENTY OF DENSE, MEATY WHITE FLESH. HERE, IT IS COMBINED WITH HOEGAARDEN WHITE BEER, A VARIETY FLAVOURED WITH GROUND CORIANDER AND ORANGE PEEL.

SERVES FOUR

INGREDIENTS

90g/3½oz/7 tbsp butter
1 onion or 3 shallots, finely chopped
a handful of chopped fresh parsley
a drizzle of vegetable oil or olive oil
4 cod fillets, each about 175g/6oz
1 bay leaf
300ml/½ pint/1¼ cups white
  beer, such as Hoegaarden, or
  dry white wine
8 lemon slices
4 thyme sprigs
60ml/4 tbsp soft white breadcrumbs
salt and ground black pepper, to taste
To garnish and serve
  chopped fresh parsley
  lemon wedges
  boiled or steamed potatoes

1 Preheat the oven to 180°C/350°F/ Gas 4. Using half the butter, grease a flameproof casserole or a frying pan that can be used in the oven.

2 Add the onion or shallots and parsley. Drizzle with the oil. Transfer the casserole or pan to the oven and cook the onion for about 4 minutes.

3 Season the cod fillets with salt and ground black pepper on both sides. Place on top of the onion and parsley mix. Add the bay leaf and pour in the beer or wine to almost cover the fish. Top each fillet with two lemon slices and a thyme sprig.

4 Return the casserole or pan to the oven and bake for 15–20 minutes, depending on the thickness of the fillets, until the fish flakes when tested with the tip of a sharp knife. Transfer the fillets to a platter, cover with foil and keep warm.

5 Put the casserole or pan over medium heat on top of the stove. Cook for about 5 minutes until the juices have reduced by about three-quarters. Add the breadcrumbs and stir until they have been absorbed.

VARIATION
You can use whichever herbs you prefer: a mixture of parsley, chopped chives and dill works well, or you could add a little tarragon (don't use too much, or it will overwhelm the flavour of the fish).

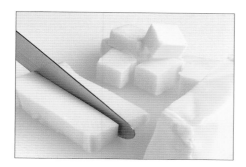

6 Cut the remaining butter into cubes and add to the sauce, a little at a time. Stir until thick and creamy. If it is too thick, add more beer or wine to thin it.

7 Check the seasoning and adjust if necessary. Pour the sauce over the fish. Garnish with parsley and lemon wedges. Serve immediately with the potatoes.

Per portion Energy 407kcal/1695kJ; Protein 27.5g; Carbohydrate 13g, of which sugars 1.4g; Fat 25.3g, of which saturates 12.5g; Cholesterol 111mg; Calcium 44mg; Fibre 0.6g; Sodium 339mg.

DE ACHTERHOEK STOCKFISH

Stockfish is cod that has been dried until it is stiff and hard, similar to salt cod. In the past, it used to be pounded with hammers for 24 hours before soaking, but today you can buy the fish ready to cook from good fish suppliers. In De Achterhoek, in the eastern part of the Netherlands, it was traditionally used as a festive dish for weddings and birthday parties, during fairs and at the end of the rye harvest.

SERVES FOUR

INGREDIENTS
  250g/9oz stockfish
  500g/1¼lb waxy potatoes
  40g/1½oz/3 tbsp butter
  4 onions, sliced
  400g/14oz/3½ cups finely shredded
    red cabbage
  1 tart apple, peeled, cored
    and quartered
  15ml/1 tbsp red wine vinegar
  2 cloves
  pinch of sugar
  salt and ground black pepper, to taste
For the mustard sauce
  25g/1oz/2 tbsp butter
  25g/1oz/¼ cup plain
    (all-purpose) flour
  400ml/14fl oz fish stock
  30ml/2 tbsp Dutch or Dijon mustard

1 Soak the stockfish in a large bowl of cold water for 24 hours, changing the water two or three times.

2 Drain the fish, pull off the skin and remove the bones.

3 Cut the fish into 15cm/6in long strips, then roll up the strips and tie with kitchen string.

4 Bring a pan of salted water to the boil, add the fish rolls and poach for 45–60 minutes, until the fish is cooked through.

5 Cook the potatoes in salted boiling water for 20–25 minutes, until tender.

6 Meanwhile, melt the butter in a large, heavy frying pan with 200ml/7fl oz water. Add the onions and cook over low heat, stirring occasionally, for 10 minutes, until lightly browned.

7 Put the cabbage, apple, vinegar, cloves and sugar in a pan, season with salt and pepper to taste, and cook over medium heat for 20 minutes, until tender.

8 To make the sauce, melt the butter in a small pan over low heat. Stir in the flour and cook, stirring constantly, until lightly coloured.

9 Gradually stir the stock into the sauce and simmer, stirring constantly, for a further minute until slightly thickened. Stir in the mustard.

10 Drain the potatoes. Transfer the fish and vegetables to a warm serving dish. Serve immediately with the sauce in a sauceboat handed separately.

VARIATION
Instead of vinegar, you can add a dash of red wine with a tablespoon of currants to the cabbage at Step 7.

Per portion Energy 440kcal/1846kJ; Protein 28.1g; Carbohydrate 48.8g, of which sugars 20.1g; Fat 16.7g, of which saturates 8.8g; Cholesterol 72mg; Calcium 145mg; Fibre 6.6g; Sodium 376mg.

RED GURNARD WITH ASPARAGUS

MAINTAINING THE STANDARD AND VIBRANCY OF ANY NATIONAL CUISINE INVOLVES MORE THAN REPRODUCING SUCCESSFUL RECIPES OF THE PAST. IT IS ALSO IMPORTANT TO ADAPT TO MODERN TRENDS AND RESEARCH. THIS RECIPE OF GURNARD WITH ASPARAGUS AND CELERIAC SAUCE IS BASED ON ONE BY JONNIE BOER, ONE OF THE MOST CREATIVE CONTEMPORARY CHEFS IN THE NETHERLANDS, WHO RUNS THE RENOWNED RESTAURANT DE LIBRIJE IN OVERIJSSEL IN THE EAST OF THE COUNTRY.

SERVES FOUR

INGREDIENTS
  8 red gurnards, 100g/3¾oz each
  150g/5oz powdered *droge worst* or
    other dried sausage
  30ml/2 tbsp white breadcrumbs
  salt and ground black pepper,
    to taste
For the asparagus
  8 white asparagus spears, trimmed
  15g/½oz/1 tbsp butter
  30ml/2 tbsp lemon juice
For the celeriac sauce
  50g/2oz celeriac, diced
  150ml/¼ pint/⅔ cup fish stock
  50ml/2fl oz/¼ cup double
    (heavy) cream
  50ml/2fl oz/¼ cup sour cream

1 First, prepare the garnish. Peel the asparagus carefully with a vegetable peeler from the tip. Poach gently in boiling, salted water for 10 minutes.

2 Remove the pan from the heat and leave to rest in the cooking liquid for at least 20 minutes, then drain well.

3 Place in a dish, add the butter and lemon juice, season to taste with salt and pepper and keep warm.

COOK'S TIP
Droge worst is a dried pork sausage, heavily flavoured with cloves. It is thinly sliced and dried until crisp in a medium oven, then processed to a powder.

4 To make the sauce, put the celeriac, stock and double cream in a pan and cook for 15–20 minutes, until tender.

5 Transfer the mixture to a blender and process until smooth, then pass through a sieve (strainer) into a clean pan. Bring to the boil, add the sour cream and season to taste. Remove the pan from the heat and keep warm.

6 Preheat the oven to 160°C/325°F/ Gas 3. Cut off the gurnard tails from just behind the last fin. Discard the heads and front parts of the fish.

7 Heat a non-stick frying pan, add the fish, in batches if necessary, and cook until lightly browned on both sides. Remove the fish from the pan.

8 Mix together the powdered sausage and breadcrumbs. Coat the fish with the mixture and place on a baking sheet. The coating will cling better to the fish if you make ten shallow incisions with a very sharp knife on the top side.

9 Bake for 6–12 minutes, until the flesh flakes easily when tested with a fork. Serve immediately with the asparagus and celeriac sauce.

Per portion Energy 489kcal/2043kJ; Protein 44.8g; Carbohydrate 11.2g, of which sugars 3g; Fat 29.7g, of which saturates 11.2g; Cholesterol 55mg; Calcium 218mg; Fibre 1.5g; Sodium 600mg.

ZANDER WITH PARSLEY SAUCE

DURING WORLD WAR II, THE DUTCH WERE ABLE TO BUY FISH WITHOUT COUPONS AS WELL AS CATCH IT FOR THEMSELVES, SO FRESHWATER FISH BECAME A DELICACY IN THOSE TIMES OF HARDSHIP WHEN THERE WAS LITTLE ELSE ON OFFER. RECIPES FOR ZANDER, ALSO KNOWN AS PIKE PERCH, ARE DESCRIBED IN SEVERAL WARTIME COOKBOOKS. THIS VERSION IS INSPIRED BY A POPULAR INTERPRETATION OF THIS RECIPE BY THE CHEF ALBERT TIELEMANS.

SERVES FOUR

INGREDIENTS

    4 zander or pike-perch fillets,
      each about 250g/9oz, head
      and bones reserved
    1 onion
    1 carrot
    1 parsley sprig
    6 black peppercorns
    5ml/1 tsp ground mace
    15ml/1 tbsp chopped fresh thyme
    300g/11oz potatoes, sliced
    300g/11oz celeriac, diced
    200g/7oz carrots, sliced
    200g/7oz mangetouts (snow peas)
    200g/7oz leeks, sliced
    75g/3oz/6 tbsp butter
    50g/2oz/½ cup plain
      (all-purpose) flour
    30ml/2 tbsp milk
    30ml/2 tbsp finely chopped
      fresh parsley
    salt and ground black pepper, to taste

1 Put the fish head and bones in a pan with the onion, carrot, parsley and peppercorns. Add 400ml/14fl oz/ 1⅔ cups water and bring to the boil. Cover and simmer for 20 minutes.

2 Strain the stock into a pan and bring to just below boiling point. Sprinkle the skin of the fish with the mace and thyme and season. Fold the fillets in half, skin side inwards, and tie with kitchen string. Add the fillets to the stock and poach for 10 minutes.

3 Remove the fish from the pan with a slotted spoon. Cut off and discard the string and keep the fish warm. Reserve the stock.

4 Put the potatoes and celeriac into a large pan of boiling water and cook for 15–20 minutes, until tender.

5 Cook the carrots, mangetouts and leeks in separate pans of boiling water, each with 15g/½oz/1 tbsp of the butter, until tender.

6 Drain the potato and celeriac mixture and mash well. Season to taste with salt, then stir in 25g/1oz/2 tbsp of the remaining butter.

7 Spoon the potato and celeriac mash into a piping (pastry) bag and pipe a decorative ring on a serving plate. Place the fish in the middle.

8 Drain the carrots, mangetouts and leeks and arrange between the fish on the plate.

9 Melt the remaining butter in a small pan. Stir in the flour and cook over low heat, stirring constantly, until it is just coloured. Then gradually stir in the reserved fish stock.

10 Continue cooking the sauce, stirring constantly, until it thickens. Stir in the milk and parsley, pour the sauce over the fish and serve immediately.

Per portion Energy 565kcal/2362kJ; Protein 52.1g; Carbohydrate 30.7g, of which sugars 9g; Fat 26.7g, of which saturates 15.5g; Cholesterol 177mg; Calcium 151mg; Fibre 5.8g; Sodium 398mg.

STEAMED MUSSELS WITH CELERY

ONE OF THE BEST WAYS OF PREPARING THIS NATIONAL DISH IS TO SIMPLY STEAM THE MUSSELS IN THEIR OWN JUICES WITH CELERY AND ONIONS: À LA MARINIÈRE OR À LA NATURE. THIS ALLOWS THE DELECTABLE FLAVOUR OF THE MUSSELS TO SHINE THROUGH. IN BELGIUM, THE MUSSELS ARE TRADITIONALLY SERVED IN INDIVIDUAL CASSEROLES WHOSE LIDS CAN BE INVERTED TO MAKE A CONTAINER FOR THE EMPTY SHELLS. FRIES AND PICKLES OR MAYONNAISE MAKE IDEAL ACCOMPANIMENTS.

2 Melt the butter in a large, heavy pan over medium heat. Add the onions. Sauté for 5 minutes until softened and glazed. Add the celery and sauté for 5 minutes more. Add the mussels and season generously with salt and pepper.

3 Cover the pan and place over high heat for 3–4 minutes or until the mussels open, shaking the pan occasionally to distribute the steam.

4 Discard any mussels that have failed to open. Taste the liquid in the pan and adjust the seasoning if necessary, then spoon the mussels and the liquid into bowls or pots.

5 Sprinkle with parsley and serve with fries or crusty bread. Offer pickles, mayonnaise or mustard vinaigrette on the side.

SERVES FOUR

INGREDIENTS
    4kg/9lb live mussels
    40g/1½oz/3 tbsp butter, softened
    2 onions, roughly chopped
    3–4 celery sticks, roughly chopped
    salt and ground white pepper, to taste
    chopped fresh parsley, to garnish
To serve
    Belgian fries (*see* page 191) or bread
    Belgian pickles or Mayonnaise
        (*see* page 33)

VARIATION
Additional flavourings include leek or carrot slices, chopped garlic, thyme and/or bay leaves.

1 Scrub the mussels under cold running water until the shells are shiny black and smooth. Remove any 'beards', if present. If any of the shells are cracked or broken, discard them, along with any mussels that are open and that do not snap shut if tapped.

Per portion Energy 393kcal/1658kJ; Protein 46.5g; Carbohydrate 17.3g, of which sugars 6g; Fat 15.5g, of which saturates 6.2g; Cholesterol 181mg; Calcium 183mg; Fibre 1.9g; Sodium 1048mg.

MUSSEL MEAL

THIS DISH FROM ZEEUWS VLAANDEREN IN SOUTHERN ZEELAND COMBINES THE TASTE FOR FENNEL SHARED BY ALL DUTCH CHILDREN WITH AN ADULT PASSION FOR WINE AND FRENCH PERNOD. THE ZEELAND CUISINE HAS BEEN INFLUENCED BY THE HUGUENOT REFUGEES WHO MOVED THERE IN THE 17TH CENTURY, AND WHO GAVE THEIR LOCAL DISHES A FRENCH TOUCH. THE MUSSELS SHOULD BE EATEN BY PICKING THEM UP WITH AN EMPTY SHELL, AND THEN DIPPING THEM INTO THE SAUCE.

SERVES TWO

INGREDIENTS
  2 fennel bulbs, trimmed
    and quartered
  2 celery sticks, coarsely chopped
  1 onion, coarsely chopped
  1 bay leaf
  1 thyme sprig
  300ml/½ pint/1¼ cups dry
    white wine
  2kg/4½lb live mussels
  15ml/1 tbsp finely chopped
    fresh chervil
  15ml/1 tbsp Pernod
  white pepper
To serve (optional)
  white bread
  gherkins
  mayonnaise flavoured with Pernod
  fries
  winter salad (*see* Cook's tip)

3 Meanwhile, scrub the mussels and remove any 'beards', if present. Discard any mussels with broken shells or that do not shut immediately when tapped.

4 Add the mussels to the pan, season with pepper, cover and cook over high heat, shaking the pan, for 3–4 minutes, until the shells have opened. Remove and discard any mussels that remain closed. Sprinkle with chervil and Pernod.

5 Serve the mussels immediately with white bread, gherkins and mayonnaise flavoured with Pernod. Alternatively, do it the Belgian way and serve the mussels with a generous supply of fries. You can also serve the dish with a winter salad.

VARIATION
The more traditional national way to eat mussels in the Netherlands uses the following recipe: Prepare and cook the vegetables and herbs in 150ml/¼ pint/⅔ cup water or white wine (*see* Step 1), substituting celery leaves and a carrot for the fennel and celery sticks. Then, prepare and cook the mussels (*see* Steps 2 to 3). Serve the mussels from the pan with a selection of mayonnaise sauces flavoured with mustard, tomato purée (paste), chopped herbs, capers or crème fraîche.

1 Put the fennel, celery, onion, bay leaf and thyme in a large, heavy pan, pour in the wine and simmer for about 20 minutes, until tender.

2 Bring the liquid to the boil and cook until reduced by half.

COOK'S TIP
For a winter salad, mix thin strips of carrot in a dressing of two parts olive oil to one part wine vinegar, seasoned with pepper, salt and a pinch of sugar. Toss with sliced iceberg lettuce and strips of red cabbage.

Per portion Energy 179kcal/752kJ; Protein 5.7g; Carbohydrate 30.3g, of which sugars 5.2g; Fat 4.8g, of which saturates 2.5g; Cholesterol 34mg; Calcium 104mg; Fibre 0.8g; Sodium 301mg.

POULTRY AND
GAME DISHES

Chicken, pheasant, partridge, duck, rabbit and venison are
all celebrated in a number of warming and hearty dishes
throughout Belgium and the Netherlands, and hunting is still
a popular pastime. Among the many regional dishes are a
number of roasts, stews and braises, often combined with local
beer and a range of seasonal vegetables, such as Rabbit in
Cherry Beer and Ardennes-style Venison Stew.

CHICKEN WITH FOREST MUSHROOMS

THIS DELICIOUS, EARTHY STEW DATES FROM A TIME WHEN CHICKEN WAS A RARE TREAT IN BELGIUM, AND WAS TRADITIONALLY SERVED IN AUTUMN, WHEN WILD MUSHROOMS WERE ABUNDANT. THE ADDITION OF ABBEY BEER AND A LOCALLY DISTILLED GENEVER MAKE IT EXTRA SPECIAL.

SERVES FOUR–SIX

INGREDIENTS

  1 good quality chicken, about
    1.6kg/3½lb
  15g/½oz/2 tbsp plain
    (all-purpose) flour
  40g/1½oz/3 tbsp butter
  30ml/2 tbsp vegetable oil or olive oil
  3 onions, halved and sliced
  1 garlic clove, crushed
  450g/1lb/6 cups wild mushrooms, sliced
  30ml/2 tbsp Hasseltse genever or gin
  15ml/1 tbsp soft light brown sugar
  30ml/2 tbsp red wine vinegar
  100ml/3½fl oz/scant ½ cup
    chicken stock
  500ml/17fl oz/generous 2 cups
    Abbey beer
  1 bouquet garni (*see* Cook's tip on
    page 144)
  salt and ground black pepper

1 Cut the chicken in four or six pieces and season with salt and pepper. Coat lightly with flour, shaking off the excess.

2 Melt 30ml/2 tbsp of the butter with 15ml/1 tbsp of the vegetable or olive oil in a large, heavy frying pan. Add the chicken and brown on both sides over medium heat for about 10 minutes or until golden. Lift out the chicken and transfer it to a bowl or plate.

3 Sauté the onions in the fat remaining in the pan for 3 minutes or until translucent. Stir in the garlic and mushrooms and fry for about 5 minutes, adding more butter and oil as needed, until the onions are golden.

4 Stir in the genever or gin and cook for 2 minutes more, to reduce slightly. Using a slotted spoon, scoop out the onion mixture and add it to the chicken.

5 Add the sugar and vinegar to the pan and whisk over medium heat for 1–2 minutes or until dissolved. Return the chicken and vegetables to the pan and pour over the chicken stock and beer.

6 Tuck the bouquet garni among the chicken pieces, cover and simmer over low heat for 1 hour, until the chicken falls off the bone.

7 With a slotted spoon, transfer the chicken and vegetables to a heated serving platter. Discard the bouquet garni. Cover the chicken with foil to keep it warm.

8 Skim the fat from the surface of the sauce, then boil it for 5 minutes, until reduced by about one-third. Check the seasoning, pour the sauce over the chicken and serve.

VARIATION
If preferred, the dish can be prepared in a flameproof casserole and baked in a preheated 180°C/350°F/Gas 4 oven for 1 hour. Finish the sauce on the stove.

Per portion Energy 563kcal/2336kJ; Protein 33.2g; Carbohydrate 10.2g, of which sugars 6.6g;Fat 40.9g, of which saturates 12.1g; Cholesterol 174mg; Calcium 44mg; Fibre 1.8g; Sodium 177mg.

GHENT-STYLE CHICKEN STEW

WATERZOOI (MEANING BOILED OR STEWED IN WATER), IS A CENTURIES-OLD SOUP OR STEW THAT IS ASSOCIATED WITH THE CITY OF GHENT. ORIGINALLY PREPARED WITH FISH FROM THE CITY'S NETWORK OF RIVERS AND CANALS, THE CHICKEN VERSION HAS NOW BECOME THE MORE POPULAR CHOICE.

SERVES FOUR–SIX

INGREDIENTS
1 chicken, about 1.6kg/3½lb
chicken stock, to cover the meat
 (*see* method)
2 sprigs of thyme
2 bay leaves
1 clove
10 peppercorns
1 garlic clove, crushed
40g/1½oz/3 tbsp unsalted butter
 or vegetable oil
3 carrots, finely chopped
2 onions, finely chopped,
2 leeks, white part only,
 thinly sliced
¼ celeriac or 2 celery sticks,
 finely chopped
6 small potatoes, quartered
2 egg yolks
200ml/7fl oz/scant 1 cup double
 (heavy) cream
salt and ground black pepper, to taste
pinch of grated nutmeg
lemon juice, for squeezing (optional)
a handful of fresh parsley, chopped,
 to garnish

1 Rinse the chicken and trim off any excess fat. Place the whole bird in a large pot and pour over chicken stock to two-thirds cover. Add the thyme, bay leaves, clove, peppercorns and crushed garlic. Bring to the boil.

2 Reduce the heat, cover and simmer for 1–1½ hours, until the meat begins to fall from the bones. Lift the chicken out of the pan and leave to cool slightly.

COOK'S TIP
Belgian gastronomes rave about *Mechelse koekkoek*, or *Coucou de Malines*, a breed of chicken from Mechelen with a fabulous flavour. This is due to the fact that it doesn't have a true fat layer. Instead, fat stores are distributed throughout the meat, making it juicy and tender. If you can't buy this type of chicken, use any good-quality bird.

3 Remove the skin, take the meat off the bones and cut it into bitesize pieces. Cover and set aside. Skim the fat from the surface of the stock, then pour it into a jug (pitcher) and set aside.

4 Melt the butter in the clean pan. Add all the vegetables except the potatoes and fry over low heat for 10 minutes, stirring frequently, until softened. Pour in the reserved stock and the potatoes, bring to the boil and cook for 10–15 minutes, until the potatoes are tender.

5 Mix the egg yolks and cream in a bowl. Remove the pan from the heat, add the chicken pieces and gradually stir the cream mixture into the stew. Return the pan to the heat and cook, stirring constantly, for 5 minutes, until thickened. Do not let it boil.

6 Season the stew to taste with salt, pepper and grated nutmeg. Add lemon juice if you like. Ladle into bowls, sprinkle with chopped parsley and serve immediately.

Per portion Energy 660kcal/2739kJ; Protein 33.7g; Carbohydrate 16.7g, of which sugars 1.9g; Fat 51.3g, of which saturates 22.7g; Cholesterol 287mg; Calcium 44mg; Fibre 1g; Sodium 187mg.

CHICKEN PIE

THIS DUTCH CHICKEN PIE, KIEKENPASTEY, *WAS TRADITIONALLY A SWEET DISH CONTAINING GINGER, CINNAMON, SAFFRON AND PLENTY OF SUGAR. LATER, THE INGREDIENTS INCLUDED COCKS' COMBS, SWEETBREADS AND CHESTNUTS IN AN OPEN PASTRY CASE. THIS RECIPE HAS BEEN ADAPTED FOR THE MODERN KITCHEN AND IS SERVED AS A SPECIAL TREAT AT EASTER.*

SERVES SIX

INGREDIENTS
  375g/13oz/3¼ cups strong white
    bread flour, plus extra for dusting
  1 sachet easy-blend (rapid-rise)
    dried yeast
  150ml/¼ pint/⅔ cup lukewarm water
  2.5ml/½ tsp sugar
  1 egg, lightly beaten
  50g/2oz/¼ cup butter, softened,
    plus extra for greasing
  5ml/1 tsp salt
For the filling
  1 chicken, about 800g/1¾ lb
  15ml/1 tbsp lemon juice
  50g/2oz/¼ cup butter
  150g/5oz minced (ground) veal
  pinch of freshly grated nutmeg
  300g/11oz pork sausage
  150g/5oz oyster mushrooms, diced
  8 canned artichoke bottoms, drained
  60ml/4 tbsp breadcrumbs
  5 small (US medium) eggs
  60ml/4 tbsp chopped celery leaves
  2 spring onions (scallions), chopped
  100ml/3½fl oz/scant ½ cup
    whipping cream
  milk, for glazing
  salt and ground black pepper
For the sauce
  250ml/8fl oz/1 cup whipping cream
  15ml/1 tbsp cornflour (cornstarch)
  30ml/2 tbsp chopped fresh chives

1 To make the dough, sift the flour into a large bowl and make a well in the centre. Add the yeast and water and mix gently, gradually incorporating all of the flour. Stir in the sugar, cover with a clean dish towel and leave to rise for 15 minutes.

2 Add the egg and butter to the dough and knead. Add the salt and, if necessary, a little more lukewarm water or flour. Turn out the dough on to a lightly floured surface and knead until it is smooth and elastic and does not stick to your hands.

3 Shape the dough into a ball, return to a clean bowl, cover with a dampened dish towel and leave to rise at room temperature for about 1½ hours, until doubled in volume.

4 Make the filling. Cut the chicken into eight pieces and rub with lemon juice, salt and pepper. Melt the butter in a casserole over high heat. Add the chicken, in batches if necessary, and cook, turning often, for 10 minutes, until browned. Transfer the chicken to a plate and remove the casserole from the heat.

5 Mix the veal with the nutmeg, season and form the mixture into small balls. Return the casserole to the heat, add the meatballs and sausage and cook, turning frequently, for 10 minutes, until browned all over. Return the chicken, cover and simmer for 25 minutes.

6 Remove the meat. Reduce the cooking liquid until it sizzles. Add the mushrooms, and cook for 4–5 minutes. Using a slotted spoon, remove them from the casserole. Discard the fat.

7 Cut the chicken meat from the bones and dice. Thickly slice the sausage. Pat the artichoke bottoms dry with kitchen paper and stuff with the mushrooms.

8 Preheat the oven to 200°C/400°F/Gas 6. Grease a 25cm/10in round non-stick springform cake tin (pan). Cut off one-third of the dough, knead it on a floured surface and form into a ball. Set aside. Knead the larger piece; form into a ball.

9 Roll out the larger ball to a 35cm/14in round. Line the tin; the dough may hang over the rim. Roll out the smaller ball to a 25cm/10in round. Using a heart-shaped cutter, stamp out six hearts.

10 Sprinkle the breadcrumbs over the base and put the artichokes on top. Spoon the chicken, meatballs and sausage in between the artichoke hearts. Using a spoon, make five hollows and break the eggs into them. Season, sprinkle with celery and spring onions and pour in the cream.

11 Cover with the remaining dough. Press the edges together and cut off surplus dough. Brush the top with milk, arrange the hearts and brush with milk. Bake for 1 hour. Halfway through, spray with water and cover with baking parchment.

12 For the sauce, heat the cream in a pan. Mix the cornflour with 30ml/2 tbsp water, then stir into the cream. Season and stir in the chives. Carefully remove the pie from the tin, slice and serve with the sauce.

Per portion Energy 982kcal/4093kJ; Protein 39.4g; Carbohydrate 65.3g, of which sugars 3.8g; Fat 64.3g, of which saturates 32.1g; Cholesterol 245.5mg; Calcium 184.8mg; Fibre 3.1g; Sodium 699.8mg.

GRANNY'S CHICKEN

MANY FARMERS MADE THEIR LIVING ON THE FERTILE SOIL RUNNING ALONGSIDE THE BIG RIVERS OF THE NETHERLANDS. THIS DISH, KIP VAN GROOTJE, WOULD HAVE BEEN A TYPICAL ONE IN A FARMING FAMILY, WITH THE WIFE CATCHING A CHICKEN AND HER HUSBAND SLAUGHTERING IT FOR HER. THE CHICKEN IS STUFFED WITH ONION AND LEMON BALM AND SLOW-ROASTED IN A CLAY POT BEFORE BEING SERVED WITH POACHED PEARS AND SLICED POTATOES AND ONIONS FLAVOURED WITH BACON.

SERVES FOUR

INGREDIENTS
   butter, for greasing
   1.2kg/2½lb chicken
   2 onions
   a large bunch of lemon balm, plus
     extra leaves to garnish (optional)
   800g/1¾lb waxy potatoes
   100g/3¾oz/scant ⅔ cup diced
     lean smoked bacon
   salt and ground black pepper
To serve
   1kg/2¼lb red cooking pears
   1 vanilla pod (bean), split in half
   45ml/3 tbsp sugar
   dash of red wine
   45ml/3 tbsp potato flour

1 First, make the accompaniment. Peel the pears and remove the calyx from the base, but leave the stalks on.

2 Place the pears in a heavy pan with the vanilla pod and sugar, add water almost to cover and bring to the boil.

3 Lower the heat, cover and simmer for 1 hour. Add the wine to the pan, re-cover and simmer for a further 2 hours.

COOK'S TIP
Lemon balm, used in this recipe to stuff the chicken, is easy to grow in a herb garden. According to the German medieval abbess Hildegard von Bingen, the herb is not only tasty but also good for your nerves.

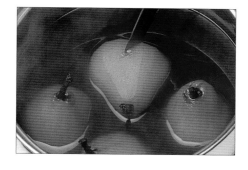

4 Test the pears with a knife to check they are tender. Using a slotted spoon, transfer to a dish, standing them upright.

5 Measure 500ml/17fl oz/generous 2 cups of the cooking liquid, pour it into a clean pan and bring to the boil.

6 Mix the potato flour to a paste with 90ml/6 tbsp cold water in a bowl and stir into the cooking liquid. Cook, stirring, until the liquid starts to thicken, then remove from the heat. Pour the sauce over the pears and cool.

7 To cook the chicken, soak a *tontopf* pot or other unglazed clay pot in cold water for 15 minutes. Dry the inside and grease generously with butter.

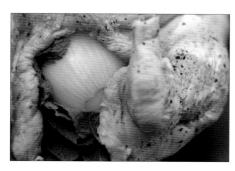

8 Stuff the chicken with the whole onion and lemon balm. Rub with salt and pepper.

9 Place the chicken in the pot, cover with the lid and place in the cold oven. Set the temperature to 240°C/475°F/ Gas 9 and cook for 30 minutes.

10 Meanwhile, chop the remaining onion, slice the potatoes and season with salt and pepper.

11 Remove the pot from the oven and arrange the potato slices around the chicken. Sprinkle the diced bacon and chopped onion on top.

12 Cover the pot and return it to the oven for 45 minutes. Remove the lid from the pot and cook the chicken for a further 5–10 minutes, until browned.

13 Serve the chicken straight from the pot or transfer it to a serving platter. Garnish with lemon balm leaves, if you like, and hand the poached pears around separately.

Per portion Energy 829kcal/3466kJ; Protein 47.4g; Carbohydrate 79.2g, of which sugars 40.2g; Fat 37.3g, of which saturates 11.1g; Cholesterol 213mg; Calcium 69mg; Fibre 7.9g; Sodium 573mg.

BRABANT-STYLE PHEASANT

In the Middle Ages, when hunting was a favourite pursuit of the wealthy and game was reserved for nobles, pheasant tended to be served only at upper class tables. Today, the bird has wider appeal and dishes like this one often feature on gastronomic menus in the Ardennes, especially during the shooting season in autumn. Wild pheasants are the best option, but farmed birds, which have a less gamey flavour, can be used instead.

SERVES FOUR

INGREDIENTS
15ml/1 tbsp vegetable oil, plus extra
  for greasing
2 young pheasants, cleaned and
  pan ready
115g/4oz/½ cup butter
200g/7oz bacon slices
8 Belgian endives (chicory),
  cores and any tough outer
  leaves removed
pinch of sugar
salt and ground black pepper
celeriac or parsnip purée, to serve

1 Preheat the oven to 180°C/350°F/
Gas 4. Grease a roasting pan lightly with
oil. Season the pheasants generously
inside and out with salt and ground
black pepper. Put 2.5ml/½ tsp butter
in the cavity of each bird.

2 Heat 60ml/4 tbsp of the remaining
butter with the oil in a heavy frying
pan that is large enough to hold both
pheasants. Add the birds, placing them
on their sides. Fry over medium heat for
about 10 minutes, turning the pheasants
until they are golden brown on all sides.

COOK'S TIPS
• Wrapping the pheasant in bacon will
help to keep it moist while roasting.
• If you wish to test the pheasants with
a meat thermometer, the internal
temperature when they are cooked
should be 65°C/149°C.

3 Lift out the birds and set the pan
aside. When the birds are cool enough
to handle, wrap them in bacon, tying it
on with kitchen string (twine).

4 Put the pheasants in the greased
roasting pan, cover with foil or a lid,
and roast in the oven for 45 minutes.

5 Meanwhile, return the frying pan
to the heat, reheat the fat, then add
the endives in a single layer. Pour in
enough water to come halfway up the
endives. Dot with 5ml/1 tsp butter and
season with salt and pepper. Bring to
the boil, reduce the heat, cover and
simmer for 20 minutes.

6 Using tongs, turn the endives over,
replace the lid and simmer for a further
15–20 minutes, until tender.

7 When the pheasants are cooked,
transfer them on to a chopping board.
Slit the string, remove the bacon and
set it aside, then cover the birds with
foil and leave to rest for 10 minutes.

8 Lift the endives out of the frying pan
and put them on a plate. Pour their
cooking liquid into the roasting pan.
Place the pan over medium-high heat
and boil the liquid, stirring frequently,
for 8 minutes.

9 Meanwhile, return the endives to
the frying pan, sprinkle with the sugar
and cook until the endives are
caramelized on both sides.

10 Add the remaining butter to the
reduced sauce in the roasting pan and
stir over the heat for 4 minutes or until
it thickens. The reserved bacon can be
chopped or crumbled and added to the
sauce, if you like.

11 Carve the birds and arrange on a
platter. Arrange the endives around the
meat and spoon the sauce over. Serve
with the celeriac or parsnip purée.

Per portion Energy 896kcal/3738kJ; Protein 90.4g; Carbohydrate 1.9g, of which sugars 1.9g; Fat 58.7g, of which saturates 26.5g; Cholesterol 88mg; Calcium 160mg; Fibre 0.9g; Sodium 1211mg.

GUELDERS GOOSE BOARD

IN THE NETHERLANDS, GEESE WERE ALWAYS RAISED FOR CHRISTMAS DINNER AND WERE ESPECIALLY ASSOCIATED WITH THE PROVINCE OF GELDERLAND, WHERE THIS DISH OF MARINATED ROASTED GOOSE AND ALL THE TRIMMINGS COMES FROM. THOSE WHO WERE TOO POOR WOULD BUY A RAFFLE TICKET IN THE LOCAL BAR OR BUTCHER'S TO TRY TO WIN A BIRD. AFTER ITS SLAUGHTER, ITS HEAD WAS NAILED TO THE WALL AND, WHEN EVERYONE HAD EATEN, THEY WOULD CALL OUT, 'THANK YOU MOTHER GOOSE!'

SERVES FOUR

INGREDIENTS
    4 goose legs, halved
    75ml/5 tbsp brandy
    30ml/2 tbsp lemon juice
    5ml/1 tsp grated lemon rind
    salt and ground black pepper
For the sauce
    30ml/2 tbsp plain (all-purpose) flour
    200ml/7fl oz/scant 1 cup chicken
      stock
To serve
    12 pitted prunes
    45ml/3 tbsp brandy
    450g/1lb can chestnuts purée
    15–30ml/1–2 tbsp whipping cream
    400g/14oz Brussels sprouts, trimmed
    12 shelled walnuts
    salt

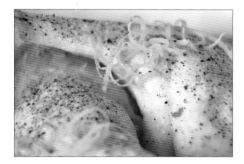

1 Place the halved goose legs in a non-metallic dish. Mix together the brandy, lemon juice and rind in a bowl, season with pepper and pour over the legs, turning to coat. Cover and marinate in the refrigerator for 12 hours.

2 Meanwhile place the prunes for the accompaniments in a bowl, pour in the brandy and leave to soak.

MENU IDEAS FOR A DUTCH CHRISTMAS FEAST:
First course: Queen's Soup
Main course: Guelders Goose Board
Dessert: mature (sharp) Gouda cheese, followed by Bavarois with Candied Fruit
Wine: St Émilion

3 Pat the goose legs dry with kitchen paper. Reserve the marinade. Rub the legs with salt and cook in a dry frying pan over medium heat, turning often, for 10 minutes, until browned.

4 Lower the heat, partially cover the pan and cook the goose for about 2 hours, until the juices run clear when the thickest part of the legs is pierced with the point of a knife. Transfer to a plate, cover and keep warm. Reserve the pan of goose fat.

5 To make the garnish, mix the chestnut purée with 15ml/1 tbsp of the reserved goose fat and the cream in a pan and season with salt. Cook over low heat, stirring frequently, until smooth.

6 Meanwhile, cook the trimmed Brussels sprouts in a pan of boiling water for 3–5 minutes, until tender-crisp. Drain and keep warm.

7 Drain the prunes, reserving the brandy, and stuff with the walnuts.

8 To make the sauce, drain off all but 60ml/4 tbsp of the goose fat from the pan. (You could store the remainder in the refrigerator for roasting potatoes, if you like.)

9 Heat the fat in the pan, stir in the flour and cook, stirring constantly, until lightly browned. Gradually stir in the chicken stock and reserved marinade and simmer gently, stirring frequently, for 10 minutes. Finally, stir in the reserved brandy.

10 To serve, spoon the chestnut purée mixture into a piping (pastry) bag and pipe neat mounds around the rim of a large serving plate. Place the prunes in between the purée and the Brussels sprouts in the middle. Arrange the legs on top and spoon a little of the sauce over them. Serve immediately, with the remaining sauce in a separate dish.

Per portion Energy 1033kcal/4312kJ; Protein 57.7g; Carbohydrate 62.1g, of which sugars 21.9g; Fat 55.8g, of which saturates 2.9g; Cholesterol 4mg; Calcium 135mg; Fibre 11.3g; Sodium 268mg.

BRAISED PARTRIDGE WITH CABBAGE

FOR THIS CLASSIC DISH FROM THE HISTORIC CITY OF SAINT HUBERT, PARTRIDGES ARE LAYERED WITH SAVOY CABBAGE OR BRUSSELS SPROUTS AND COOKED IN STOCK AND BEER. WILD PARTRIDGES ARE NO LONGER VERY COMMON IN BELGIUM, BUT FARMED BIRDS ARE AVAILABLE IN SPECIALITY STORES.

SERVES FOUR

INGREDIENTS

2 mature partridges, cleaned and
  ready to cook
115g/4oz/½ cup butter
1 large Savoy cabbage, sliced
200g/7 oz rindless smoked streaky
  (fatty) bacon
4 small pork sausages
4 small smoked sausages
pinch of freshly grated nutmeg
250ml/8fl oz/1 cup hot chicken stock
750ml/1¼ pints/3 cups dark Abbey
  beer or more hot chicken stock
2 bay leaves
4 juniper berries
salt and ground black pepper
boiled or mashed potatoes, to serve

1 Cut each partridge in half down the centre. Season with salt and pepper.

2 Melt the butter in a large, heavy frying pan over medium-high heat. Add the partridges and brown them on both sides. Cover the pan with foil or a lid and cook over low heat for 30 minutes.

3 Meanwhile, bring a large pan of water to the boil. Stir in 15ml/1 tbsp salt. Add the cabbage and blanch it for 3 minutes, then drain and pat dry with kitchen paper.

4 Lift the partridges out of the frying pan and put them on a plate. Set aside. Reheat the fat in the pan and add the bacon and both types of sausage. Fry, stirring occasionally, for 5 minutes, until the bacon is crisp and the sausages are fully cooked.

5 Preheat the oven to 160°C/325°F/ Gas 3. Grease a baking dish that is large enough to hold the pheasant halves in a single layer. Spread half the cabbage on the base and season it with salt, pepper and nutmeg.

6 Place the partridges on top and arrange the bacon and sausages in between. Cover with the rest of the cabbage and season again with salt, pepper and nutmeg.

7 Pour over the hot chicken stock and beer (or both quantities of stock). Add the bay leaves and juniper berries, cover the dish and bake in the oven for 1 hour. Check the meat is cooked.

8 Taste the cooking juices and adjust the seasoning if necessary. Mound the cabbage on a heated platter and arrange the partridges on top, with the bacon and sausages around the side. Serve immediately with boiled or mashed potatoes.

Per portion Energy 1016kcal/4227kJ; Protein 79.7g; Carbohydrate 15.2g, of which sugars 10g; Fat 66.2g, of which saturates 29g; Cholesterol 139mg; Calcium 219mg; Fibre 2.9g; Sodium 1633mg.

DUCK BREAST WITH TURNIPS

WHETHER WILD OR FARMED, DUCK IS OFTEN SERVED AT FESTIVE OCCASIONS IN BELGIUM. IN THIS RECIPE, DUCK BREASTS ARE COMBINED WITH TURNIPS, A ROOT VEGETABLE THAT HAS BEEN USED FOR CENTURIES; IT WAS A STAPLE IN MEDIEVAL STEWS AND HOTPOTS BEFORE THE ARRIVAL OF THE POTATO.

SERVES FOUR

INGREDIENTS

4 duck breast fillets, skin on
15ml/1 tbsp clear honey
1kg/2¼lb fresh young turnips
50g/2oz/¼ cup unsalted butter
15ml/1 tbsp sherry vinegar
salt and ground black pepper
chopped fresh chervil or parsley,
　to garnish

1 Rinse the duck breast fillets and pat them dry with kitchen paper. Trim off any sinew. Using a sharp knife, cross hatch the fatty skin on each breast and rub with honey on both sides. Take care to cut right through the fatty skin without piercing the meat.

COOK'S TIPS
• Select breast that have a fatty skin, as this will protect the meat from drying out.
• Cook duck breasts like you would a steak, so that it is pink and tender in the middle.

2 Scrub, rinse and dry the turnips and slice them thinly. Melt the butter in a frying pan over medium-high heat. Add the prepared turnips and fry for about 10 minutes, stirring occasionally, until they start to brown.

3 Meanwhile, put the duck breast fillets, skin-side down, in a large non-stick frying pan. Cook over medium heat for about 5 minutes or until the fat runs and the skin becomes crisp and golden. Drain off any excess fat. Season to taste.

4 Using tongs, turn the duck breast fillets over and cook the other side for 5–6 minutes. Do not overcook the meat. Season again. Remove from the heat, cover with foil or a lid and set aside for 4–5 minutes.

5 Add the sherry vinegar to the turnips and stir over the heat for 3 minutes, until reduced. Season to taste and spoon on to warm plates.

6 Slice the duck breast fillets thinly and fan over the turnips, spooning a little of the juices from the pan on top. Garnish with the chopped herbs and serve.

Per portion Energy 591kcal/2446kJ; Protein 13.7g; Carbohydrate 14.7g, of which sugars 14.2g; Fat 53.7g, of which saturates 18.1g; Cholesterol 27mg; Calcium 134mg; Fibre 6g; Sodium 191mg.

DUCK STEW <u>FROM THE</u> HAGUE

IN THE 19TH CENTURY, TURBOT AND DUCK WERE COMMONLY AVAILABLE AND INEXPENSIVE IN THE NETHERLANDS, UNLIKE TODAY WHEN THEY ARE SEEN AS MORE LUXURIOUS INGREDIENTS. INDEED, SUCH WAS THE FREQUENCY OF THEIR APPEARANCE ON MENUS THAT A DUTCH COOKBOOK OF THE EARLY 20TH CENTURY ADVISED: 'DO NOT ALWAYS ENTERTAIN YOUR GUESTS WITH THE SAME STARTER, CHICKEN SOUP, TURBOT OR BRAISED DUCK'. THIS DISH OF TENDER DUCK LEGS STEWED WITH RED WINE AND SERVED WITH A GREEN OLIVE SAUCE IS A MODERN INTERPRETATION OF A HANDWRITTEN RECIPE FROM THE EXERCISE BOOK OF A HAGUE COOK SCHOOL PUPIL OF THE SAME PERIOD.

SERVES FOUR

INGREDIENTS
   4 duck legs
   100g/3¾oz onion, chopped
   500ml/17fl oz/generous 2 cups
      red wine
   bouquet garni, consisting of 2
      tarragon sprigs, 2 parsley sprigs
      and 1 thyme sprig
   salt and ground black pepper
For the sauce
   200g/7oz/3½ cups pitted
      green olives
   200g/7oz leeks, sliced
   200g/7oz mushrooms, sliced
   2 garlic cloves, finely chopped
   25g/1oz/¼ cup plain
      (all-purpose) flour
To serve
   4 slices white bread,
      cut into triangles
   parsley sprigs
   tarragon sprigs
   a bowl of watercress

3 Season the duck with salt and ground black pepper, add the onion and cook, stirring occasionally, for 5 minutes, until softened. Pour in the wine and add the bouquet garni.

4 Cover and simmer the duck gently for 1¼ hours, until it is tender and cooked through. Add a little water, if necessary, to prevent the duck from drying out.

5 Remove and discard the bouquet garni. Transfer the duck legs to a chopping board. Reserve the cooking liquid. Cut the meat off the bones in large pieces.

7 Stir in the flour and cook, stirring, for 2 minutes. Gradually, stir in the reserved cooking liquid. If the sauce seems too thick, stir in a little water to thin it down.

8 Add the olives and duck meat to the sauce and heat through gently.

9 Transfer the duck and sauce to a platter and keep warm. Meanwhile, preheat the grill (broiler).

10 Brush one side of the bread triangles with a little of the reserved duck fat and cook the bread under the grill until browned.

11 Turn them over, brush with a little more duck fat and grill until the second sides are browned.

12 Arrange the toasted bread triangles around the stew and garnish with parsley and tarragon sprigs. Serve immediately with watercress.

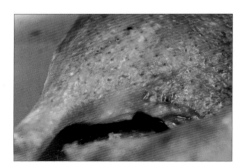

1 Heat a flameproof casserole without any added fat, then add the duck legs, skin side down, and cook over low heat for about 10 minutes, until well browned. Turn the legs over and cook until the other side is well browned.

2 Drain off and reserve all but about 15ml/1 tbsp of the fat.

6 To make the sauce, place the olives in a small pan of boiling water and cook for 5 minutes, then drain. Heat 15ml/ 1 tbsp of the reserved duck fat in a pan. Add the leeks and mushrooms and cook over low heat, stirring occasionally, for 5 minutes, until soft. Add the garlic and cook for a further minute.

COOK'S TIPS
• Store any remaining duck fat from this recipe in a sealed container, such as a jar, in the refrigerator and use it at a later date for roasting potatoes.
• Keep an eye on the toast when you are grilling (broiling) it, as it will burn quickly; do not walk off and leave it.

Per portion Energy 353kcal/1476kJ; Protein 29.7g; Carbohydrate 9.6g, of which sugars 2.9g; Fat 15g, of which saturates 2.8g; Cholesterol 151mg; Calcium 78mg; Fibre 3.5g; Sodium 1293mg.

RABBIT IN CHERRY BEER

RABBIT AND HARE ARE CENTRAL TO BELGIAN CUISINE. THERE ARE HUNDREDS OF WAYS OF COOKING THEM, OFTEN WITH TRADITIONAL BEERS, FRESH OR DRIED FRUITS, SPICES AND LOCALLY PRODUCED MUSTARDS. THIS RECIPE COMES FROM THE BRUSSELS AREA, WHERE KRIEK (SOUR CHERRY) BEER IS PRODUCED. IN COMBINATION WITH THE CANNED SOUR CHERRIES, THE BEER GIVES THE SLOW-COOKED DISH A SWEET-SOUR FLAVOUR THAT ECHOES THE COOKING STYLE OF BELGIUM'S MEDIEVAL PAST. THERE ISN'T A LOT OF MEAT ON A RABBIT, SO YOU SHOULD ASK FOR ONE THAT IS BIG ENOUGH TO SERVE FOUR.

SERVES FOUR

INGREDIENTS

1 ready-to-cook rabbit, cut into
  pieces, about 675g/1½lb
  total weight
40g/1½oz/3 tbsp butter
15ml/1 tbsp vegetable oil
1 large onion, roughly chopped
2 carrots, finely chopped
2 celery sticks, finely chopped
2 bay leaves
3 sprigs of thyme
10 peppercorns
250ml/8fl oz/1 cup *Kriek*
  Lambic beer
15ml/1 tbsp clear honey
15ml/1 tbsp red wine vinegar
1 x 470g/1lb ¾oz can or jar sour
  cherries in syrup (*see* Cook's tip)
50g/2oz/½ cup plain
  (all-purpose) flour
salt and ground black pepper
parsley sprigs, to garnish
boiled potatoes, potato croquettes
  or crusty dark bread, to serve

1 Season the rabbit pieces with salt and pepper. Melt 30ml/2 tbsp of the butter in a large, heavy frying pan over medium heat. When it foams, add the oil.

COOK'S TIP

If you cannot locate sour cherries labelled as such, buy canned or bottled Morello cherries.

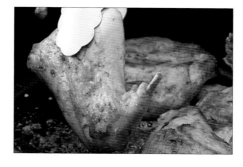

2 Add the pieces of rabbit and fry, turning occasionally, for 8 minutes or until browned on all sides. Lift out the rabbit and place on a platter.

3 Add the onion to the fat remaining in the pan. Sauté for 3–4 minutes until glazed, then stir in the carrots and celery. Continue cooking, stirring constantly over medium heat, for about 12 minutes, until the vegetables have browned slightly.

4 Return the rabbit to the pan and spoon the vegetables over. Season again and stir to combine. Tuck the bay leaves, thyme and peppercorns among the rabbit portions.

5 Pour over the beer, honey and vinegar to just cover the rabbit and vegetables. Add a little of the syrup from the canned cherries, if you like. Cover and simmer for 1 hour or until the rabbit meat starts to fall off the bones.

6 Lift out the rabbit pieces and put them on a heated serving platter. Cover to keep warm. Remove the vegetables and herbs with a slotted spoon and discard them.

7 Reheat the pan juices and sprinkle over the flour. Cook for 1 minute, stirring constantly to incorporate all the brown bits from the base of the pan. Cook the sauce, stirring frequently, until reduced by half.

8 Drain the cherries, reserving the syrup, and stir them in. Simmer for 10 more minutes. Add a little of the syrup to thin the sauce, if necessary. Swirl the remaining butter into the sauce. Return the pieces of rabbit to the pan and reheat gently in the sauce.

9 Taste and adjust the seasoning, then serve at once with boiled potatoes, potato croquettes or crusty dark bread.

Per portion Energy 471kcal/1975kJ; Protein 32.7g; Carbohydrate 39.1g, of which sugars 27.2g; Fat 19.6g, of which saturates 9g; Cholesterol 168mg; Calcium 75mg; Fibre 2.4g; Sodium 111mg.

RABBIT IN SOUR SAUCE

THIS DISH DATES FROM A TIME WHEN POOR PEOPLE IN THE PROVINCE OF LIMBURG WOULD BRAVELY GO OUT RABBIT POACHING, IN SPITE OF THE RISK OF HARSH PUNISHMENT FROM THE LANDOWNERS. REFERRED TO AS KNIEN IN 'T ZOER *IN THE LIMBURG DIALECT, THIS IS A VERY OLD DISH, A VERSION OF WHICH WAS FIRST FOUND IN A DUTCH COOKBOOK PUBLISHED IN 1593. THE SAUCE DERIVES ITS SPECIAL FLAVOUR FROM THE SPICE CAKE,* DEVENTER KOEK.

SERVES TWO

INGREDIENTS
   150g/5oz pitted prunes
   300ml/½ pint/1¼ cups tea
   3 onions
   40g/1½oz/3 tbsp butter
   1 ready-to-cook rabbit, cut
      into pieces, about 675g/1½lb
      total weight
   100ml/3½fl oz/scant ½ cup red
      wine vinegar
   5ml/1 tsp soft dark brown sugar
   1 bay leaf
   300g/11oz waxy potatoes, diced
   300g/11oz tart apples
   sugar, to taste
   pinch of ground cinnamon
   40g/1½oz spice cake, preferably
      Deventer koek
   10ml/2 tsp apple spread
   30ml/2 tbsp cowberries or
      cranberries (optional)
   salt and ground black pepper

1 Put the prunes in a small bowl, pour in the tea and leave to soak for at least 1 hour or overnight.

2 Slice two onions into rings and finely chop the third.

COOK'S TIP
Cowberries are also called lingonberries, mountain cranberries and red whortleberries. They are slightly acidic, which helps to cut through the richness and sweetness of this dish.

3 Melt the butter in a large pan. Add the onion rings and cook over low heat, stirring occasionally, for about 10 minutes, until the onions are lightly browned. Remove from the pan with a slotted spoon and set aside.

4 Increase the heat to medium, add the pieces of rabbit to the pan and cook, turning occasionally, for about 10 minutes, until the rabbit pieces are browned all over.

5 Add the chopped onion to the rabbit, season with salt and pepper and cook for a further 2–3 minutes.

6 Pour in the red wine vinegar and 100ml/3½fl oz/scant ½ cup water. Add the brown sugar and bay leaf. Stir to combine, lower the heat, cover and simmer for 1 hour.

7 Meanwhile, cook the diced potatoes in a large pan of lightly salted boiling water for 10–15 minutes, until tender. Drain well.

8 Peel and core the apples, then slice thinly and cook in a large pan with sugar to taste until soft but not disintegrating. Add the potatoes and warm through.

9 Using a slotted spoon, remove the rabbit from the pan and place on a warm serving plate. Top with the onion rings. Spoon the apple and potato mixture around the meat and surround with the prunes. Sprinkle the potatoes and apples with cinnamon.

10 Crumble the cake into the cooking liquid remaining in the pan and whisk until smooth. Whisk in the apple spread. Add the berries, if using, and warm through. Spoon the sauce over the meat and serve immediately.

Per portion Energy 831kcal/3497kJ; Protein 52.3g; Carbohydrate 102.3g, of which sugars 70.9g; Fat 26g, of which saturates 14.4g; Cholesterol 217mg; Calcium 213mg; Fibre 12.7g; Sodium 289mg.

JUGGED HARE

HUNTING WAS ALWAYS THE PRESERVE OF THE UPPER CLASSES IN THE NETHERLANDS, AND A SMALLHOLDER OR TENANT OF A RICH LANDOWNER COULD RISK LOSING HIS FARM IF CAUGHT POACHING. THIS SIMPLE HARE STEW WOULD ALMOST CERTAINLY HAVE BEEN THE RESULT OF SUCH A RISKY ENTERPRISE, AND WOULD HAVE BEEN COOKED WITH WATER INSTEAD OF WINE AND COMBINED WITH WILD BERRIES.

SERVES FOUR

INGREDIENTS
  1.6kg/3½lb hare (jack rabbit),
    cut into pieces
  300ml/½ pint/1¼ cups red wine
    or water
  50ml/2fl oz/¼ cup red wine vinegar
  1 onion, chopped
  2 bay leaves
  10ml/2 tsp black peppercorns, crushed
  40g/1½oz/3 tbsp butter
  7.5ml/1½ tsp sugar
  40g/1½oz/⅓ cup plain
    (all-purpose) flour
  50ml/2fl oz/¼ cup whipping cream
  salt and ground black pepper
For the sauce
  400g/14oz/3¼ cups cowberries
    or cranberries
  200g/7oz/1 cup sugar
  1 cinnamon stick
To serve
  Brussels sprouts
  knob (pat) of butter
  freshly grated nutmeg
  mashed potato rosettes

1 Rinse the hare and rub the pieces all over with salt and pepper. Pour the wine or water and vinegar into a large, non-metallic bowl. Add the onion, bay leaves and peppercorns. Add the hare, turning to coat, cover and leave to marinate in the refrigerator overnight.

2 Remove the pieces of hare from the marinade and pat dry with kitchen paper. Reserve the marinade.

3 Melt the butter in a pan, add the hare and cook over medium heat, turning often, for about 10 minutes, until lightly browned on all sides. Pour in the marinade, add the sugar and bring to the boil. Lower the heat, cover and simmer for 2 hours, until very tender.

4 Meanwhile, make the sauce. Put the berries, sugar and cinnamon stick in a small, heavy pan and cook over low heat, stirring occasionally, for 10–15 minutes, until thick and pulpy.

5 Remove the cinnamon stick and spoon the mixture into individual pots. Leave to cool.

6 Using a slotted spoon, remove the pieces of hare from the pan and place them on a warm serving dish. Set aside and keep warm.

7 Strain the cooking liquid into a clean pan and return it to the heat. Blend the flour with a little water and stir it into the cooking liquid. Simmer, stirring, for 3–4 minutes, until thickened.

8 Remove the pan from the heat and stir in the cream. Spoon a little of the sauce over the pieces of hare and pour the remainder into a sauceboat.

9 Cook the Brussels sprouts in a pan of boiling water for 3–5 minutes, until they are tender-crisp (don't overcook). Drain them well, toss lightly with butter and sprinkle with nutmeg.

10 Serve the hare surrounded by potato rosettes and accompanied by the pots of berry sauce, Brussels sprouts and cream sauce.

VARIATION
You could cheat and use good-quality store-bought cranberry sauce instead of making your own.

Per portion Energy 997kcal/4199kJ; Protein 89.4g; Carbohydrate 72.7g, of which sugars 64.7g; Fat 35.4g, of which saturates 8.5g; Cholesterol 22mg; Calcium 126mg; Fibre 2.1g; Sodium 195mg.

ARDENNES-STYLE VENISON STEW

November is prime game season in Belgium. Months before, lovers of good food go on gastronomic weekends in the Belgian Ardennes so that they can sample the superb dishes that are only available at this time. Game is often marinated in wine and spices before being cooked. This way of preserving and tenderizing meat is one of the world's oldest culinary techniques. It is used to great advantage in this delectable venison and mushroom stew, promoting its complex flavours and tempting aromas.

SERVES FOUR–SIX

INGREDIENTS
1.6kg/3½lb stewing venison, cubed
150g/5oz bacon (optional)
25g/1oz/2 tbsp butter
15ml/1 tbsp vegetable oil or olive oil
1 onion, finely chopped
15g/½oz/2 tbsp plain (all purpose) flour
45ml/3 tbsp brandy
150g/5oz packet dried mixed
  wild mushrooms
bouquet garni (*see* Cook's tip)
15ml/1 tbsp cornflour (cornstarch),
  mixed to a paste with
  45ml/3 tbsp water
30ml/2 tbsp red wine vinegar
salt and ground black pepper
For the marinade
1 onion, roughly chopped
1 carrot, roughly chopped
2 garlic cloves, crushed
20 juniper berries
3 bay leaves
4 cloves
1 sprig of thyme
1 litre/1¾ pints/4 cups red wine
15ml/1 tbsp vegetable or olive oil
To serve
Poached Apples with Berry Compote
  (*see* page 184)
boiled new potatoes with butter and
  chopped parsley

1 First, make the marinade. Mix all the ingredients in a medium pan. Bring the mixture to the boil, then reduce the heat and simmer for 15 minutes. Pour into a non-reactive bowl. Cover and leave to cool.

2 Add the venison cubes to the bowl of cooled marinade and stir to coat thoroughly. Replace the cover and marinate the meat for 12–48 hours in a cold place or the refrigerator, stirring occasionally.

3 Using a slotted spoon, lift out the meat and dry well on kitchen paper. Strain the marinade into a jug (pitcher) and set aside.

4 If using the bacon, dice it finely and cook in a large heavy pan or flameproof casserole over medium heat until the fat runs, then increase the heat and cook for about 4 minutes more, until crisp. Remove from the pan and set aside.

5 Add the butter and oil to the frying pan or casserole and heat until the butter melts. Add the chopped onion and sauté over medium high heat for 4–6 minutes until glazed and golden brown. Using a slotted spoon, transfer the onion to a platter.

6 Add the venison in batches to the fat remaining in the pan and brown over fairly high heat for about 4 minutes to seal. As each batch browns, remove it from the pan.

7 When the final batch has browned, return all the venison to the pan, sprinkle with the flour and season with salt and pepper, stirring until the flour has been absorbed. Add the brandy and cook, stirring, for 1 minute more.

8 Add the mushrooms, bouquet garni, onions and bacon (if using). Pour the reserved marinade into the pan and bring to simmering point. Cook over low heat on top of the stove for 1–1½ hours, until the meat is very tender.

9 Taste and adjust the seasoning and remove the bouquet garni. Skim the fat from the surface.

10 Stir the cornflour mixture in a small bowl, then add it to the pan, stirring. Cook for 10–15 minutes more, stirring frequently, until the liquid thickens.

11 Spoon the stew on to warmed serving plates and serve with Poached Apples with Berry Compote and boiled new potatoes with butter and parsley.

COOK'S TIP
To make the bouquet garni, tie 6 parsley sprigs, 2 bay leaves and 2–3 fresh sprigs of thyme together with kitchen string (twine). Leave a trailing end long enough to tie to the pan handle, so that the bouquet garni can easily be retrieved at the end of the cooking time.

Per portion Energy 474kcal/1996kJ; Protein 60.7g; Carbohydrate 8.7g, of which sugars 3.3g; Fat 9.6g, of which saturates 4.3g; Cholesterol 142mg; Calcium 44mg; Fibre 1.1g; Sodium 188mg.

MEAT DISHES

Along with potatoes and vegetables, meat is the basis of most main meals for many Dutch and Belgian people. Pork and beef are by far the most popular types, and all cuts are used, from stewing meat and sausages to roasting joints and the finest steaks. Many dishes incorporate flavourings, such as condiments, spices or alcohol, as well as vegetables and dried beans and peas. Meatballs are especially popular, and appear in a number of guises, including Bird's Nests, which are similar to Scotch eggs.

PORK CHOPS IN MUSTARD SAUCE

Ever since the days when every rural family kept a pig, pork has been a favourite meat in Belgium and there are numerous pork dishes in the culinary repertoire. Many of these recipes, such as this one, include mustard, which is also a popular accompaniment for cheeses and cold meats. The tradition of fine mustard-making was established in Belgium in the 13th century, and continues to the present day.

SERVES FOUR

INGREDIENTS

    4 pork loin chops, about
      2.5cm/1in thick
    25g/1oz/2 tbsp unsalted butter
    5ml/1 tsp vegetable oil or
      olive oil
    4 shallots, chopped
    200ml/7fl oz/scant 1 cup white wine
      or Belgian blond beer
    200ml/7fl oz/scant 1 cup double
      (heavy) cream
    30ml/2 tbsp good-quality mustard
    salt and ground black pepper
    30ml/2 tbsp chopped fresh parsley,
      to garnish
    green beans, Brussels sprouts and
      boiled potatoes, to serve

1 Season the pork chops with salt and pepper. Heat a heavy frying pan over medium to high heat. Add the butter and oil and swirl to coat. Add the chops and fry them for 4 minutes on each side or until cooked to your taste. Using tongs, transfer the chops to a platter, cover and keep warm.

2 Reheat the fat remaining in the frying pan and sauté the chopped shallots for 3–5 minutes, stirring frequently, until softened.

3 Add the wine or beer. Cook, stirring well to incorporate the sediment on the base of the pan, for about 2 minutes, then whisk in the cream and mustard and bring to the boil.

4 Reduce the heat and simmer the sauce for about 3 minutes, until it is slightly thickened. Season to taste.

5 Pour the sauce over the pork chops. Garnish with parsley and serve with the beans, Brussels sprouts and potatoes.

COOK'S TIP
Pork chops can easily be overcooked and become dry. Thinner cuts will take less time and can be cooked at a higher heat. For thicker cuts, reduce the heat and increase the cooking time.

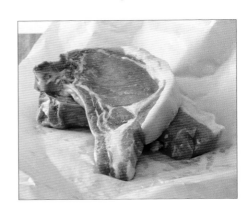

Per portion Energy 551kcal/2285kJ; Protein 33.7g; Carbohydrate 3.1g, of which sugars 2.6g; Fat 41.4g, of which saturates 22.4g; Cholesterol 176mg; Calcium 50mg; Fibre 0.2g; Sodium 378mg.

FIVE BREAKS

IN THE 19TH CENTURY, A LOVELORN YOUNG DUTCHMAN IS KNOWN TO HAVE DECLARED TO HIS SWEETHEART, 'I HAVE BEEN IN LOVE WITH YOU FOR YEARS AND I AM PREPARED TO WORK FIVE BREAKS AND MORE, IF ONLY I CAN HAVE YOU'. A NORMAL WORKING DAY HAD FOUR BREAKS — SHORT PERIODS OF REST — SO THE NAME OF THIS DISH IMPLIES THAT EATING IT WILL ENABLE YOU TO DO MORE THAN IS REQUIRED. ORIGINATING IN UTRECHT, IT COMPRISES BEANS, VEGETABLES, APPLES AND BACON.

SERVES FOUR

INGREDIENTS
    250g/9oz/scant 1½ cups dried brown
      beans, soaked overnight in cold
      water to cover
    1kg/2¼lb waxy potatoes, quartered
    4 onions, sliced
    500g/1¼lb large carrots, sliced
    2 tart apples, peeled, quartered
      and cored
    15ml/1 tbsp cornflour (cornstarch)
    25g/1oz/2 tbsp butter
    100g/3¾oz/scant ⅔ cup diced
      smoked bacon
    salt and ground black pepper

1 Drain and rinse the beans, place in a pan, cover with cold water and bring to the boil. Lower the heat and cook for 50 minutes.

2 Add the potatoes, onions and carrots to the pan, top up the pan with boiling water if necessary to keep the vegetables covered, and cook for about 15 minutes, until just tender.

3 Add the apples and simmer for a further 5 minutes. Drain well, reserving the cooking liquid. Transfer the mixture to a serving dish and keep warm.

4 Mix the cornflour with 30ml/2 tbsp water to a paste in a small bowl, then stir into the reserved cooking liquid in the pan. Heat, stirring constantly, until the sauce is thickened.

5 Stir the butter into the sauce and season to taste with salt and pepper. Pour the sauce into a sauceboat.

6 Cook the bacon in a dry frying pan over medium heat until crisp. Sprinkle it over the top of the bean mixture and serve immediately with the sauce.

VARIATION
Although the authentic Dutch dish includes bacon, you could omit it for a vegetarian version of the dish.

Per portion Energy 544kcal/2299kJ; Protein 24.1g; Carbohydrate 91.9g, of which sugars 22.9g; Fat 11.5g, of which saturates 5.3g; Cholesterol 27mg; Calcium 131mg; Fibre 17g; Sodium 493mg.

BEANS WITH PORK AND NUTMEG

THIS TRADITIONAL DUTCH WINTER MEAL WAS ORIGINALLY MADE FROM GREEN BEANS PRESERVED IN SALT ALONG WITH DRIED WHITE BEANS. APPARENTLY, THE SIGHT OF THE COMBINATION OF WHITE AND GREEN BEANS IN MIDWINTER USED TO PROVOKE THE WILDEST FANTASIES ABOUT NAKED BODIES CAVORTING IN SPRING MEADOWS. AS A RESULT, THE DISH WAS ALSO FONDLY REFERRED TO AS 'NAKED BOTTOMS ON GRASS', 'NAKED MISSIES IN THE GREEN' OR 'BABES IN THE GRASS'. IT IS USUALLY SERVED WITH A SLICED WARM SMOKED SAUSAGE ON TOP AND FLAVOURED WITH PAPRIKA AND NUTMEG.

SERVES FOUR

INGREDIENTS
  400g/14oz/2 cups dried white beans,
    soaked overnight in cold water,
    and drained
  1 bay leaf
  800g/1¾ lb runner (green) beans, sliced
  200g/7oz lean pork, diced
  50g/2oz/⅓ cup diced lean
    smoked bacon
  1 onion, chopped
  60ml/4 tbsp breadcrumbs
  30ml/2 tbsp mild paprika
  20g/¾oz/1½ tbsp butter
  pinch of freshly grated nutmeg
  30ml/2 tbsp cornflour (cornstarch)
  1 carrot, thinly sliced
  salt and ground black pepper

1 Put the beans in a pan, add 1.2 litres/ 2 pints/5 cups water and the bay leaf, bring to the boil and cook for 1 hour, until tender.

2 Cook the green beans in a small pan of boiling water for about 10 minutes, until tender. Drain well, reserving the cooking liquid.

3 Put the pork, bacon and onion in a food processor and process until finely minced (ground). Scrape into a bowl and knead with the breadcrumbs and salt and pepper.

4 Form the mixture into 30 small balls. Spread out the paprika in a dish and roll the balls through it. Flatten them and snip the rims in four places.

5 Melt the butter in a non-stick frying pan. Add the balls and cook over low heat for a few minutes on each side until evenly browned. Remove with a slotted spatula.

6 Drain the white beans, reserving the cooking liquid.

7 Mix the reserved cooking liquid from the green and white beans together, measure and make up to 500ml/ 17fl oz/generous 2 cups with water, if necessary.

8 Pour the liquid into the frying pan that the 'flowers' were cooked in, add the nutmeg, season with salt and bring to the boil over low heat.

9 Mix the cornflour with 60ml/4 tbsp cold water to a paste in a small bowl and stir into the liquid. Cook, stirring constantly, until thickened.

10 Ladle some of the sauce into a flameproof dish and add the mixed beans. Top with the 'flowers' and garnish them with the carrot. Warm through in the oven, then serve, handing the remaining sauce separately.

VARIATIONS
• You could use drained, canned white beans, if you prefer, although the flavour will not be as good.
• Instead of the 'flowers', you could cook 3–4 good-quality sausages, then slice them and serve in the same way.

Per portion Energy 457kcal/1937kJ; Protein 29.2g; Carbohydrate 70.1g, of which sugars 9.2g; Fat 8.7g, of which saturates 3.8g; Cholesterol 17mg; Calcium 189mg; Fibre 20.1g; Sodium 360mg.

KALE <small>WITH</small> SMOKED SAUSAGE

ANY DISH WITH MASHED POTATOES AND COOKED VEGETABLES IS A TRADITION OF THE 'POTTAGE' — MEAT, VEGETABLES AND DRIED BEANS COOKED IN ONE POT — COMMON IN THE MIDDLE AGES, AND WHICH HAS DEVELOPED INTO THE SIGNATURE DISH OF THE NETHERLANDS. THIS ONE USES KALE AND SMOKED SAUSAGE.

3 Put the drained kale and the sausage on top, cover and cook over medium heat for 30 minutes.

4 Remove the sausage and drain the vegetables in a colander.

5 Return the vegetables to the pan, mash well and stir in the milk and butter until smooth.

6 Season to taste with salt and serve with the sausage and some butter on top.

SERVES FOUR–FIVE

INGREDIENTS
    1.6kg/3½lb curly kale, tough stalks
      removed, finely shredded
    1kg/2¼lb potatoes, peeled
    1 smoked sausage, about 300g/11oz
    100ml/3½fl oz/scant ½ cup milk
    25g/1oz/2 tbsp butter
    salt
    butter, to serve

VARIATION
You could substitute the kale with shredded Savoy or other cabbage or spinach, if you prefer.

1 Cook the kale in a little boiling water for 10 minutes, then drain well.

2 Put the potatoes in a large pan and half cover with water.

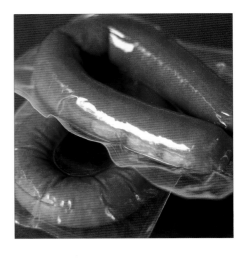

Per portion Energy 452kcal/1894kJ; Protein 14.3g; Carbohydrate 56.2g, of which sugars 20.2g; Fat 20.1g, of which saturates 9.0g; Cholesterol 35.8mg; Calcium 222.6mg; Fibre 9.0g; Sodium 569.4mg.

SAUERKRAUT WITH SMOKED SAUSAGE AND BACON

EVERY DUTCH MASH IS EATEN WITH A WELL (KUILTJE) IN THE MIDDLE. WHEN PRESENTED WITH A PLATE OF MASH, THE DINER (OFTEN A CHILD) MAKES A WELL, LADLES IN BUTTER OR GRAVY, AND THEN SPOONS UP THE MASH UNTIL THE DIKE BURSTS. HERE IT IS SERVED WITH BACON AND SMOKED SAUSAGE.

SERVES FOUR–FIVE

INGREDIENTS

400g/14oz unsmoked bacon
1kg/2¼ lb potatoes, quartered
4 black peppercorns, crushed
a pinch of salt
800g/1¾ lb natural sauerkraut
  (fermented rather than pickled)
1 smoked sausage, about 300 g/11oz
50ml/2fl oz/¼ cup milk
25g/1oz/2 tbsp butter
butter, to serve

1 Bring a large, shallow pan of water to the boil. Add the bacon and cook for 5 minutes.

2 Add the potatoes, peppercorns, a pinch of salt and sufficient water to cover.

VARIATION
If you can't find or don't like sauerkraut, you could sauté some shredded cabbage in a frying pan with 15ml/1 tbsp oil and a knob of butter and use that instead. Rather than adding it to the pan in Step 3, stir it into the mashed potato in Step 5, after you have made a smooth mixture.

3 Separate the strands of sauerkraut with a fork, pile it on to the potatoes and put the sausage on top. Simmer gently for 30 minutes.

4 Remove the bacon and sausage. Drain the vegetables, reserving the cooking liquid, and return them to the pan.

5 Mash the potatoes and sauerkraut and add the milk, butter and sufficient cooking liquid to make a smooth mixture. Serve with the sausage and bacon on top.

Per portion Energy 547.6kcal/2284kJ; Protein 24.5g; Carbohydrate 41.5g, of which sugars 5.9g; Fat 32.5g, of which saturates 13.8g; Cholesterol 77.6mg; Calcium 137.8mg; Fibre 5.8g; Sodium 2718mg.

BLOOD SAUSAGE WITH ONIONS

BLOOD SAUSAGES, ALSO CALLED BLOED WORST, ZWARTE PENS, BEULING OR BOUDIN NOIR, DATE BACK TO THE 14TH CENTURY. LIKE BLACK PUDDING, THEY ARE MADE BY MIXING THE BLOOD FROM FRESHLY SLAUGHTERED PIGS WITH SPICES, CEREAL, SALT AND SOMETIMES ONIONS. THE DELICACY IS VERY POPULAR IN BELGIUM, ESPECIALLY AS A WINTER DISH, WHEN BLOOD SAUSAGES ARE TRADITIONALLY SERVED WITH MUSTARD OR PICKLES, DARK RYE BREAD AND BAKED APPLES.

SERVES FOUR

INGREDIENTS

    25g/1oz/2 tbsp butter
    2 onions, halved and thinly sliced
    500g/1¼lb cooking apples, peeled,
      cored, halved and sliced
    a pinch each of sugar, ground
      cinnamon and grated nutmeg
    4 medium blood sausages
    salt and ground black pepper
    mustard, Belgian pickles and dark rye
      bread, to serve

1 Melt the butter in a large frying pan that has a lid. Add the onions and cook over medium heat for 8–12 minutes, until they start to soften.

2 Add the apple slices to the pan, then sprinkle with the sugar to promote caramelization, and sauté for 5 minutes more, stirring frequently.

3 Add the cinnamon and grate the nutmeg into the pan. Season.

4 Add the sausages to the pan, cover and cook for 10 minutes, stirring occasionally to prevent the apples from sticking to the pan.

5 Remove the lid from the pan and carefully turn the sausages over, using tongs, a fish slice or a spatula to avoid puncturing them.

6 Give the apple and onion mixture a gentle stir, cover the pan again and cook for 5 minutes more or until the sausages are well done.

7 Serve the blood sausage and onions immediately with the mustard or pickles and a few slices of dark rye bread to mop up the juices.

Per portion Energy 340kcal/1420kJ; Protein 9g; Carbohydrate 29.5g, of which sugars 15.5g; Fat 21.6g, of which saturates 9.6g; Cholesterol 64mg; Calcium 115mg; Fibre 3.2g; Sodium 748mg.

ENDIVE, HAM AND CHEESE GRATIN

ENDIVES, WHICH ARE SOMETIMES CALLED CHICORY, ARE BELGIUM'S 'WHITE GOLD'. THE STYLISH VEGETABLE IS DEEPLY ROOTED IN THE COUNTRY'S GASTRONOMY AND ITS FAME IS SPREADING FAST. THIS IS DUE IN PART TO ITS SLEEK, TORPEDO-LIKE APPEARANCE, BUT ALSO TO THE TEXTURE AND THE UNIQUE, SOMEWHAT BITTER TASTE. THIS CLASSIC DISH IS POPULAR IN WINTER, THE TRADITIONAL TIME FOR HARVESTING ENDIVES. IT IS USUALLY SERVED WITH MASHED POTATOES OR CRUSTY BREAD.

SERVES FOUR–EIGHT

INGREDIENTS
  40g/1½oz/3 tbsp butter, plus extra
    for greasing
  8 small Belgian endives (UK chicory)
  8 thin slices of cooked ham
  salt and ground black pepper
For the sauce
  65g/2½oz/5 tbsp butter
  40g/1½oz/6 tbsp plain
    (all-purpose) flour
  500ml/17fl oz/generous 2 cups
    creamy milk
  150g/5oz/1¼ cups grated Gruyère
    or Emmenthal cheese
  pinch of grated nutmeg
  salt and ground white pepper,
    to taste

1 Melt the butter in a large frying pan over medium heat. Add the endives and let them brown lightly on all sides. Reduce the heat, cover and cook for about 20 minutes.

2 When the endives are tender when pierced with a thin-bladed knife, lift them out of the pan and drain well on layered kitchen paper. If necessary, squeeze out extra liquid when they have cooled slightly.

3 Preheat the oven to 200°C/400°F/ Gas 6. Make the sauce. Melt the butter in a small pan over medium heat. Stir in the flour and cook, stirring constantly with a wooden spoon, for 1 minute.

4 Gradually add the milk to the pan, whisking vigorously until the sauce boils and thickens. Reduce the heat and simmer for 2–3 minutes, still whisking, then stir in three quarters of the grated cheese. Add nutmeg, salt and white pepper to taste.

5 Butter an ovenproof baking dish that is large enough to hold the endives in one layer. Wrap each endive in a slice of ham and place in the dish. Pour the sauce over and top with the remaining cheese.

6 Bake for about 25 minutes or until heated thoroughly. Just before serving, brown the topping under a hot grill (broiler), taking care not to let it burn.

COOK'S TIPS
• The endives can be steamed or boiled instead of braised.
• Do not leave the dish in the oven for too long or the fat in the cheese will curdle and the water released by the endives will thin the sauce.

Per portion Energy 251kcal/1036kJ; Protein 8.1g; Carbohydrate 11g, of which sugars 4g; Fat 20.3g, of which saturates 12.8g; Cholesterol 55mg; Calcium 253mg; Fibre 1.5g; Sodium 244mg.

BIRDS' NESTS WITH PINK POTATO PURÉE

THIS TRADITIONAL BELGIAN EASTER TREAT RESEMBLES THE BRITISH DISH CALLED SCOTCH EGGS. IT ORIGINATED IN MEDIEVAL TIMES AS A WAY OF PRESERVING THE EGGS THAT WERE DENIED TO CATHOLICS DURING THE LENTEN FAST, FOR CONSUMPTION AT A LATER DATE. WHEN THE DEEP-FRIED BALLS ARE CUT IN HALF, THEY LOOK LIKE BIRDS' NESTS, HENCE THE NAME. CHILDREN LOVE THEM, ESPECIALLY WHEN THEY ARE SERVED, AS HERE, WITH TOMATO SAUCE AND PINK POTATO PURÉE.

SERVES FOUR

INGREDIENTS
　4 eggs
　225g/8oz/1 cup minced (ground) beef
　225g/8oz/1 cup minced
　　(ground) pork
　1 shallot, finely chopped
　a pinch each of grated nutmeg
　　and dried thyme
　45ml/3 tbsp chopped fresh parsley
　1 egg, beaten
　egg white and fresh white
　　breadcrumbs, for coating
　15g/½oz/1 tbsp butter
　15ml/1 tbsp vegetable oil or olive oil
　chopped fresh parsley, to garnish
For the tomato sauce
　400g/14oz can chopped tomatoes
　15g/½oz/1 tbsp butter
　15ml/1 tbsp vegetable oil or olive oil
　2–3 shallots or 1 onion, chopped
　1 garlic clove, finely chopped
　30ml/2 tbsp tomato purée (paste)
　30ml/2 tbsp sherry or Madeira
　1 bay leaf
　5ml/1 tsp paprika
　salt and ground black pepper
For the potato purée
　500g/1¼lb potatoes, peeled
　500ml/17fl oz/generous 2 cups milk
　40g/1½oz/3 tbsp unsalted butter
　30ml/2 tbsp tomato purée
　pinch of grated nutmeg

1 Put the eggs in a pan with water to cover. Bring to the boil and cook for 10 minutes. Drain and cool in iced water.

2 As soon as the eggs are cold, remove them from the water, shell them and set them aside until required.

3 Put the minced beef and pork in a large bowl. Add the chopped shallot, nutmeg, thyme, parsley and egg. Mix thoroughly with clean hands until it holds together.

4 Divide the meat mixture into four equal portions and knead each one around a hard-boiled egg to make an even coating 2cm/¾in thick.

5 Put the egg white and breadcrumbs in separate shallow dishes. Dip each covered egg in egg white, then roll in breadcrumbs until the outside is evenly and well coated.

6 Melt the butter in the oil in a large frying pan over medium heat. Add the covered eggs and brown on all sides.

7 Reduce the heat, cover and cook for 30 minutes.

8 Meanwhile, make the sauce. In a pan, melt the butter in the oil. Add the chopped shallots or onion and sauté for 3 minutes. Add the garlic and sauté gently for 3 minutes more.

9 Add the tomatoes and tomato purée. Simmer for 5 minutes, then add the sherry or Madeira and the bay leaf. Season and add the paprika. Cook over low heat for 20 minutes.

10 Meanwhile, make the potato purée. Put the potatoes in a pan with lightly salted water to cover. Bring to the boil, reduce the heat and cook for 25 minutes, until tender. Drain the potatoes, return them to the pan and place over the heat to dry. Mash with the milk, butter, tomato purée and nutmeg.

11 Pile the potato purée in the centre of warm plates. Surround with most of the sauce. Cut the meatballs in half and arrange two on the sauce on each of the plates. Spoon the remaining sauce over. Garnish with the parsley and serve.

Per portion Energy 734kcal/3067kJ; Protein 39.1g; Carbohydrate 41g, of which sugars 13.1g; Fat 46.5g, of which saturates 20.5g; Cholesterol 359mg; Calcium 234mg; Fibre 2.9g; Sodium 496mg.

MEATBALL AND BROWN BEAN PIE

THIS PIE WAS ORIGINALLY MADE OF VERY SIMPLE INGREDIENTS, MOSTLY LEFTOVERS. SO, THE CRUST OF BREADCRUMBS OR CRUSHED RUSKS HIDES THE HUMBLE DISH BENEATH. THE DUTCH NAME FOR THIS DISH IS PHILOSOPHER, OR FILOSOOF, A REFERENCE TO WHAT WAS SEEN AS A PHILOSOPHER'S TENDENCY TO DISGUISE SIMPLE TRUTHS. THIS VERSION DATES FROM THE 1950S.

SERVES FOUR

INGREDIENTS
  250g/9oz lean minced (ground) beef
  250g/9oz lean minced (ground) pork
  1 large (US extra large) egg, beaten
  25g/1oz/½ cup crushed rusks or
    dry breadcrumbs
  2.5ml/½ tsp freshly ground nutmeg
  30ml/2 tbsp mild paprika
  40g/1½oz/3 tbsp butter
  1 onion, chopped
  150g/5oz mushrooms
  40g/1½oz/⅓ cup plain
    (all-purpose) flour
  50ml/2fl oz/¼ cup Madeira
  480g/17oz can brown beans
  30ml/2 tbsp chopped fresh parsley
  800g/1¾lb waxy potatoes
  salt and ground black pepper
For the topping
  25g/1oz/2 tbsp butter, melted
  30ml/2 tbsp crushed rusks or
    breadcrumbs
To serve
  Brussels sprouts
  apple sauce

1 Put the meat in a bowl with the egg, rusks, nutmeg, 2.5ml/½ tsp black pepper and salt. Knead until combined.

2 Form the meat, egg and rusk mixture into about 30 small balls. Spread out the paprika in a dish and roll the meatballs in it to coat.

3 Melt the butter in a large frying pan, add the meatballs and cook over high heat, stirring and turning frequently, for about 8 minutes, until browned on all sides. Add the onion and mushrooms to the pan and cook, stirring frequently, for 2–3 minutes.

4 Sprinkle in the flour and cook, stirring constantly, for 2–3 minutes, until it is lightly coloured.

5 Gradually stir in 400ml/14fl oz/1⅔ cups water, then stir in the Madeira. Season with salt and pepper. Lower the heat, cover and simmer for 10 minutes.

6 Drain and rinse the beans and transfer to an ovenproof dish. Sprinkle with parsley. Preheat the oven to 200°C/400°F/Gas 6.

7 Par-boil the potatoes in boiling water for 5–7 minutes, then drain well.

8 Slice the potatoes and arrange, overlapping slightly, on top of the pie. Drizzle with the melted butter and sprinkle with the pepper, salt and the rusks or breadcrumbs.

9 Bake for 40–45 minutes until golden brown on top. Serve immediately with Brussels sprouts sprinkled with toasted almonds and apple sauce.

VARIATION
To top the pie with mashed potatoes, cook 800g/1¾lb potatoes in boiling water for about 25 minutes, until tender. Drain well and pass through a potato ricer or mash by hand. Beat in 2.5ml/½ tsp each salt, paprika and grated nutmeg, 2.5ml/½ tsp ground black pepper, 2 egg yolks and 25g/1oz/2 tbsp butter. Add some milk if necessary. Spread over the pie, sprinkle with rusks and drizzle with melted butter before baking.

Per portion Energy 774kcal/3247kJ; Protein 42.4g; Carbohydrate 77g, of which sugars 9.4g; Fat 33.9g, of which saturates 16g; Cholesterol 161mg; Calcium 185mg; Fibre 11.1g; Sodium 813mg.

ENDIVE AND MEATBALLS

COOKED ENDIVE IS ALWAYS SERVED WITH MEATBALLS (GEHAKTBAL) IN THE NETHERLANDS. THE MEATBALL, ONCE KING OF PUBS AND SANDWICH BARS, IS THE MOST POPULAR MEAT DISH IN THE COUNTRY TODAY. EVERY WEDNESDAY, DUTCH BUTCHERS HAVE MINCED MEAT ON SPECIAL OFFER AND THIS IS TAKEN FULL ADVANTAGE OF BY STUDENTS, WHO WILL TREAT THEMSELVES TO THIS TRADITIONAL DISH.

SERVES FOUR

INGREDIENTS
- 500g/1¼lb lean minced (ground) beef
- 1 large (US extra large) egg
- 25g/1oz/½ cup crushed rusks or dry breadcrumbs
- 2.5ml/½ tsp freshly ground nutmeg
- 2.5ml/½ tsp black pepper
- salt
- 30ml/2 tbsp plain (all-purpose) flour
- 65g/2½oz/5 tbsp butter, plus extra for greasing
- pinch of burnt sugar, caramel sugar or gravy browning
- 8 waxy potatoes, halved
- 1kg/2¼lb frisée lettuce, coarsely sliced
- 15ml/1 tbsp cornflour (cornstarch)

1 Put the minced beef, egg, crushed rusks, nutmeg and black pepper and a pinch of salt in a bowl and knead until thoroughly combined. Form the mixture into four smooth balls without any cracks. Place the flour in a shallow dish and roll the meatballs through it to coat.

2 Melt 40g/1½oz/3 tbsp of the butter in a non-stick frying pan. Add the meatballs and cook them over medium heat, turning frequently, for 10 minutes, until browned on all sides.

COOK'S TIP
You could combine the meatball ingredients with more breadcrumbs to make the mixture go further.

3 Pour in 400ml/14fl oz/1⅔ cups water and add the sugar and potatoes. Lower the heat, cover the pan and simmer for 20 minutes.

4 Cook the endive in a little boiling water for 10 minutes, then drain well and toss with the remaining butter. Grease a shallow ovenproof dish with butter and spread out the endive in the base.

5 Using a slotted spoon, remove the meatballs and potatoes from the frying pan. Reserve the cooking liquid.

6 Put the meatballs in the middle of the endive in the ovenproof dish, surround them with the potatoes and sprinkle the top with nutmeg.

7 Mix the cornflour with 30ml/2 tbsp water to a smooth paste in a small bowl. Stir the mixture into the cooking liquid in the frying pan and heat gently, stirring constantly, until the mixture is thickened.

8 Ladle a little of the sauce over the meat balls and pour the rest into a warmed sauceboat. Serve the endive and meatballs immediately with the extra sauce.

Per portion Energy 544kcal/2262kJ; Protein 29.9g; Carbohydrate 29.3g, of which sugars 2.8g; Fat 36.9g, of which saturates 18.1g; Cholesterol 157mg; Calcium 96mg; Fibre 3.1g; Sodium 274mg.

BLIND FINCHES WITH CARROTS

THERE ARE NUMEROUS EXPLANATIONS AS TO HOW THIS CLASSIC DISH GOT ITS NAME. SOME SAY IT DATES FROM A PERIOD WHEN UPPER CLASS BELGIANS REGULARLY DINED ON FINCHES. PEASANTS — WHO COULD ONLY AFFORD MEAT ONCE A WEEK ON SUNDAYS — COULD NOT MAKE THE DISH, SO THEY INVENTED THEIR OWN VERSION, USING VEAL AND MINCED BEEF OR PORK INSTEAD OF BIRDS. THEY CALLED IT 'BLIND FINCHES' BECAUSE, ALTHOUGH THE PIECES OF MEAT WERE VAGUELY BIRD-SHAPED, THEY HAD NO EYES. READY-TO-COOK BLIND FINCHES ARE ON SALE IN MOST BELGIAN BUTCHER'S SHOPS, BUT IT IS FUN AND EASY TO MAKE YOUR OWN AT HOME.

SERVES FOUR

INGREDIENTS
 4 x 90g/3½ oz sirloin or flank beef
  or veal steaks
 15g/½ oz/1 tbsp butter
 15ml/1 tbsp oil
 2 shallots or 1 small onion,
  finely chopped
 1 garlic clove, finely chopped
 500g/1¼ lb young carrots,
  finely chopped
 1 bay leaf
 2 thyme sprigs
 150ml–250ml/5–8fl oz/⅔–1 cup
  good quality Belgian beer
 5ml/1 tsp Tierenteyn or Dijon mustard
 salt and ground black pepper
 chopped fresh parsley, to garnish
For the filling
 225g/8oz/1 cup minced (ground)
  pork or a mixture of pork and beef
 1 egg yolk
 5ml/1 tsp dried sage
 2 shallots, finely chopped
 15ml/1 tbsp chopped fresh parsley
 5ml/1 tsp grated nutmeg
 15–45ml/1–3 tbsp breadcrumbs

1 Put all the ingredients for the filling in a large bowl, using just enough of the breadcrumbs to bind the mixture. Mix well. Dampen hands by running them under cold water, then roll the filling into four oval shapes of equal size. Set aside.

2 Put each steak between two sheets of clear film (plastic wrap) and pound it with a meat mallet or rolling pin until it is 5mm/¼in thick and large enough to wrap a portion of filling.

3 Fold the steak over the filling and tuck the ends in to make a parcel. Tie with kitchen string (twine) to maintain the shape.

4 Heat the butter and the oil in a large, heavy frying pan over medium heat. When it is hot, but not smoking, add the meat rolls and cook for about 10 minutes, turning occasionally until browned on all sides. Using tongs, transfer the rolls to a plate and cover with foil to keep warm.

5 Add the shallots or onion to the fat remaining in the pan and gently sauté for about 5 minutes to soften but not brown them.

6 Stir in the garlic, carrots, bay leaf and thyme, then return the beef rolls to the pan, season well and pour in the beer. Bring to the boil, then reduce the heat, cover and simmer for 10 minutes.

7 Turn the beef rolls over, stir the mustard into the vegetables, replace the lid and simmer for 8–10 minutes more or until the carrots are tender and the meat rolls and their filling are cooked through.

8 Remove the string from the beef rolls and divide among warmed plates.

9 Remove the herbs from the carrot mixture, then spoon it on to the plates. Sprinkle with chopped parsley and serve.

COOK'S TIP
You could make the finches in advance, putting them in the refrigerator at the end of Step 3 until required.

Per portion Energy 340kcal/1419kJ; Protein 25g; Carbohydrate 18.2g, of which sugars 12g; Fat 17.9g, of which saturates 6.4g; Cholesterol 131mg; Calcium 66mg; Fibre 3.9g; Sodium 450mg.

CAPTAIN'S DINNER

KAPUCIJNERTAFEL, OR 'MARROWFAT PEA TABLE', IS THE POLITE NAME OF THIS DISH, BUT DUTCH PEOPLE TEND TO USE THE SAILOR'S SLIGHTLY MORE COARSE NAME RAASDONDERS. WHATEVER THE NAME, THIS MASCULINE DISH WAS ALREADY ON THE SUNDAY MENU OF THE DUTCH EAST INDIES COMPANY IN THE 17TH CENTURY AND IT IS STILL POPULAR AMONG EXPATRIATES.

SERVES FOUR

INGREDIENTS
  500g/1¼lb dried marrowfat peas
For the apple sauce
  cooking apples
  cinnamon stick
  sugar, to taste
  dash of lemon juice
For the endive salad
  2 raw endives
  oil
  vinegar
For the accompaniments, choose from
  crisply fried thin bacon slices
  small meatballs
  fried small pork chops
  warm boiled potatoes
  golden brown fried onion rings
  finely chopped raw onions
  mustard
  piccalilli
  Amsterdam onions and cocktail onions
  sweet-sour gherkins

1 Soak the peas overnight in 2 litres/3½ pints/8¾ cups cold water. Drain and rinse well.

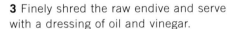

2 Put the peas in a pan, add cold water to cover and bring to the boil. Lower the heat and cook, uncovered, for about 45 minutes, until tender. Drain and keep warm while you prepare your chosen accompaniment(s).

3 Finely shred the raw endive and serve with a dressing of oil and vinegar.

4 To make apple sauce, peel, quarter and core the cooking apples.

5 Place the apples in a pan with a cinnamon stick, sugar to taste and just enough water to cover the base of the pan. Add some lemon juice, if you like.

6 Cook the sauce over low heat, stirring occasionally, until pulpy. Remove from the heat and cool before serving.

VARIATION
Use fresh green marrowfat peas, which need no soaking, if you like. Boil them for 15 minutes, or until tender.

Per portion Energy 162kcal/690kJ; Protein 11.6g; Carbohydrate 27.6g, of which sugars 3.4g; Fat 1.4g, of which saturates 0.2g; Cholesterol 0mg; Calcium 28mg; Fibre 3.6g; Sodium 680mg.

Hotch Potch with Beef

This delicious dish celebrates the end of the Spanish siege of the city of Leyden in 1574. The people were freed by a confederacy of nobles called the Watergeuzen, or 'Sea Beggars', who treated them to a meal of herring and white bread as well as an olla podrida, a stew of highly seasoned meat and vegetables left behind by the fleeing Spaniards.

SERVES FOUR

INGREDIENTS
    500g/1¼lb lean boneless
      beef flank
    5ml/1 tsp salt
    1kg/2¼lb potatoes, sliced
    800g/1¾lb carrots, diced
    500g/1¼lb onions, finely chopped

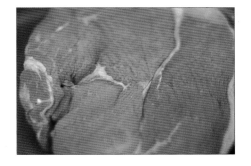

1 Put the beef in a large pan, then add the salt and pour in 300ml/½ pint/1¼ cups water.

2 Bring to the boil, then lower the heat, cover the pan with a lid and simmer for 2 hours, until the meat is tender.

3 Remove the beef from the pan. Add the potatoes, carrots and onions to the liquid and place the beef on top. Cover the pan with a lid and simmer for 30 minutes.

4 Pour off the cooking liquid from the vegetables through a colander into a bowl positioned underneath. Reserve the liquid.

5 Remove the beef to a chopping board and cut it into slices.

6 Mash the vegetables and potatoes, adding a little of the cooking liquid.

7 Season the mashed vegetables with salt to taste and pile on to plates.

8 Top the vegetables with the sliced meat and serve immediately.

Per portion Energy 536kcal/2250kJ; Protein 36.2g; Carbohydrate 71.9g, of which sugars 29.3g; Fat 13.4g, of which saturates 5.2g; Cholesterol 73mg; Calcium 122mg; Fibre 10.1g; Sodium 655mg.

AMSTERDAM BEEF ROLL

THE ROLLADE, OR ROLLED BEEF, IS THE DUTCH MEAT OF CHOICE FOR SPECIAL OCCASIONS. FRESHLY
PREPARED BY THE BUTCHER, THE ROLL MAY CONSIST OF BEEF, VEAL OR PORK. THIS RECIPE WAS
ORIGINALLY CALLED ROLLENDE, MEANING ROLLED LOIN. THE DISTINCTIVE AMSTERDAM ONIONS
LEND A UNIQUE TASTE TO THE GRAVY, HENCE THE NAME.

SERVES FOUR

INGREDIENTS
  50g/2oz/¼ cup butter
  1kg/2¼lb rolled beef, spiced
    with white pepper, freshly
    grated nutmeg, ground mace
    and ground gloves
  1 x 450g/1lb jar Amsterdam onions
  300ml/½ pint/1¼ cups red wine
    or water
  15ml/1 tbsp cornflour (cornstarch)
  30ml/2 tsp sugar
  1.5kg/3¾lb young marrowfat peas,
    or garden peas, shelled weight
    500g/1¼lb
  100g/3¾oz thinly sliced
    smoked bacon
  800g/1¾lb small potatoes
  2 spring onions (scallions),
    thinly sliced
  salt and ground black pepper,
    to taste
  apple sauce, to serve

1 Start preparing this dish the day before you intend to serve it. Melt the butter in a flameproof casserole over medium heat until lightly browned. Add the beef and cook on all sides, including the ends, until browned.

2 Lower the heat, add 30ml/2 tbsp of the juice from the onion jar, cover and simmer gently, turning the beef occasionally, for 2 hours. Transfer the beef to a plate, leave to cool, then cover with clear film (plastic wrap) and chill in the refrigerator overnight.

3 Transfer the cooking juices to a small bowl, leave to cool, then cover with clear film and chill in the refrigerator overnight. The next day, skim off and discard any fat from the surface. Reserve the solidified fat.

4 Remove and discard the string from the roll of beef. Cut it into 5mm/¼in thick slices, then reassemble into a roll shape and tie with kitchen string (twine).

5 Add the wine or water to the cooking liquid, pour into a large pan and bring to the boil.

6 Mix the cornflour with 30ml/2 tbsp water to a paste in a small bowl.

7 Stir the cornflour mixture into the cooking liquid. Cook, stirring constantly, for 1 minute and season to taste. Add the beef to the pan and warm through over a low heat for 20 minutes.

8 Heat half the reserved fat in a frying pan. Drain the onions, pat them dry with kitchen paper and add them to the pan.

9 Cook over low heat, stirring occasionally, for 10 minutes, until they are evenly browned. Sprinkle with the sugar, shake the pan well, remove from the heat and keep warm.

10 Cook the peas in a small pan of boiling water for 15 minutes. Drain, garnish with onions and keep warm.

11 Dry-fry the bacon in a heavy frying pan until crisp. Remove from the pan and drain on kitchen paper.

12 Cook the potatoes in boiling water for 15 minutes, until tender. Drain well and pat dry with kitchen paper.

13 Melt the remaining reserved fat in a frying pan, add the potatoes and cook, turning frequently, until browned all over.

14 To serve, remove and discard the kitchen string. Arrange the meat on a plate. Surround with onions, potatoes and peas, and garnish with fried bacon.

15 Ladle some sauce over the meat. Pour the rest in a sauceboat. Serve immediately with apple sauce as a side dish.

COOK'S TIP
The Amsterdam onions can be replaced with large sweet cocktail onions. These should have a small amount of tumeric powder or kurkuma added (enough so they look a pale yellow) and should be left in the refrigerator for 12 hours.

Per portion Energy 913kcal/3813kJ; Protein 74.5g; Carbohydrate 66.7g, of which sugars 19.8g; Fat 40.4g, of which saturates 18.2g; Cholesterol 185mg; Calcium 89mg; Fibre 9.5g; Sodium 650mg.

FLEMISH-STYLE BEEF STEW WITH BEER

THIS STEW IS ONE OF THE MOST FAMOUS OF ALL THE TRADITIONAL FLEMISH DISHES. THE TASTE VARIES FROM REGION TO REGION, DEPENDING ON WHICH TYPE OF BEER IS USED TO FLAVOUR AND TENDERIZE THE MEAT. THE TASTE IS ALSO INFLUENCED BY THE ADDITION OF BREAD OR SPICE CAKE, SPREAD WITH MUSTARD. THIS IS INITIALLY PLACED ON TOP OF THE STEW, BUT GRADUALLY DISSOLVES INTO IT TO FORM A THICK SAUCE. IT MAKES A DELICIOUS, HEARTY MEAL.

3 Add the onion to the fat remaining in the pan and cook gently for 6–8 minutes, until translucent, then add the garlic and fry for 3 minutes more.

4 Return the meat to the frying pan and stir well to combine with the onions.

5 Pour in the beer and bring the mixture to just below boiling point. Add the bouquet garni, vinegar and brown sugar.

6 Cover the pan, reduce the heat and simmer for 1½ hours or until meat has become tender.

SERVES FOUR–SIX

INGREDIENTS
  500g/1¼lb stewing beef, cubed
  20g/¾oz/3 tbsp plain (all-purpose)
    flour, for dusting
  25g/1oz/2 tbsp butter
  30ml/2 tbsp vegetable oil
  1 large onion, chopped
  2 garlic cloves, crushed
  330ml/11½fl oz dark Belgian beer,
    such as Chimay
  bouquet garni (*see* Cook's tip on
    page 144)
  30ml/2 tbsp red wine vinegar
  30ml/2 tbsp soft light brown sugar
  2 slices of rustic bread or spice cake
  30ml/2 tbsp Dijon mustard
  handful of fresh parsley, chopped
  salt and ground black pepper
To serve
  fries or bread and Belgian pickles

1 Season the beef cubes with salt and pepper, then coat them in the flour.

2 Heat a large, heavy frying pan that has a tight-fitting lid. Melt the butter and the oil over medium to high heat. Add the cubed beef in batches and brown over fairly high heat for about 4 minutes to seal. As each batch browns, remove the cubes from the pan and place them on a plate.

7 Spread the bread or spice cake thickly with mustard and place it on top of the stew, mustard side down.

8 Replace the lid and simmer the stew for 20–30 minutes more, stirring occasionally until the meat is very tender. The bread or cake will absorb some of the pan juices and dissolve to thicken the stew.

9 Taste and adjust the seasoning if necessary. Remove the bouquet garni and stir in the parsley. Serve with potato purée, fries or bread, with pickles.

COOK'S TIP
The addition of vinegar helps to tenderize the meat during the cooking process, while the soft light brown sugar enhances the flavour and colour of the finished dish.

Per portion Energy 317kcal/1324kJ; Protein 21.6g; Carbohydrate 19.8g, of which sugars 8.9g; Fat 15.7g, of which saturates 5.9g; Cholesterol 57mg; Calcium 47mg; Fibre 1.1g; Sodium 314mg.

MAASTRICHT FARE

THE PEOPLE IN THE SOUTHERN PROVINCE OF LIMBURG CALL THEMSELVES 'BURGUNDIANS', AND MANY OF THE FRENCH CASTLES STILL REMAIN. THOSE WHO WORKED IN THE CASTLE KITCHENS LEARNED HOW TO PREPARE SOPHISTICATED DISHES AND PASSED THIS KNOWLEDGE DOWN THROUGH THE GENERATIONS, SO THE MAASTRICHT CUISINE HAS A QUALITY THAT IS UNSURPASSED ELSEWHERE IN THE NETHERLANDS. CLOSE CONTACT BETWEEN LIMBURG AND GERMANY AND BELGIUM ALSO HELPED DEVELOP NEW CULINARY IDEAS.

SERVES FOUR

INGREDIENTS
20 ready-to-eat prunes
100ml/3½fl oz/scant ½ cup
  brandy
2.5ml/½ tsp grated lemon rind
65g/2½oz/5 tbsp butter
600g/1lb 6oz braising veal, diced
200ml/7fl oz/scant 1 cup stock
30ml/2 tbsp lemon juice
1 thyme sprig
1 bay leaf
200ml/7fl oz/scant 1 cup
  whipping cream
5ml/1 tsp potato flour or cornflour
  (cornstarch)
salt and ground black pepper
chopped fresh parsley, to garnish
To serve
  young peas
  carrots
  small new potatoes

1 Put the prunes in a bowl, add the brandy and lemon rind, cover and soak overnight.

2 Melt the butter in a pan, add the veal and cook over medium heat for about 10 minutes, until evenly browned.

3 Season and add the stock, lemon juice, thyme and bay leaf. Lower the heat, cover and simmer for about 1 hour, until tender.

4 Arrange the vegetables in a ring on a warm serving plate. Using a slotted spoon, transfer the veal to the centre of the plate and keep warm.

5 Bring the cooking liquid to the boil and reduce slightly, then stir in the cream. Remove and discard the thyme and bay leaf. Season with salt and pepper.

6 Mix the potato flour or cornflour with 15ml/1 tbsp cold water to a paste and stir into the sauce until it is thickened and smooth. Add the prunes with their soaking liquid and warm through.

7 Pour the sauce over the veal, sprinkle the vegetables with chopped parsley and serve immediately.

Per portion Energy 610kcal/2536kJ; Protein 34.4g; Carbohydrate 19.9g, of which sugars 18.7g; Fat 37.9g, of which saturates 22.4g; Cholesterol 213mg; Calcium 86mg; Fibre 3.5g; Sodium 286mg.

MUM'S BRAISING STEAK

TRADITIONALLY, DUTCH BEEF IS LEAN. THIS IS NOT BECAUSE OF MODERN CONCERNS ABOUT EATING TOO MUCH FAT — STEAK WAS USUALLY BROWNED IN LAVISH QUANTITIES OF BUTTER — BUT BECAUSE THE MEAT COMES FROM DAIRY CATTLE. GREEN BEANS ARE AMONG THE MOST POPULAR VEGETABLES IN THE NETHERLANDS AND, COMBINED WITH BRAISING STEAK, THEY MAKE A CLASSIC SUNDAY DISH.

SERVES FOUR

INGREDIENTS

4 pieces of braising steak, each
   about 175–225g/6–8oz
75g/3oz/6 tbsp butter
1 leek, sliced
1 bay leaf
pinch of ground cloves
10ml/2 tsp cornflour (cornstarch)
   (optional)
500g/1¼lb green beans
pinch of freshly grated nutmeg
salt and ground black pepper
boiled potatoes sprinkled with
   freshly grated nutmeg (optional),
   to serve

1 Rub the meat all over with salt and pepper. Melt 50g/2oz/4 tbsp of the butter in a frying pan. Add the pieces of steak and cook over medium-low heat for about 5 minutes on each side, until well browned.

2 Add the leek and cook, stirring from time to time, for 2–3 minutes, until softened but not coloured.

3 Stir in 200ml/7fl oz/scant 1 cup water, scraping up the sediment from the pan with a wooden spoon. Add the bay leaf and ground cloves. Lower the heat, cover and simmer gently, turning the meat every 30 minutes, for about 2–3 hours, until tender.

4 Cook the beans in a pan of boiling water for 15 minutes. Drain and place the beans in a serving dish. Toss with the remaining butter, sprinkle with nutmeg and keep warm.

5 If you would like to thicken the gravy, mix the cornflour with 20ml/4 tsp cold water to a paste in a small bowl and then stir into the pan.

6 Transfer the mixture to a warm dish and serve with the beans and potatoes.

VARIATIONS

• 7.5ml/1½ tsp vinegar used to be added to the water for braising the steak. Nowadays, red wine often replaces the water.
• For an alternative way to serve the beans, first rinse the cooked beans in a colander. Cook 50g/2oz/⅓ cup finely diced smoked bacon and one small finely chopped onion in a frying pan, stirring occasionally, for 5 minutes. Add the cooked beans to the pan and warm the mixture through.

Per portion Energy 457kcal/1902kJ; Protein 46.8g; Carbohydrate 5.4g, of which sugars 4g; Fat 27.7g, of which saturates 14.7g; Cholesterol 166mg; Calcium 69mg; Fibre 3.7g; Sodium 243mg.

STEAK WITH FRIES

BESIDES MUSSELS, BELGIUM'S OTHER NATIONAL DISH IS STEAK FRITES — BEEF STEAK WITH FRENCH FRIES. STEAK IS SERVED IN A VARIETY OF WAYS, WITH ALL SORTS OF SAUCES, BUT NEVER WITHOUT FRIES — THE TWO ARE INSEPARABLE IN THE NATIONAL PSYCHE. THE BEST BEEF IN BELGIUM COMES FROM THE WHITE BLUE BREED OF CATTLE, WHOSE MEAT IS LEAN AND TENDER, WITH SUPERIOR FLAVOUR.

SERVES FOUR

INGREDIENTS

  50g/2oz/¼ cup unsalted butter
  15ml/1 tbsp vegetable oil
  4 Belgian White Blue beef steaks or
    prime sirloin steaks, each about
    125g/4¼oz, at room temperature
    (*see* Cook's tip)
  salt and ground black pepper
  30ml/2 tbsp beef stock
  Belgian Fries (*see* page 191), to serve

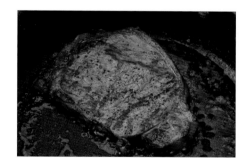

1 Heat 40g/1½oz/3 tbsp of the butter and the oil in a large, heavy frying pan over high heat. When it is hot, add the steaks and sear them for 1 minute on each side, using tongs to turn them.

VARIATION

To make steak in green peppercorn cream sauce, fry the steaks in 30ml/2 tbsp clarified butter for 3 minutes on one side until well browned, then turn them over and fry for 3 more minutes for rare steak or 4–7 minutes for medium rare. Pour a splash of cognac into the pan and set this alight carefully with a long safety match. Shake the pan. When the flames die down, remove the steaks and keep warm. Add to the pan 30ml/2 tbsp drained and rinsed bottled green peppercorns, then whisk in 200ml/7fl oz/scant 1 cup double (heavy) cream. Add a further 30ml/2 tbsp butter and cook over low heat, swirling the pan, until the sauce thickens. Add 5ml/1 tsp extra cognac to the sauce, season and pour over the steaks. Garnish with watercress and serve with fries.

2 Reduce the heat to medium and fry the steaks for a further 3–5 minutes on each side, depending on the thickness of the meat and how you like it. Season the steaks on both sides, then transfer them to individual plates. Cover with foil to keep warm.

3 Pour the stock into the frying pan and heat it, stirring and scraping the pan to incorporate the sediment on the base.

4 Add the remaining butter and continue stirring the sauce for 2 minutes. Pour over the steaks and serve immediately, with fries.

COOK'S TIP

Remove the steaks from the refrigerator 1 hour before cooking and let them come to room temperature. This results in juicier meat that will cook evenly.

Per portion Energy 287kcal/1192kJ; Protein 29.5g; Carbohydrate 0.1g, of which sugars 0.1g; Fat 18.7g, of which saturates 9.3g; Cholesterol 90mg; Calcium 9mg; Fibre 0g; Sodium 163mg.

VEAL TONGUE WITH MADEIRA SAUCE

Tongue doesn't appeal to everybody, but it is a delicious meat, tender and full of flavour. This recipe is a Belgian classic, served on special occasions. Preparation should begin the day before you intend to serve it. It is a favourite with connoisseurs and a revelation to those who have never encountered it before.

4 Lift out the tongue, rinse under cold water, drain and dry. Strain the stock into a measuring jug (cup). When the tongue is cool enough to handle, peel off the skin, trim the base of gristle and fat, then cut evenly into 1cm/½in slices. Fan these on a serving platter, cover and keep warm.

5 Slice the mushroom caps. Heat the oil in a frying pan and sauté the mushrooms for 8–10 minutes, until softened. Sprinkle with the lemon juice and season to taste.

6 Melt the butter in another frying pan. Sauté the remaining onion for 5–8 minutes until aromatic, then add the remaining garlic and sauté for 3 minutes more. Sprinkle over the flour and cook for 2 minutes, stirring.

7 Stir in the tomato purée, then gradually add 400ml/14fl oz/1⅔ cups of the reserved stock, stirring until the mixture thickens. Simmer for 5 minutes, stir in the mushrooms and Madeira and cook for 2 minutes more. Pour over the tongue and garnish with parsley. Serve.

SERVES FOUR–SIX

INGREDIENTS
  1kg/2¼lb veal tongue
  1 celery stick, diced
  1 carrot, diced
  1 onion, finely diced
  3 garlic cloves, crushed
  2 bay leaves
  15 peppercorns
  2 sprigs of fresh thyme
  250g/9oz/3½ cups button (white) mushrooms, caps and stems separated
  15ml/1 tbsp vegetable oil or olive oil
  15ml/1 tbsp lemon juice
  50g/2oz/¼ cup unsalted butter
  15g/½oz/2 tbsp plain (all-purpose) flour
  45ml/3 tbsp tomato purée (paste)
  100ml/3½fl oz/scant ½ cup Madeira
  salt and ground black pepper
  chopped parsley, to garnish

1 Rinse the tongue and put it in a large bowl with salted water to cover. Cover the bowl and leave to soak for 6–8 hours or overnight.

2 Rinse the tongue again, drain and place in a large pan or stockpot. Pour in water to cover, add 15ml/1 tbsp salt and bring to the boil. Reduce the heat, simmer for 10 minutes, then drain and rinse. Put the tongue back in the pan and cover with fresh water.

3 Add the celery and carrot, with half the chopped onion and a third of the crushed garlic. Toss in the peppercorns, thyme and mushroom stems. Season with salt. Bring to the boil, then reduce the heat, cover and simmer for 1½–2 hours or until the skin of the tongue comes away easily when prodded with a fork.

Per portion Energy 443kcal/1834kJ; Protein 27g; Carbohydrate 4.4g, of which sugars 2.4g; Fat 33.3g, of which saturates 4.6g; Cholesterol 318mg; Calcium 21mg; Fibre 0.8g; Sodium 773mg.

LEG OF LAMB WITH PARSLEY

THIS DISH, DATING FROM 1761, IS VERY TYPICAL OF TRADITIONAL DUTCH COOKING. AT THAT TIME, THE MEAT WOULD HAVE BEEN ROASTED ON A SPIT, BUT HERE IT IS COOKED IN A THOROUGHLY MODERN WAY IN A ROASTING BAG. IT IS SERVED WITH CAULIFLOWER, THE NUMBER ONE DUTCH VEGETABLE. IT IS ALSO GOOD WITH CRUSTY BREAD AND A GLASS OF RED CÔTES DU RHÔNE.

SERVES FOUR

INGREDIENTS
- 1kg/2¼lb boned leg of lamb
- salt
- 2 shallots, finely chopped
- 60ml/4 tbsp finely chopped fresh parsley
- 1 cauliflower, cut into florets
- pinch of freshly grated nutmeg

1 Put a wide, flat, ovenproof dish in the oven and preheat the oven to 200°C/400°F/Gas 6.

2 Using a sharp knife, make diamond-shaped incisions into the fat side of the meat. Rub the inside and outside of the lamb with salt.

4 Put the lamb into a roasting bag and seal loosely. Place the bag on the preheated dish in the oven and roast for 45 minutes.

5 Remove the lamb from the oven and increase the temperature to 240°C/475°F/Gas 9. Hold the bag over a bowl to collect the cooking juices and cut off one of the lower corners. Remove and discard the bag.

6 Return the lamb to the dish and roast for a further 15 minutes, until tender but still pink in the middle.

7 Put an ice cube in the cooking juices to help remove the fat, then strain into a sauceboat. Keep warm.

8 Meanwhile, cook the cauliflower in a pan of boiling water for 3–5 minutes, until tender-crisp. Drain well.

9 Carve the meat into thick slices and place on a serving dish. Sprinkle with nutmeg. Serve immediately, handing the sauce around separately.

3 Stuff the bone cavity with the shallots and parsley. Roll up, with the fat on the outside and tie with kitchen string (twine).

VARIATION
If you prefer your cauliflower with white sauce, cook it whole, head downwards, in a pan of boiling water for a maximum of 15 minutes. Drain, reserving 120ml/4fl oz/ ½ cup of the cooking liquid. Melt 25g/ 1oz/2 tbsp butter over low heat. Stir 30ml/2 tbsp plain (all-purpose) flour and cook, stirring, for 2 minutes. Gradually stir in 120ml/4fl oz/½ cup milk and the reserved cooking liquid. Cook, stirring constantly, until thickened and smooth. Season with salt, spoon the sauce over the cauliflower and sprinkle with freshly grated nutmeg.

Per portion Energy 500kcal/2088kJ; Protein 54.1g; Carbohydrate 5.3g, of which sugars 4.3g; Fat 29.3g, of which saturates 13.3g; Cholesterol 190mg; Calcium 75mg; Fibre 3.1g; Sodium 231mg.

HIGH MOORLAND LEG ᵒꜰ LAMB

*THE BARGERVEEN IS A NATURE RESERVE IN THE PROVINCE OF DRENTHE IN THE NORTH-EAST OF THE
NETHERLANDS, AND THE HEATH THERE IS HOME TO A LARGE HERD OF SHEEP, WHOSE MEAT HAS A UNIQUE
FLAVOUR. THE COMPANY WHO DISTRIBUTE THE MEAT ORGANIZED A REGIONAL RECIPE COMPETITION
A FEW YEARS AGO AND THIS IS AN ADAPTATION OF THE WINNING DISH BY WILLEM DE WITTE. IT
INVOLVES COATING BROWNED, ROLLED LAMB IN HAY, HEATHER AND FLOWERS AND ROASTING IT IN FOIL.*

SERVES FOUR

INGREDIENTS
   1 leg of lamb, boned, with the
      bones reserved
   2 egg whites, lightly beaten
   7.5ml/1½ tsp yellow mustard seeds,
      marinated in vinegar
   sea salt
   50g/2oz/¼ cup butter
To coat
   2 handfuls of hay
   1 handful of heather
   cumin seeds
   dried camomile flowers
   bay berries
   dried elderflowers
For the lemon thyme sauce
   2 shallots, chopped
   1 leek, chopped
   6 fresh lemon thyme sprigs
   30ml/2 tbsp plain (all-purpose) flour
   500ml/17fl oz/generous 2 cups
      gooseberry or white currant wine
   heather honey, to taste
   full-cream (whole) sheep's milk
      yogurt, to taste
   salt and pepper
To serve
   frisée lettuce
   cooked potatoes
   cooked brown beans
   crisp smoked bacon
   vinaigrette

1 Open out the leg of lamb and brush
the inside with the beaten egg whites
and mustard seeds.

2 Sprinkle the meat with salt, roll it up
and tie with kitchen string (twine), with
the fat on the outside.

3 Melt the butter in a large pan or
flameproof casserole, add the lamb
and cook, turning occasionally, for
about 15 minutes, until browned on all
sides. Meanwhile, preheat the oven to
150°C/300°F/Gas 2.

4 Mix together the hay, heather, cumin,
camomile flowers, bay berries and
elderflowers in whatever proportions you
like. Remove the lamb from the pan
and reserve the frying fat. Coat the lamb
in the aromatic hay mixture, then wrap in
a rectangle of foil and tie with string.

5 Place the parcel in a roasting pan and
roast for an hour, until cooked but still
pink in the middle.

6 Meanwhile, make the sauce. Heat the
pan of reserved fat. Add the lamb bones,
shallots, leek, lemon thyme and flour
and fry, stirring frequently, for 5 minutes.

7 Gradually stir the wine into the pan
and bring to the boil, then lower the
heat and simmer for 1 hour.

8 Strain the sauce into a clean pan
through a sieve (strainer) and boil until
reduced by half. Season and stir in
honey and yogurt to taste.

9 Remove the lamb from the oven and
leave to rest for 15 minutes.

10 Finely shred the frisée lettuce and
finely slice the potatoes.

11 Unwrap the lamb and carve it into
slices. Serve immediately with the
sauce, along with a mixture of endive,
bacon, potatoes and brown beans
tossed in a vinaigrette and seasoned
with salt and pepper.

COOK'S TIP
This dish can also be served with a salad
of raw chicory (witloof or Belgian endive).

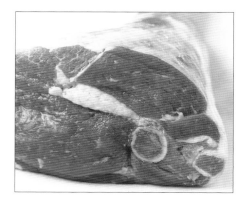

Per portion Energy 629kcal/2634kJ; Protein 75.9g; Carbohydrate 8.5g, of which sugars 2.3g; Fat 23.8g, of which saturates 9.7g; Cholesterol 265mg; Calcium 83mg; Fibre 1g; Sodium 219mg.

SALADS AND SIDE DISHES

Blessed with ideal growing conditions, Belgium and the Netherlands are home to a wealth of high-quality vegetables, including the much-prized asparagus, endive and, most notably, the potato, which is used to make the national favourites — mash and fries. The vegetables are transformed into a wide range of simple yet delicious salads, often incorporating meat, fish or eggs, and side dishes, which are often a combination of flavours, as in Brussels Sprouts and Carrot Mash.

CLASSIC TOMATO SALAD

TOMATOES ARE AN IMPORTANT CROP IN BELGIUM. DURING THE SUMMER MONTHS GREENHOUSES AND FIELDS ARE FILLED WITH TOMATOES THAT DIFFER WIDELY IN SIZE, QUALITY AND TEXTURE AND EVERY YEAR NEW VARIETIES BECOME AVAILABLE TO MEET AN INCREASING DEMAND. HOME COOKS AND RESTAURATEURS ALIKE HEIGHTEN THEIR SUMMER MENUS WITH THIS CLASSIC TOMATO SALAD.

SERVES FOUR

INGREDIENTS
4 ripe but firm tomatoes on the vine
2–3 shallots, finely chopped
45ml/3 tbsp chopped fresh parsley
    or dill
30ml/2 tbsp red wine vinegar
90ml/6 tbsp vegetable oil, olive oil
    or a mixture
salt and ground black pepper

COOK'S TIP
The fresher the tomatoes, the better this salad will be. They should be full-flavoured and firm enough to slice neatly with a serrated knife, yet not underripe. Try to make the salad when tomatoes are in season in the summer for best results.

1 Remove the stem and core from each tomato, then slice them evenly and arrange them on a serving dish. Finely chop the shallots.

2 Sprinkle the tomatoes with the shallots, season with salt and pepper and sprinkle with the parsley or dill.

3 Make a simple dressing by putting the vinegar in a small bowl and whisking in the oil. Drizzle the dressing over the tomatoes.

4 Cover with clear film (plastic wrap) and marinate for 30 minutes at room temperature before serving.

VARIATION
The herbs can be varied, depending on what you have in the garden. Tarragon makes a good addition, especially if the salad is to be served with fish.

COOK'S TIP
If you want a more refined salad, or the tomatoes have thick skins, you can remove the skin before slicing. Make a small cross at the top of the tomatoes, then put them in a heatproof bowl and cover with boiling water. Leave for about 2 minutes, lift out with a slotted spoon and peel away the skins as soon as they are cool enough to handle.

Per portion Energy 171kcal/705kJ; Protein 1.1g; Carbohydrate 3.9g, of which sugars 3.5g; Fat 16.9g, of which saturates 2g; Cholesterol 0mg; Calcium 34mg; Fibre 1.6g; Sodium 11mg.

NORTH HOLLAND SALAD

THIS MAIN DISH SALAD IS PERFECT FOR A HOT SUMMER'S DAY, WHEN THE SUBLIME NORTH HOLLAND POTATO OPPERDOEZER RONDE IS IN SEASON. A FIRM YELLOW POTATO, IT IS AN IDEAL PARTNER FOR HERRINGS, EGGS, GHERKINS AND ROUND LETTUCE, A CLASSIC VARIETY OF SALAD LEAF THAT MATCHES UP TO ANY MODERN ONE — TASTE A PIECE OF ITS HEART AND YOU WILL DISCOVER WHY.

SERVES TWO

INGREDIENTS

6–8 Opperdoezer Ronde or other
waxy potatoes, scraped clean
1 round (butterhead) lettuce,
coarse outer leaves removed
2 hard-boiled eggs, halved
100g/3¾oz extra-mature (sharp)
Gouda cheese, cut into thin strips
4 marinated herrings, drained and
cut into pieces
2 spring onions (scallions),
coarsely chopped
4 large sweet pickled gherkins,
cut into strips
45ml/3 tbsp olive oil
15ml/1 tbsp white wine vinegar
salt and ground black pepper
chopped fresh parsley, to garnish
To serve
boiled potatoes
50g/2oz/¼ cup butter, melted
mustard, oil and vinegar

VARIATION
If you don't like or can't find Gouda, you could use mature (sharp) Cheddar cheese or some shaved Parmesan instead.

1 Cook the potatoes in boiling water for about 20 minutes, until tender. Drain well and keep warm.

2 Tear the lettuce into bitesize pieces and spread out on a serving platter. Arrange the egg halves, strips of cheese and herrings on top. Sprinkle with spring onions and gherkins.

3 Whisk together the oil and vinegar in a bowl or glass, season with salt and pepper and sprinkle over the salad. Garnish with chopped parsley.

4 Serve with the potatoes and a sauceboat of the melted butter, with mustard, oil and vinegar added to taste.

COOK'S TIP
It is best not to put the salad together too far in advance or the lettuce will become limp and soggy and everything will lose its freshness.

Per portion Energy 862kcal/3577kJ; Protein 38g; Carbohydrate 21g, of which sugars 13.5g; Fat 69.8g, of which saturates 27.3g; Cholesterol 328mg; Calcium 477mg; Fibre 1.9g; Sodium 1525mg.

MECHELEN CAULIFLOWER AND SHRIMP SALAD

THE AREA OF MECHELEN IS FAMOUS FOR ITS SUPERB CAULIFLOWERS. IN THIS SIMPLE RECIPE, THE FIRM, CREAMY FLORETS OF THE VEGETABLE ARE COMBINED WITH DELICIOUS GREY SHRIMP FROM THE NORTHERN BELGIAN COAST IN A RICH, HERBY MAYONNAISE. SERVED ON A BED OF CRUNCHY LETTUCE, THIS DELIGHTFUL SALAD MAKES A NUTRITIOUS LUNCH OR DINNER.

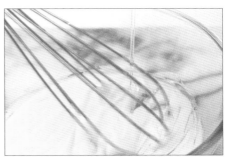

3 Make a mayonnaise by whisking the egg yolk, mustard and lemon juice in a large, clean bowl or food processor. Add the oil in a slow, steady stream, constantly whisking or processing the mixture until it thickens.

4 When the mayonnaise is smooth and silky, mix in the tomato purée and the chopped chives or dill. Season with salt and pepper and stir well.

5 Arrange the lettuce leaves on a serving platter or plate and pile up the cauliflower florets in the centre. Top with the shrimp.

6 Drizzle the herb mayonnaise over the shrimp and lettuce and garnish with the finely chopped hard-boiled egg and chopped parsley.

SERVES FOUR–SIX

INGREDIENTS
    1 medium cauliflower, outer leaves
      removed, cut into florets
    1 cos, romaine or round
      (butterhead) lettuce
    1 egg yolk
    5ml/1 tsp Dijon mustard
    juice of 1 lemon
    500ml/17fl oz/generous 2 cups
      vegetable oil
    5–10ml/1–2 tsp tomato purée (paste)
    15ml/1 tbsp finely chopped fresh
      chives or dill
    350g/12oz peeled cooked grey
      shrimp or pink salad shrimp
    salt and ground black pepper
To garnish
    1–2 hard-boiled eggs, finely chopped
    a handful of fresh parsley, chopped

1 Bring a large pan of lightly salted water to the boil, add the cauliflower and cook for 5–10 minutes or until the florets are crisp-tender Drain, rinse under cold water and drain again. Leave to cool.

2 Rinse the lettuce leaves, dry them in a salad spinner or by blotting them with a clean dish towel or kitchen paper. Tear into bitesize pieces.

COOK'S TIPS
• Do not overcook the cauliflower. Soggy florets lose colour and flavour, as well as valuable nutrients
• To keep the cauliflower white, add 15–30ml/1–2 lemon juice or 15ml/ 1 tbsp white wine vinegar to the cooking water before adding the cauliflower. Alternatively, substitute 250ml/8fl oz/ 1 cup of the cooking water with milk.

VARIATION
Any cooked shrimp or prawns can be used in this dish. Crayfish and lobster would also be delicious. They will not taste the same as grey shrimp, but they have a great flavour.

Per portion Energy 637kcal/2630kJ; Protein 17.6g; Carbohydrate 3.5g, of which sugars 3.1g; Fat 61.5g, of which saturates 7.5g; Cholesterol 109mg; Calcium 221mg; Fibre 1.9g; Sodium 2256mg.

DUTCH ASPARAGUS

In the early 20th century, a priest began cultivating the first white asparagus in Limburg to raise money for his parishioners. Now, both Limburg and Brabant have an Asparagus Society, and these organize asparagus feasts. From the middle of May the N271 in Limburg, christened the 'asparagus road', is dotted with stalls selling the vegetable.

SERVES FOUR

INGREDIENTS

2kg/4½lb finest white asparagus
25ml/1½ tbsp salt
8–12 small new potatoes, peeled
4 eggs
100g/3¾oz/scant ½ cup
  butter, melted
8 slices unsmoked cooked ham
pinch of freshly grated nutmeg
chopped fresh parsley, to garnish

1 Rinse the asparagus and trim about 2cm/¾in from the base, reserving the trimmings. Using a vegetable peeler, carefully peel the spears from the tips downwards.

2 Put the peel and trimmings in a pan and cover with a clean dish towel, leaving the sides overhanging.

3 Place the asparagus spears on the dish towel, fold in the overhang, add enough cold water to cover and the salt. Cover the pan and bring to the boil, then lower the heat and poach gently for 10 minutes.

4 Remove the pan from the heat and leave to stand for 15–20 minutes. Test the asparagus is tender by pricking the ends with a fork; they should be soft but not mushy.

5 Meanwhile, cook the potatoes in a pan of boiling water for 20 minutes, until tender. Drain and keep warm.

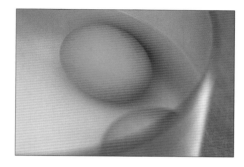

6 Hard-boil the eggs in another pan of boiling water for 10 minutes. Refresh under cold running water, then shell and halve.

7 Using a slotted spoon, remove the asparagus from the pan and drain on a dish towel. Pour the melted butter into a sauceboat.

8 Arrange the asparagus spears on individual plates and garnish with ham, hard-boiled egg halves and warm potatoes sprinkled with nutmeg and chopped parsley. Serve immediately with the melted butter.

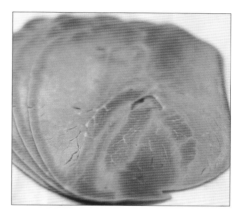

Per portion Energy 491kcal/2035kJ; Protein 31.4g; Carbohydrate 22.7g, of which sugars 11.1g; Fat 31g, of which saturates 15.7g; Cholesterol 273mg; Calcium 176mg; Fibre 9.3g; Sodium 835mg.

HUSSAR'S SALAD

THIS IS A TRADITIONAL NEW YEAR'S EVE DISH IN THE NETHERLANDS. THE NAME IS SAID TO DERIVE FROM THE HUSSARS, WHO WERE ONCE STATIONED ALL OVER THE COUNTRY, AND WERE GENERALLY UNDERFED IN THEIR BARRACKS. IN DESPERATION, THEY COURTED THE KITCHEN MAIDS OF WEALTHY FAMILIES, WHO FED THEM COLD LEFTOVERS FROM THEIR MASTERS' KITCHENS.

SERVES SIX

INGREDIENTS

1 lettuce, coarse outer
  leaves removed
600g/1lb 6oz boiled potatoes
about 45ml/3 tbsp vegetable oil
about 45ml/3 tbsp white wine vinegar
5ml/1 tsp ready-made mustard
1 tart apple
4 gherkins, chopped
60ml/4 tbsp cocktail onions, chopped
1 cooked beetroot (beet), peeled
  and diced
300g/11oz cold cooked veal or
  beef, diced
2 hard-boiled eggs, finely chopped
150–250ml/5–8fl oz/⅔–1 cup
  mayonnaise
salt and ground black pepper
15ml/1 tbsp chopped fresh parsley,
  to garnish

1 Wash the lettuce leaves thoroughly under cold running water, then line a shallow dish with them and set aside.

2 Mash the boiled potatoes with the oil, vinegar and mustard in a large bowl until smooth. Season with salt and pepper. Taste the mashed potato to check the balance of flavours and the texture are correct. You may need to add a little more oil and vinegar.

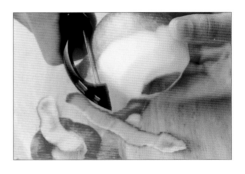

3 Peel and dice the apple. Set aside 15ml/1 tbsp each of the chopped gherkins, cocktail onions and beetroot for the garnish.

4 Carefully mix the remainder with the mashed potato, then stir in the apple, meat and eggs.

5 Make a mountain of this mixture over the lettuce leaves, and then cover with a thick coating of mayonnaise.

6 Garnish with the reserved beetroot, gherkins and onions and sprinkle with the parsley before serving.

VARIATIONS
• The modern trend is to dice the potatoes in this dish rather than mash them. This is certainly tastier, but is more time-consuming.
• Peas and carrots make good additions to the salad.

Per portion Energy 425kcal/1768kJ; Protein 16.3g; Carbohydrate 20.5g, of which sugars 5.2g; Fat 31.5g, of which saturates 6.1g; Cholesterol 111mg; Calcium 39mg; Fibre 2g; Sodium 217mg.

POTATO, BEAN AND BACON SALAD

THIS SPECIALTY SALAD COMES FROM LIÈGE, THE FRENCH-SPEAKING CENTRE OF WALLONIA. FROM MID-MAY UNTIL THE END OF OCTOBER, CRISP GARDEN GREEN BEANS ARE AT THEIR PEAK. THEY PARTNER POTATOES IN THIS CLASSIC SALAD, WHICH IS A POPULAR MENU ITEM AT RESTAURANTS AND BRASSERIES. IT MAKES A SATISFYING LUNCH AND IS USUALLY ACCOMPANIED BY A REFRESHING BELGIAN LOCAL BEER.

SERVES FOUR

INGREDIENTS
  600g/1lb 6oz potatoes, scrubbed
    but not peeled
  500g/1¼lb/3½–4 cups fine green
    beans, trimmed
  15ml/1 tbsp vegetable oil
  150g/5oz smoked bacon,
    finely chopped
  1 small onion, finely chopped
  90ml/6 tbsp red wine vinegar
  salt and ground black pepper
  15ml/1 tbsp chopped fresh parsley,
    to garnish

1 Put the scrubbed potatoes in a large pan with enough lightly salted water to cover. Bring to the boil and cook for 15–20 minutes, until tender but still fairly firm.

2 Meanwhile, cook the beans in a separate pan of lightly salted water for 5 minutes, until just tender but not overcooked and soggy.

3 Drain the beans in a colander, rinse with cold water to prevent further cooking, then pat dry with kitchen paper. Put the beans in a salad bowl and cover with foil to keep warm.

4 Heat the oil in a frying pan and fry the bacon over medium heat for 7 minutes, or until crisp. Remove with a slotted spoon and sprinkle over the beans. Cover the salad bowl with foil again. Set aside the frying pan.

5 Drain the potatoes in the colander. When they are cool enough to handle, cut into thick slices or quarters.

6 Return the frying pan to the heat. When the bacon fat is hot, add the chopped onion and fry on medium heat for 8–10 minutes until golden brown. Tip the contents of the pan over the beans and bacon, then add the potatoes. Mix gently.

7 Pour the wine vinegar into the frying pan. Boil rapidly for 2 minutes, stirring to incorporate any bits of bacon or onion that have stuck to the base. Pour over the salad. Season and toss to coat. Sprinkle with chopped parsley and serve immediately, while still warm.

Per portion Energy 246kcal/1029kJ; Protein 11.3g; Carbohydrate 29.3g, of which sugars 5.7g; Fat 10.1g, of which saturates 2.9g; Cholesterol 20mg; Calcium 60mg; Fibre 4.5g; Sodium 595mg.

PEAS AND CARROTS FLEMISH STYLE

FROM THE MIDDLE OF MAY UNTIL MID-JULY, BELGIANS INDULGE IN ONE OF THEIR FAVOURITE TREATS: FRESH PEAS. SWEET AND TENDER, THEY ARE DELICIOUS EATEN RAW, OR CAN BE ACCOMPANIED BY YOUNG CARROTS, PEARL ONIONS, GARDEN LETTUCE AND SALTY BACON OR CURED HAM, AS IN THIS CLASSIC RECIPE. THIS DISH IS ESPECIALLY POPULAR SERVED WITH ROAST PORK OR BEEF.

SERVES FOUR–SIX

INGREDIENTS

8 young carrots, thinly sliced
1.6kg/3½lb fresh peas in pods or
    500g/1¼lb/5 cups frozen peas
40g/1½oz/3 tbsp butter
115g/4oz rindless smoked bacon,
    cut into fine strips
100g/3¾oz/⅔ cup baby or small
    pearl onions, peeled and left whole
100ml/3½fl oz/scant ½ cup stock
1 small lettuce, cut in thin strips
pinch of sugar and grated nutmeg
salt and ground black pepper
chopped fresh parsley, to garnish

COOK'S TIP
Shell the peas just before cooking them. Pinch off the stem, then pull the string down the full length of the pod. The pod will pop open so the peas can be removed.

1 Bring a pan of salted water to the boil. Add the carrots and cook for 3 minutes. Remove with a slotted spoon and leave to dry.

2 Pod the peas (*see* Cook's tip) and add them to the pan of boiling water. Cook for 2 minutes, then drain and add the peas to a bowl of iced water to stop them from cooking any further. Drain and set aside.

3 Melt 25g/1oz/2 tbsp of the butter in a large frying pan. Add the bacon and sauté for 3 minutes, then add the onions and sauté for 4 minutes.

4 When the onions are translucent, add the carrots and sauté for 3 minutes until they are glazed.

5 Pour in the stock, cover and cook for 10–15 minutes, or until all the liquid has been absorbed. Add the lettuce and cook for 3–5 minutes until the strips have wilted.

6 Add the peas, with the remaining butter. Simmer for 2–3 minutes until the peas are just tender. Add the sugar and nutmeg, season and stir to mix. Spoon into a warmed bowl, garnish with parsley and serve.

VARIATION
If available, substitute smoked ham from the Ardennes or Ganda for the bacon, or use Breydel ham from Flanders. Sauté for just 1 minute, not 3.

Per portion Energy 141kcal/585kJ; Protein 9.8g; Carbohydrate 15.5g, of which sugars 7.4g; Fat 4.9g, of which saturates 1.5g; Cholesterol 10mg; Calcium 49mg; Fibre 5.8g; Sodium 311mg.

RED CABBAGE BRAISED WITH APPLES

RED CABBAGE IS A TRADITIONAL VEGETABLE WHOSE USE IS PROFOUNDLY INGRAINED IN BELGIAN CUISINE. THE FLEMISH PREDILECTION FOR MIXING SWEET AND SOUR FLAVOURS AND COMBINING VEGETABLES WITH FRUITS AND SPICES REFLECTS THE COUNTRY'S HISTORY. THE FLAVOURS ARE COMPLEX AND EARTHY, MAKING IT A GREAT COMPANION FOR HEARTY MEAT, GAME OR SAUSAGE DISHES.

SERVES FOUR

INGREDIENTS
  65g/2½oz/5 tbsp butter or 75ml/
    5 tbsp oil
  1 onion, finely chopped
  675g/1½lb red cabbage, evenly
    shredded (*see* Cook's tips)
  90–120ml/6–8 tbsp white or red
    wine vinegar
  3–4 cooking apples, peeled
    and sliced
  2 cloves
  2 fresh bay leaves
  pinch of ground cinnamon
  15–30ml/1–2 tbsp soft dark
    brown sugar
  salt and ground black pepper

1 Heat the butter or oil in a heavy flameproof casserole or pan. Add the onion and sauté, stirring frequently, for 5 minutes, or until lightly browned.

2 Add the cabbage to the casserole or pan and stir thoroughly to coat in the fat. Immediately pour in the vinegar.

3 Add the apples and cook for 3 minutes more, stirring frequently.

4 Roll each clove in a bay leaf and push down inside the casserole. Bring to the boil, then reduce the heat to low.

5 Cover the casserole or pan and simmer for 1½–2 hours, stirring occasionally, or until the cabbage is tender.

6 Check the casserole or pan from time to time to make sure that the cabbage mixture remains moist. If it seems dry, add a tablespoon of boiling water. When the cabbage is done, there should be hardly any liquid left in the bottom of the casserole.

COOK'S TIPS
• To prepare the cabbage, first remove any damaged outer leaves. Slice the cabbage in half lengthways. Cut a V-shaped wedge around the white core and remove it. Slice both pieces in half again, then slice or shred the cabbage with a sharp cook's knife.
• Adjust the amount of vinegar or sugar, depending on how tart the apples are and your personal preference.

7 Season with salt and pepper, then add the cinnamon, with brown sugar to taste. Simmer for 3 minutes more, until the sugar has dissolved completely.

8 Remove the bay leaves and cloves, transfer the cabbage into a heated bowl and serve immediately.

Per portion Energy 222kcal/924kJ; Protein 3g; Carbohydrate 22.6g, of which sugars 22g; Fat 13.8g, of which saturates 8.5g; Cholesterol 35mg; Calcium 95mg; Fibre 5.4g; Sodium 113mg.

POACHED APPLES WITH BERRY COMPOTE

THE SMALL TRAILING CRANBERRIES THAT GROW IN BELGIUM, KNOWN LOCALLY AS EITHER VEENBESSEN OR AIRELLES, ARE PALER THAN THEIR MORE ROBUST AMERICAN COUSINS AND HAVE A SLIGHTLY DIFFERENT FLAVOUR. THESE JEWEL-LIKE FRUITS ARE OFTEN PARTNERED WITH POACHED APPLES OR PEARS. IN THE ARDENNES AREA, THE COMBINATION IS REGULARLY SERVED WITH POULTRY AND GAME, ESPECIALLY WILD BOAR, AS THE SWEET AND TART COMBINATION COMPLEMENTS THE RICH MEAT WELL.

SERVES FOUR

INGREDIENTS
    2 firm, sharp, eating apples
    45ml/3 tbsp sugar
    500ml/17fl oz/generous 2 cups water
    juice of ½ lemon
For the berry compote
    250/9oz/2½ cups cranberries
    60–90ml/4–6 tbsp water
    150g/5oz/¾ cup sugar, or to taste
    5–10ml/1–2 tsp lemon juice

VARIATION
You could use firm, tart pears instead of apples for a slightly different version of this autumnal accompaniment.

1 Peel the apples and cut them in half. Cut away the stem and core from each with a paring knife and use a spoon to carefully enlarge the core space and create a cavity.

2 In a pan large enough to hold the apples in a single layer, heat the sugar with the water. Bring to the boil, stirring occasionally to make a syrup.

3 Stir in the lemon juice. Reduce the heat and place the apple halves in the pan, so they are covered with syrup. Cover and simmer for about 20 minutes or until they are tender but still hold their shape.

4 Lift out the apples with a slotted spoon and drain on a wire rack positioned over a baking sheet.

5 Make the berry compote. Rinse the cranberries in a colander and put them in a pan with the water and sugar. Bring to the boil.

6 Reduce the heat, cover and simmer for 10 minutes or until the berries have softened. Stir occasionally and skim off any foam that rises to the surface.

7 Add 5ml/1 tsp of the lemon juice, taste and adjust for sweetness. If necessary, add more sugar, heating until it dissolves.

8 Transfer the apples to a serving platter, with the hollowed-out cavities uppermost. Fill them with the berry compote. To serve warm, reheat the apples in a shallow pan for about 5 minutes. They can also be served chilled. Offer any remaining berry compote in a separate bowl.

Per portion Energy 250kcal/1069kJ; Protein 0.8g; Carbohydrate 65.6g, of which sugars 65.6g; Fat 0.2g, of which saturates 0g; Cholesterol 0mg; Calcium 33mg; Fibre 2.7g; Sodium 6mg.

RHUBARB COMPOTE

ALTHOUGH RHUBARB IS OFTEN THOUGHT OF AS A FRUIT, IT IS ACTUALLY A VEGETABLE AND IS CLOSELY RELATED TO SORREL. IT GROWS EXCEPTIONALLY WELL IN BELGIUM'S COOL CLIMATE AND IS A POPULAR INGREDIENT IN BOTH SAVOURY AND SWEET DISHES. THIS VERSATILE RHUBARB COMPOTE MAKES A TERRIFIC SAUCE FOR CHICKEN, DUCK, GAME OR PORK, BUT CAN ALSO BE USED AS A PIE FILLING OR MIXED WITH YOGURT TO MAKE A QUICK DESSERT.

SERVES FOUR

INGREDIENTS
400g/14oz rhubarb
50g/2oz/¼ cup sugar or honey
strip of pared orange or lemon rind
1 cinnamon stick
15ml/1 tbsp cornflour (cornstarch)
  mixed with 30ml/2 tbsp water
  (optional)

1 Trim the rhubarb stalks, removing the hard section at the base of each. Cut into 2.5cm/1in pieces.

2 Pour enough water into a non-reactive pan to just cover the base. Sprinkle half the sugar on top of the water. Heat gently, stirring occasionally, until the sugar has dissolved completely.

3 Add the rhubarb to the pan with the citrus rind and cinnamon stick. Bring to the boil, then reduce the heat and simmer for 15 minutes or until the rhubarb is tender.

4 If the compote needs to be thickened, stir in the cornflour mixture. Continue to simmer the mixture for about 5 minutes, stirring gently so as not to break up the rhubarb too much.

VARIATIONS
• Use a mixture of strawberries and rhubarb.
• Add 30–45ml/2–3 tbsp raisins or currants.
• Add a splash of port or red vermouth when adding the rhubarb.

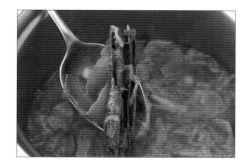

5 Remove the cinnamon stick and citrus peel. Taste the compote and add more of the sugar if needed. Serve warm, at room temperature or chilled.

Per portion Energy 43kcal/186kJ; Protein 1g; Carbohydrate 10.4g, of which sugars 10.4g; Fat 0.1g, of which saturates 0g; Cholesterol 0mg; Calcium 94mg; Fibre 1.4g; Sodium 5mg.

BRUSSELS SPROUTS AND CARROT MASH

STOEMP IS HEARTY COMFORT FOOD WITH ITS ROOTS IN ANCIENT FLEMISH PEASANT COOKING. POTATOES ARE THE BASIS OF THIS RUSTIC WINTER DISH, WHICH HAS AS MANY VARIATIONS AS THERE ARE COOKS UNDER THE BELGIAN SKY. ANY VEGETABLES THAT ARE AVAILABLE, AFFORDABLE AND IN SEASON ARE LIKELY TO END UP IN THE DISH. BUTTER, BACON, CHEESE OR CREAM ARE ADDED TO THE MIXTURE TO MAKE A CREAMY MASH, WHICH CAN BE SERVED AS A ONE-DISH MEAL OR A SIDE DISH.

2 Pour in hot water or, for more flavour, chicken stock, to cover. Add the bouquet garni. Bring to the boil, then reduce the heat, cover and simmer for about 10 minutes.

3 Cut the potatoes into even cubes and add to the pan, making sure there is still enough liquid to cover. Boil for 15 minutes more, until the potatoes are tender.

4 Drain the vegetables over a large bowl, reserving the liquid for use in another dish, such as a soup.

5 Remove the bouquet garni, add the nutmeg and mash the vegetables roughly. Add the remaining butter and season to taste. Mix well to combine and serve the mash warm.

SERVES FOUR

INGREDIENTS

115g/4oz/½ cup unsalted butter
3 shallots, finely chopped
350g/12oz/4 cups Brussels sprouts, trimmed and halved
350g/12oz carrots, sliced (about 3 cups)
250–300ml/8–10fl oz/1–1¼ cups hot water or chicken stock
bouquet garni
600g/1lb 6oz potatoes
a pinch of grated nutmeg
salt and ground black pepper, to taste

1 Melt 30ml/2 tbsp of the butter in a large frying pan and sauté the shallots for 3 minutes. Add the Brussels sprouts and carrots and sauté for 5 minutes more, seasoning with salt and pepper to taste.

Per portion Energy 386kcal/1609kJ; Protein 6.3g; Carbohydrate 34.8g, of which sugars 11.3g; Fat 25.6g, of which saturates 15.5g; Cholesterol 61mg; Calcium 59mg; Fibre 7.2g; Sodium 218mg.

POTATO, BACON AND CHEESE MASH

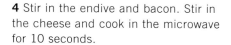

IN THE 1930S, COOKERY TEACHERS USED TO VISIT RURAL AREAS OF THE NETHERLANDS TO PASS ON THE LATEST ADVICE ABOUT PREPARING HEALTHY FOOD. THIS GOVERNMENTAL ADVICE WAS ALWAYS TAKEN BY THE LOCALS WITH A PINCH OF SALT, AS THESE RURAL COMMUNITIES KNEW THAT NOTHING COULD BE HEALTHIER AND MORE NUTRITIOUS THAN THEIR MOTHER'S POTATO MASH WITH RAW VEGETABLES, OR STAMPPOT MET RAUWE GROENTEN.

SERVES FOUR

INGREDIENTS
  1kg/2¼lb potatoes
  200g/7oz/generous 1 cup diced
    lean smoked bacon
  200g/7oz/1¾ cups diced mild
    Gouda cheese
  1kg/2¼lb curly endive, shredded
  25g/1oz/2 tbsp butter
  100ml/3½fl oz/scant ½ cup
    full-fat (whole) milk
  salt
  butter or gravy, to serve

1 Cook the potatoes in salted boiling water for 20 minutes, until tender.

2 Meanwhile, cook the bacon in a dry frying pan over low heat, turning occasionally, for about 8 minutes, until light brown and crisp. Remove from the pan and crumble.

3 Drain the potatoes, return to the pan and mash with the butter and enough of the milk to make a smooth purée.

4 Stir in the endive and bacon. Stir in the cheese and cook in the microwave for 10 seconds.

5 Serve immediately. All mash is eaten with a well in the centre for a knob (pat) of butter or spoonful of gravy.

VARIATIONS
• Curly green endive is a great favourite among the Dutch, but other members of the chicory family, such as frisée and radicchio, are also popular in this dish.
• Turnip tops (greens), nettles, spinach, purslane and watercress can also be served in this way.

Per portion Energy 368kcal/1543kJ; Protein 14.6g; Carbohydrate 48.5g, of which sugars 6.2g; Fat 16g, of which saturates 7.4g; Cholesterol 41.2mg; Calcium 101.2mg; Fibre 4.7g; Sodium 848.7mg.

HOT LIGHTNING

THIS DISH IS MADE IN DIFFERENT WAYS THROUGHOUT THE NETHERLANDS. IN GRONINGEN (NORTH) SWEET APPLES ARE USED, AND IN LIMBURG (SOUTH) THE COOKED APPLES AND POTATOES ARE SIMPLY SCOOPED TOGETHER. THERE, THE DISH IS LOVINGLY CALLED 'HEAVEN AND EARTH', OR HIMMEL EN EEËD.

SERVES FOUR

INGREDIENTS

   1kg/2¼lb potatoes, quartered
   500g1¼lb eating apples, peeled,
     cored and cut into large chunks
   250g/9oz cooking apples
   40g/1½oz/3 tbsp butter
   salt and ground black pepper
   fried black pudding (blood sausage)
     or smoked bacon and butter,
     to serve

1 Put the potatoes in a large pan, half cover with water, pile the apples on top and add 25g/1oz/2 tbsp of the butter. Bring the pan to the boil, lower the heat, cover and simmer for about 30 minutes.

2 Drain, reserving the cooking liquid. Mash with the remaining butter, adding some of the cooking liquid if necessary.

3 Season the dish to taste with salt and pepper and then serve with either black pudding or bacon and butter.

Per portion Energy 315kcal/1334kJ; Protein 4.8g; Carbohydrate 57g, of which sugars 20g; Fat 9.1g, of which saturates 5.4g; Cholesterol 21.2mg; Calcium 24.2mg; Fibre 5.5g; Sodium 91.7mg.

POTATO PURÉE

WHEN SERVING A FESTIVE DISH, SUCH AS GAME, THIS LUXURY PURÉE IS PIPED ON THE RIM OF A SHALLOW OVEN PLATE IN THE NETHERLANDS. IT ALSO SURROUNDS COOKED CHICORY, IS ROLLED INTO SLICES OF COOKED HAM, OR IS ALTERNATIVELY COVERED WITH A CHEESE SAUCE AND BAKED.

SERVES FOUR

INGREDIENTS
750g/1lb 10oz peeled floury
    potatoes, cut into quarters
2.5ml/½ tsp salt
2.5ml/½ tsp paprika
2.5ml/½ tsp nutmeg
2.5ml/½ tsp black pepper
2 egg yolks
knob (pat) of butter
milk

1 Preheat the oven to 220°C/425°F/ Gas 7. Grease an ovenproof dish with butter or line a baking sheet with baking parchment.

COOK'S TIP
The egg yolks enrichen and thicken this potato purée, but you could omit them if you prefer.

2 Cook the potatoes in a large pan of lightly salted water for about 15 minutes, until tender. Drain well.

3 Pass the potatoes through a ricer or alternatively mash with a hand-held electric mixer, but take care as a mixer can produce a purée that is too sticky.

4 Stir in salt, spices, yolks, butter and some milk if the purée seems too thick.

5 While still warm, pipe or spread the purée with a fork into the prepared ovenproof dish. Alternatively, pipe rosettes on to the baking sheet lined with baking parchment.

6 Bake the purée in the oven for 20 minutes, then serve immediately.

Per portion Energy 174kcal/732kJ; Protein 4.5g; Carbohydrate 28.4g, of which sugars 2.3g; Fat 5.4g, of which saturates 2.3g; Cholesterol 106mg; Calcium 24mg; Fibre 1.8g; Sodium 236mg.

POTATO GRATIN

BELGIANS ARE POTATOHOLICS AND HAVE BEEN EVER SINCE THE STARCHY VEGETABLE WAS FIRST INTRODUCED TO EUROPE. POTATOES THRIVE ON BELGIAN SOIL AND WERE VITAL IN STAVING OFF STARVATION DURING THE WORLD WARS I AND II, WHEN FOOD WAS SCARCE. DURING THOSE HARD TIMES, BELGIANS CREATED MANY INVENTIVE POTATO DISHES, AND CONTINUE TO DO SO TODAY.

2 Pour the milk and cream into a pan large enough to hold all the potato slices. Add the potatoes and stir gently to mix them with the liquid. Bring to the boil, then add the bay leaf and nutmeg, with salt and white pepper to taste. Reduce the heat and simmer for about 10 minutes, stirring occasionally.

3 Remove the pan from the heat. Set aside 15ml/1 tbsp of the cheese for the topping, and add the rest to the potatoes. Stir gently with a wooden spoon, so as not to break them up.

SERVES FOUR

INGREDIENTS
   butter, for greasing
   1 garlic clove, cut in half
   450g/1lb potatoes
   300ml/½ pint/1¼ cups creamy milk
   100ml/3½ fl oz/scant ½ cup double
    (heavy) cream
   1 bay leaf
   5ml/1 tsp grated nutmeg
   115g/4oz/1 cup grated aged
    Gruyère cheese
   salt and ground white pepper
   30ml/2 tbsp chopped fresh flat
    leaf parsley or chives to garnish

1 Preheat the oven to 200°C/400°F/Gas 6. Grease a baking dish with butter and rub the surface all over with the cut halves of garlic. Discard the garlic. Peel the potatoes, slice them thinly, rinse in cold water and pat dry.

VARIATION
Sliced turnips, shallots or leeks (white part only) can be added to the gratin.

4 Spoon the mixture carefully into the greased dish, distributing the potatoes evenly. Remove the bay leaf. Sprinkle the reserved grated cheese on top.

5 Bake for 45–60 minutes until the potatoes are tender, the topping is golden and most of the liquid has been absorbed.

6 Remove from the oven and leave to stand for 10 minutes. Sprinkle with parsley or chives and serve.

COOK'S TIP
The gratin can be made ahead of time and reheated in a hot oven (240°C/475°F/Gas 9) for about 10 minutes.

Per portion Energy 372kcal/1547kJ; Protein 12.1g; Carbohydrate 22g, of which sugars 5.3g; Fat 26.1g, of which saturates 16.6g; Cholesterol 73mg; Calcium 320mg; Fibre 1.1g; Sodium 258mg.

BELGIAN FRIES

EVERY VILLAGE OR TOWN IN BELGIUM HAS FRITERIE *OR* FRITKOT *STANDS SELLING FRIES IN TIGHT PAPER CONES, SERVED WITH A VARIETY OF CONDIMENTS, INCLUDING MAYONNAISE AND BELGIAN PICKLES. THE KEY TO THESE CRISP, TASTY AND GREASE-FREE FRIES IS THE USE OF A SPECIFIC TYPE OF POTATO — BINTJE — AND A COOKING METHOD THAT INVOLVES DOUBLE FRYING IN CLEAN OIL OR SUET.*

SERVES FOUR–SIX

INGREDIENTS
1kg/2¼lb maincrop potatoes
(*see* Cook's tips)
peanut or other vegetable oil,
for frying
salt
Mayonnaise (*see* page 33) and/or
Belgian pickles, to serve

1 Line a baking sheet with kitchen paper. Peel the potatoes, cut them in 1cm/½in thick slices, then stack the slices and cut them in 1cm/½in batons.

2 Place in a bowl of cold water to remove some of the starch and to keep them from turning brown.

3 Half-fill a heavy pan with oil. If using a deep-fryer, fill it to the level recommended in the instruction book. Heat the oil to 160°C/325°F or until a cube of bread, added to the oil, turns golden in about 45 seconds.

4 While the oil is heating, drain the potatoes and dry them in a clean cloth. This will prevent the oil from spitting when they are added.

5 Add the potatoes, in small batches, to the frying basket. Fry for 4–8 minutes, depending on the thickness and variety, shaking the pan occasionally. After this preliminary cooking, the fries should be cooked through but not yet golden. Lift them out, shake off the excess oil, then spread them on the paper-lined baking sheet. Leave to cool slightly.

6 Reheat the oil, this time to 180°C/350°F. Return the par-cooked potatoes to the oil in small batches and fry for 4 minutes until golden and crisp.

7 Drain on fresh kitchen paper, season and serve with mayonnaise or pickles.

COOK'S TIPS
• Potatoes that are suitable for making chips or fries vary from country to country, so ask your supplier which are most suitable. In Belgium, the best variety is said to be Bintje, while English cooks swear by Maris Piper, King Edward or Sante. In America, Russet Burbank potatoes are widely used for fries.
• Whether you cut the potatoes by hand or use a chip cutter, try to ensure they are of uniform thickness.
• Don't cut the potatoes too thinly or they will absorb a lot of fat and have less flavour.
• Don't fry too many potatoes at one time or the temperature of the fat will drop.

Per portion Energy 467kcal/1957kJ; Protein 5.5g; Carbohydrate 56.7g, of which sugars 2.2g; Fat 18.3g, of which saturates 9.7g; Cholesterol 0mg; Calcium 23mg; Fibre 3.5g; Sodium 517mg.

DESSERTS AND DRINKS

Belgians and the Dutch love fine foods, and this is nowhere more apparent than in their beautifully crafted desserts, confections and drinks. From substantial puddings and flavoursome fruit-based desserts to iced and chilled treats, often made with chocolate, there is always something tempting on offer. To finish the meal there are luxurious chocolates and a range of coffees, some made with alcohol, and/or liqueurs, including the famous advocaat.

MACAROON PUDDING <u>WITH</u> VANILLA

WITH THE CULTIVATION OF SUGAR BEET IN THE NETHERLANDS THE DUTCH DEVELOPED A VERY SWEET TOOTH. NO MEAL COULD BE CONSIDERED FINISHED WITHOUT A DESSERT. THE DUTCH WORD 'PUDDING' IS BORROWED FROM THE ENGLISH, WHOSE EXPERIMENTS WITH SWEET FILLINGS IN MOULDS BEGAN THE RICH HISTORY OF THE SWEET PUDDING IN EUROPE. HERE IS A DUTCH VARIATION ON THIS THEME.

3 Make alternating layers of bread, cookies and raisins in the prepared mould, pouring a little of the egg mixture over each layer. Finish with a layer of bread. Close the lid of the mould. Steam the pudding in a double boiler for 1½ hours.

4 Meanwhile, make the vanilla sauce. Pour the milk into a pan, add the vanilla pod and salt and bring to the boil. Lower the heat and simmer for 15 minutes.

5 Whisk the egg yolks with the sugar in a bowl, stir in a little of the hot milk, then stir in the remainder. Return to the pan and heat gently, stirring constantly, until thickened. Remove the pan from the heat and discard the vanilla pod.

6 Remove the mould from the double boiler and leave to stand for a few minutes. Take off the lid and invert the pudding on to a serving plate. Pour the warm sauce over the pudding, decorate with cookies and raisins and serve.

SERVES SIX

INGREDIENTS
    butter, for greasing
    breadcrumbs, for sprinkling
    125g/4¼oz day-old white bread,
      crusts removed
    100g/3¾oz Bitter Cookies or
      macaroons, plus extra to decorate
    5 eggs
    75g/3oz/scant ½ cup sugar
    pinch of grated lemon rind
    pinch of ground cinnamon
    500ml/17fl oz/generous 2 cups milk
    100g/3¾oz/¾ cup raisins in brandy,
      Country Lads' (*see* page 214), plus
      extra to decorate
For the vanilla sauce
    500ml/17fl oz/generous 2 cups milk
    ½ vanilla pod (bean), split
    pinch of salt
    4 egg yolks
    40g/1½oz/3 tbsp sugar

1 Grease a heatproof 1-litre/1¾-pint/ 4-cup mould with a lid with butter and sprinkle with breadcrumbs, tipping out any excess.

2 Cut the bread into wide strips and place in a dish with the cookies or macaroons. Beat the eggs with the sugar, lemon rind, cinnamon and milk in a bowl and pour a little of this mixture over the cookies and bread. Leave to soak.

Per portion Energy 419kcal/1767kJ; Protein 15.7g; Carbohydrate 56.8g, of which sugars 39.8g; Fat 13.7g, of which saturates 5.1g; Cholesterol 303mg; Calcium 298mg; Fibre 0.7g; Sodium 302mg.

BREAD PUDDING FROM BRUSSELS

LIKE BREAD PUDDINGS THE WORLD OVER, THIS WAS ORIGINALLY INVENTED TO USE UP STALE BREAD. OVER THE CENTURIES, THE 'POOR MAN'S PUDDING' BECAME MORE REFINED. MILK OR CREAM WERE USED INSTEAD OF WATER, CAKE REPLACED BREAD, AND FRUITS AND EVEN LIQUEURS WERE ADDED. IN THIS VERSION, PEPERKOEK, A TRADITIONAL BELGIAN HONEY SPICE CAKE, IS ADDED TO THE MIX.

SERVES FOUR

INGREDIENTS
225g/8oz day-old white bread (about 8 slices), cubed
115g/4oz Belgian spice cake or more day-old bread, cubed
500ml/17fl oz/generous 2 cups full-fat (whole) milk
100g/3¾oz/⅔ cup raisins
15–30ml/1–2 tbsp dark rum
175g/6oz/¾ cup packed brown sugar
4 eggs, at room temperature
8g/⅓oz sachet vanilla sugar or 5ml/ 1 tsp vanilla extract
1.5ml/¼ tsp ground cinnamon
10ml/2 tsp melted unsalted butter, cooled, plus extra for greasing
icing (confectioners') sugar, for dusting
whipped cream, to serve

1 Place the bread and spice cake in a large bowl. Pour the milk into a pan, add the brown sugar and heat, stirring, until all the sugar has dissolved.

2 Ladle the milk over the bread and cake, cover and leave to soak for 2 hours.

3 Meanwhile, put the raisins in a small bowl and pour over the rum. Cover and set aside to plump up. Preheat the oven to 180°C/350°F/Gas 4. Grease a 25cm/10in round baking dish.

4 Whisk the eggs in a large bowl. Add the vanilla sugar or extract, with the cinnamon, then whisk in the melted and cooled butter.

5 Mash the soaked bread and cake with a potato masher, or press the mixture through a sieve (strainer).

VARIATION
Experiment with different types of bread, such as brioche, fruit bread or gingerbread. The crusts can be removed or left on, and the bread can be sliced, cubed or crumbed, depending on your preference.

6 Add the mashed bread and cake to the egg mixture, along with the soaked raisins and any remaining rum. Mix well.

7 Spoon the pudding mixture into the prepared baking dish and level the surface with a spoon.

8 Place in a roasting pan and pour in boiling water to come halfway up the sides of the dish. Bake for 40–45 minutes until golden and a skewer inserted in the centre comes out clean.

9 Leave to cool slightly. Serve dusted with icing sugar and whipped cream.

Per portion Energy 463kcal/1952kJ; Protein 18.1g; Carbohydrate 65.9g, of which sugars 26.2g; Fat 14.2g, of which saturates 6g; Cholesterol 213mg; Calcium 282mg; Fibre 1.8g; Sodium 596mg.

POACHED PEARS IN SPICED RED WINE

UNTIL THE 16TH CENTURY, PEARS WERE USED ONLY FOR COOKING IN EUROPE. POACHED PEARS, LIKE THE ONES HERE, WERE OFTEN SOLD BY STREET VENDORS. A POPULAR BELGIAN EXPRESSION, WARNING THAT AN APPARENTLY PROFITABLE SITUATION MAY HAVE UNEXPECTED CONSEQUENCES, RECALLS THIS WITH THE WORDS: 'MET DE GEBAKKEN PEREN BLIJVEN ZITTEN' ('GETTING STUCK WITH UNSOLD COOKED PEARS').

SERVES FOUR

INGREDIENTS
  2 firm ripe cooking pears
  500ml/17fl oz/generous 2 cups
    red wine
  100g/3¾oz/½ cup sugar
  pared rind of 1 orange
  2 whole cloves
  1 cinnamon stick
  1 peppercorn
  4 mint leaves, to decorate
  ice cream or whipped cream, to serve

VARIATION
To enrich the syrup, whisk in 15ml/1 tbsp brandy before spooning it over the pears.

1 Peel the pears, cut them in half and scoop out the cores to leave a neat, round cavity in each. Put the pear halves in a shallow pan and pour over the wine to cover them completely. Sprinkle with the sugar.

2 Pierce the strip of orange rind with the cloves. Add to the pan with the cinnamon stick and peppercorn. Bring to the boil, then reduce the heat, cover the pan and simmer for 30–45 minutes (*see* Cook's tip).

3 Using a slotted spoon, lift the pears out and place them on a serving platter or in individual bowls.

4 Increase the heat under the pan and boil the wine mixture for about 10 minutes, until it has reduced by half and become syrupy.

5 Lift out and discard the orange rind, cinnamon stick and peppercorn. Spoon the syrup over the pears. Leave to cool.

6 Serve at room temperature or chill until required, periodically basting the pears with the syrup so they develop a warm glossy red hue.

7 Trim the rounded side of each pear half if necessary so that it lies flat, with the cavity uppermost. Fill the cavities with ice cream or whipped cream, decorate with the mint leaves and serve immediately.

COOK'S TIP
Use a skewer to check that the pears are cooked. They should be soft enough for a skewer to slide in, but not so soft that they are in danger of breaking up. The cooking time required will depend on the variety of pear used, and the ripeness.

Per portion Energy 378kcal/1595kJ; Protein 1g; Carbohydrate 65.7g, of which sugars 65.7g; Fat 0.2g, of which saturates 0g; Cholesterol 0mg; Calcium 53mg; Fibre 3.9g; Sodium 22mg.

CHERRY FLANS

DUTCH CHERRIES ARE CALLED MAY CHERRIES, BECAUSE THIS IS WHEN THE TREES AND ORCHARDS ARE IN FULL BLOSSOM. IN THE CHERRY-PICKING SEASON FROM JUNE TO JULY IT IS COMMON FOR PEOPLE TO MAKE SPECIAL TRIPS TO THE ORCHARDS, SITTING ON MAKESHIFT BENCHES WHILE INDULGING IN THE DELICIOUS FRUIT. THE IDEA FOR THESE FLANS COMES FROM AN 18TH-CENTURY RECIPE.

SERVES TWO

INGREDIENTS
45ml/3 tbsp sugar
150g/5oz cherries, pitted
butter, for greasing
30ml/2 tbsp plain (all-purpose) flour
pinch of salt
1 egg
15ml/1 tbsp milk
7.5ml/1½ tsp potato flour
15ml/1 tbsp brandy or Kirsch
whipped cream, to serve (optional)

1 Pour 100ml/3½fl oz/scant ½ cup water into a pan, add 30ml/2 tbsp of the sugar and bring to the boil, stirring until the sugar has dissolved.

2 Add the cherries and simmer for 10 minutes. Drain well, reserving the syrup.

3 Preheat the oven to 200°C/400°F/ Gas 6. Grease two 10cm/4in non-stick flan tins (pans) with butter. Reserve two cherries for decoration. Divide the remainder between the flan tins.

VARIATION
To make a pear flan, halve and core 2 pears and poach in a mixture of 150ml/ 10 tbsp white wine, sugar and ground cinnamon until tender. Transfer to a small ovenproof dish. Boil the cooking liquid until reduced to a syrup and pour it over the pears. Whisk two eggs with 60ml/4 tbsp breadcrumbs and spread over the pears. Bake in a preheated oven at 200°C/400°F/ Gas 6 for 15 minutes.

4 Mix together the remaining sugar, the flour and salt in a bowl. Beat in the egg to make a smooth batter, then stir in the milk. Pour the batter over the cherries and bake for 25 minutes.

5 Bring the reserved syrup to the boil. Mix the potato flour with 15ml/1 tbsp water to a paste, stir into the syrup and immediately remove the pan from the heat. Leave to cool completely, then stir in the brandy or Kirsch.

6 Turn out the flans and serve warm with the sauce and reserved cherries, or cold with the sauce and whipped cream.

COOK'S TIP
When served directly from the oven the flans will be beautifully puffed up, and this is the best way to present and serve them. Do not chill them.

Per portion Energy 246kcal/1039kJ; Protein 6g; Carbohydrate 47.1g, of which sugars 32.8g; Fat 3.2g, of which saturates 0.9g; Cholesterol 96mg; Calcium 71mg; Fibre 1.3g; Sodium 41mg.

RICE PORRIDGE WITH BRAISED PRUNES

RICE PORRIDGE — OR RIJSTPAP AS IT IS KNOWN IN BELGIUM — IS THOUGHT TO HAVE ORIGINATED IN THE 16TH CENTURY, WHEN EMPEROR CHARLES V'S SOLDIERS RETURNED FROM FIGHTING THE OTTOMAN EMPIRE, BRINGING WITH THEM RICE AND EXOTIC SPICES SUCH AS CINNAMON AND SAFFRON. THE PRUNES HARK BACK TO MEDIEVAL TIMES, WHEN FRESH FRUITS WERE NOT AVAILABLE IN WINTER.

3 Add the milk, rice, cinnamon stick, saffron and salt to the pan, with the vanilla pod, if using. Bring to the boil, reduce the heat, cover and simmer for 30 minutes, stirring occasionally with a wooden spoon.

4 When the rice is tender, but still retains some 'bite', stir in the sugar. If you are using vanilla extract or vanilla sugar instead of the split bean, stir it into the mixture. Simmer for a further 5 minutes.

5 When all the milk has been absorbed and the rice porridge is thick and creamy, remove the cinnamon stick and vanilla pod (if using). Spoon into dessert bowls and top each portion with 15–30ml/1–2 tbsp of the prunes. Serve warm or cold.

VARIATION

For a simpler version of *rijstpap*, simply top each portion with soft light brown sugar instead of the prunes.

SERVES FOUR–SIX

INGREDIENTS
  150g/5oz/⅔ cup medium grain rice,
    such as paella rice
  1 litre/1¾ pints/4 cups full cream
    (whole) milk
  1 cinnamon stick
  pinch of crushed saffron threads
  pinch of salt
  1 vanilla pod (bean), split, or 5ml/
    1 tsp pure vanilla extract, or
    1 x 8g/⅓oz sachet vanilla sugar
  75g/3oz/6 tbsp sugar
For the prunes
  400g/14oz/1¾ cups dried prunes,
    soaked in water for 3–4 hours
  strip of pared unwaxed lemon rind
  400ml/14fl oz/1⅔ cups dark abbey
    beer, such as Chimay or Leffe
  1 cinnamon stick
  75g/3oz/scant ½ cup soft light
    brown sugar

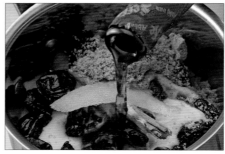

1 Start by preparing the prunes. Drain them and put them in a pan with the lemon rind, beer, cinnamon stick and sugar. Simmer, uncovered, for 30 minutes or until they are soft and tender and the cooking liquid is very syrupy.

2 Meanwhile, put the rice in a colander and rinse under cold water. Rinse a heavy pan in cold water, tip out the excess but do not dry the pan as this will help prevent the rice from sticking.

Per portion Energy 412kcal/1734kJ; Protein 9.4g; Carbohydrate 76.2g, of which sugars 56.3g; Fat 6.9g, of which saturates 4.2g; Cholesterol 23mg; Calcium 241mg; Fibre 3.8g; Sodium 85mg.

MOULDED RICE PUDDING

CREAMY COOKED RICE (RIJSTEBRIJ) WAS A CLASSIC DISH FOR SUNDAYS IN THE NETHERLANDS, ALWAYS SERVED WITH A WELL OF BUTTER AND SPINKLED WITH SUGAR AND CINNAMON. THIS ELEGANT VERSION IS SURE TO BECOME A FAMILY FAVOURITE, ESPECIALLY IF IT IS MADE IN A DECORATIVE MOULD. THE MOST POPULAR SHAPE FOR THIS RECIPE IS CREATED WITH A TURBAN-SHAPED MOULD.

SERVES FOUR

INGREDIENTS
    500ml/17fl oz/generous 2 cups milk
    1 vanilla pod (bean)
    65g/2½oz/⅓ cup short grain rice
    pinch of salt
    4 gelatine leaves
    1 egg, separated
    65g/2½oz/⅓ cup sugar

1 Rinse out a pan with cold water, pour in the milk, add the vanilla pod and bring to the boil.

2 Gradually pour in the rice, with the salt, in a steady stream so that the milk continues to boil. Stir, lower the heat and simmer, stirring occasionally, for about an hour, until the rice is tender.

3 Soak the gelatine leaves in a bowl of cold water. Beat the egg yolk in another bowl. Reserve 5ml/1 tsp of the sugar.

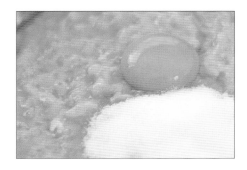

4 Stir the remaining sugar into the cooked rice, then stir in the egg yolk. Remove the pan from the heat.

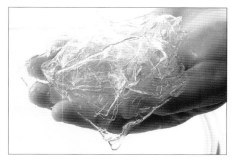

5 Squeeze out the gelatine and stir it into the hot rice mixture until it is dissolved. Remove the vanilla pod. Leave to stand until just starting to set.

6 Whisk the egg white with the reserved sugar until very stiff. Fold into the cooled rice mixture.

7 Rinse out a 750ml/1¼-pint/3-cup mould, spoon in the rice mixture and chill until set.

8 To serve, carefully invert the rice pudding on to a plate. Arrange sliced fruit or apricots in brandy (*boerenmeisjes* or Country Girls) on the sides to decorate (*see* page 214).

COOK'S TIP
If you are using canned fruit to decorate the rice pudding, you can thicken the juice by heating it with some potato flour or cornflour (cornstarch). Leave the sauce to cool completely before serving in a sauceboat with the rice pudding, or the pudding will melt when the hot sauce is added.

Per portion Energy 205kcal/866kJ; Protein 8.8g; Carbohydrate 35.8g, of which sugars 22.9g; Fat 3.6g, of which saturates 1.7g; Cholesterol 55mg; Calcium 169mg; Fibre 0g; Sodium 72mg.

THE HAGUE BLUFF

THE INGREDIENTS IN THIS FLUFFY DISH, CREATED IN THE HAGUE, ARE SIMPLE AND ECONOMICAL. BEFORE THE AGE OF FOOD PROCESSORS, EVERY DUTCH CHILD WAS HAPPY TO BEAT THE MIXTURE, KNOWING THEY WOULD BE REWARDED. THE BLUFF IS OFTEN SERVED WITH A SPONGE FINGER, A WAFER OR AN OBLONG RUSK WITH A LAYER OF SUGAR AND CINNAMON. HERE, IT IS SERVED ON A LAYER OF SEMOLINA PUDDING.

SERVES FOUR

INGREDIENTS
    500ml/17fl oz/generous 2 cups
       full cream (whole) milk
    65g/2½oz/scant ½ cup semolina
    pinch of salt
    25g/1oz/2 tbsp vanilla sugar
    2 egg yolks, lightly beaten
For the bluff
    1 egg white
    150ml/¼ pint/⅔ cup
       redcurrant juice
    50g/2oz/¼ cup sugar

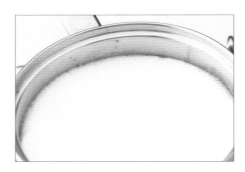

1 Bring the milk to the boil in a medium pan. Mix together the semolina, sugar and salt.

2 Pour the mixture into the boiling milk, whisking constantly. Cook over low heat, stirring constantly, for 5 minutes, until thickened.

3 Whisk in the egg yolks and cook, stirring constantly, for a few minutes more. Remove the pan from the heat.

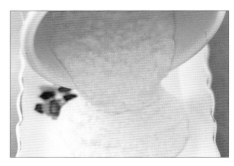

4 Rinse a large flat serving dish with cold water, pour on the mixture and leave it to cool completely.

5 Make the bluff just before serving. First of all whisk together the egg white, redcurrant juice and sugar in a large bowl until the mixture is very stiff, using a hand-held blender or whisk.

6 Using a large spoon, make one or more mounds of the bluff all over the surface of the cool semolina.

7 Touch the bluff or bluffs lightly with the back of the spoon and raise the spoon to bring the bluff(s) to a peak and make an attractive pointed cap. Serve immediately.

Per portion Energy 278kcal/1181kJ; Protein 8.4g; Carbohydrate 52.9g, of which sugars 40.3g; Fat 5.2g, of which saturates 2.1g; Cholesterol 108mg; Calcium 188mg; Fibre 0.4g; Sodium 80mg.

SEMOLINA PUDDING <u>WITH</u> REDCURRANT SAUCE

THIS IS ONE OF THE SIMPLEST OF ALL DUTCH PUDDINGS, BUT IT DOES NEED CONCENTRATION TO MAKE BECAUSE IF IT IS OVERCOOKED, IT BECOMES REALLY RUBBERY AND UNPALATABLE. THE ADDITION OF BUTTER, AN EGG AND GROUND ALMONDS TO THE BASIC SEMOLINA MIXTURE ADDS RICHNESS, WHILE THE REDCURRANT SAUCE PROVIDES A CONTRAST IN TEXTURE AND CUTS THE SWEETNESS.

SERVES FOUR

INGREDIENTS
  800ml/1⅓ pints/3½ cups milk
  lemon rind of half a lemon
  75g/3oz/½ cup semolina
  65g/2½ oz/⅓ cup sugar
  pinch of salt
  1 egg, beaten
  15g/½ oz/1 tbsp butter
  40g/1½ oz/⅓ cup coarsely
    ground almonds
  drop of almond extract or bitter
    almond oil, optional
For the redcurrant sauce
  250ml/8fl oz/1 cup redcurrant juice
  1 cinnamon stick
  45ml/3 tbsp potato flour
  65g/2½ oz/⅓ cup sugar, or to taste

1 Rinse out a heavy pan with cold water, pour in the milk, add the lemon rind and bring to the boil.

2 Mix together the semolina, sugar and salt and sprinkle into the milk, stirring constantly. Then cook over low heat, stirring constantly, for about 5 minutes, until thickened. Discard the lemon rind.

3 Whisk the egg into the mixture and cook for a few minutes more. Stir in the butter, almonds and almond extract, if using, and remove the pan from the heat.

4 Rinse out a 1-litre/1¾-pint/4-cup mould with cold water and pour in the semolina mixture. Leave to cool, then chill in the refrigerator until set.

5 Meanwhile, make the redcurrant sauce. Pour the redcurrant juice into a pan, add 250ml/8fl oz/1 cup water and the cinnamon and bring to the boil. Lower the heat and simmer for 30 minutes.

6 Mix the potato flour with 90ml/6 tbsp cold water to a paste in bowl, stir into the sauce and cook, stirring constantly, until thickened. Add sugar to taste.

7 To serve, turn out the pudding on to a platter, then pour a little of the sauce over it. Serve the remainder of the sauce in a sauceboat.

VARIATIONS
• To make an alternative redcurrant sauce, spoon 450g/1lb of redcurrant jelly or strained jam into a pan, add the juice of two lemons and 150ml/¼ pint/⅔ cup boiling water. Bring to the boil, stirring constantly, and continue to stir until smooth. Remove the pan from the heat, leave to cool, then chill in the refrigerator until required.
• In the province of Brabant a popular sauce to serve with semolina pudding is made from blackberries, blackcurrants or blueberries, simply cooked with a little sugar to taste and not thickened with potato flour.

Per portion Energy 398kcal/1679kJ; Protein 12.9g; Carbohydrate 59.3g, of which sugars 34.1g; Fat 13.9g, of which saturates 4.9g; Cholesterol 67mg; Calcium 297mg; Fibre 1.2g; Sodium 141mg.

DUTCH CUSTARD

THIS IS THE MOST COMMON TYPE OF DUTCH DESSERT. ALTHOUGH IT BEARS A CLOSE RESEMBLANCE TO ENGLISH CUSTARD, IT IS NOT EXACTLY THE SAME, THICKENED NOT ONLY WITH EGGS, BUT ALSO WITH CORNFLOUR. MANY OF THE COMMERCIALLY PRODUCED RECIPES CONTAIN CHEMICAL ADDITIVES AND ARTIFICIAL COLOURS. THIS RECIPE (VLA) PROVIDES THE AUTHENTIC FLAVOUR OF THE CLASSIC DISH.

3 Bring the vanilla-flavoured milk back to the boil, then remove the pan from heat. Stir the cornflour mixture into the pan and return to very low heat. Cook, stirring frequently, for 3 minutes.

4 Remove and discard the vanilla pod. Cover the surface of the custard with clear film (plastic wrap) to prevent a skin from forming and leave to cool.

SERVES FOUR

INGREDIENTS
500ml/17fl oz/generous 2 cups milk, plus extra to taste
½ vanilla pod (bean)
40g/1½oz/⅓ cup cornflour (cornstarch)
40g/1½oz/scant ¼ cup sugar
2 large (US extra large) egg yolks

1 Rinse out a pan with cold water, pour in 400ml/14fl oz/1⅔ cups of the milk, add the vanilla pod and bring to the boil. Simmer gently over low heat for a few minutes.

2 Meanwhile, mix together the cornflour and sugar in a small bowl, add the egg yolks and stir to form a very smooth paste. Stir in the remaining milk, ensuring it is smooth, and strain into a clean, heatproof bowl.

5 Using a hand-held mixer whisk the mixture with cold milk to create the required consistency, which is usually a cross between a sauce and a dessert. Chill before serving.

VARIATIONS
• Soak Bitter Cookies (*see* page 222) in rum in serving dishes, then cover with *vla*.
• Heat some *vla* and melt dark (bittersweet) chocolate in it. Mix with cold *vla* and leave to cool. Serve on slices of spice cake.
• To make pears on velvet, mix the *vla* with advocaat and serve with halved ripe pears, covered with redcurrant sauce.
• Mix the *vla* with ground cinnamon and some whipped cream.

COOK'S TIP
You can use the two left over egg whites to make meringues (*schuimpjes*) as a garnish for *vla*. Heat the oven to 140°C/275°F/Gas 2. Whip the egg whites until they are very stiff, then add 100g/3¾oz/scant 1 cup icing (confectioners') sugar and some vanilla extract. Pipe rosettes on to a baking tray lined with baking parchment. Bake them in the oven for 1½ hours until they have become yellow brown.

Per portion 163kcal/689kJ; Protein 5.8g; Carbohydrate 25.5g, of which sugars 16.3g; Fat 5g, of which saturates 2.1g; Cholesterol 108mg; Calcium 169mg; Fibre 0g; Sodium 64mg.

BAVAROIS WITH GLACÉ FRUIT

A SAVOURY VERSION OF THIS DUTCH PUDDING WAS CALLED 'CHIPOLATA' IN 19TH-CENTURY COOKBOOKS, A WORD TAKEN FROM THE FRENCH CHIPOLATA, A PORK SAUSAGE. A SWEET VERSION FOR LENT THEN EVOLVED INTO THIS GLORIOUS BAVAROIS WITH GLACÉ FRUIT, CREATED BY PARISIAN CHEFS WHO WORKED FOR BAVARIAN PRINCES IN THE 18TH CENTURY.

SERVES SIX

INGREDIENTS
- 8 sponge fingers, about 50g/2oz
- 100ml/3½fl oz/scant ½ cup Maraschino, plus extra for sprinkling
- 12g/¼oz or 6 gelatine leaves
- 300ml/½ pint/1¼ cups milk
- 1 vanilla pod (bean), split in half
- 2 eggs, separated
- 75g/3oz/scant ½ cup sugar
- 65g/2½oz/⅓ cup glacé (candied) red and green cherries
- 25g/1oz/2½ tbsp candied orange peel, diced
- 250ml/8fl oz/1 cup whipping cream

To decorate
- 120ml/4fl oz/½ cup whipping cream
- 15ml/1 tbsp caster (superfine) sugar

1 Place the sponge fingers side by side on a plate and pour over the Maraschino. Place the gelatine in a small bowl of cold water and leave to soak for 5 minutes.

2 Put the milk and vanilla pod in a heavy pan and bring to the boil. Simmer for a few minutes.

3 Beat the egg yolks with the sugar in a bowl, stir in a little of the hot milk and stir until smooth, then pour in the remaining milk.

4 Return to the pan and cook over very low heat, stirring constantly, for a few minutes until slightly thickened. Do not allow to boil or the eggs will curdle.

5 Remove the pan from the heat, squeeze out the gelatine and dissolve it in the warm custard. Remove and discard the vanilla pod. Leave the custard to cool and begin to set.

6 Dice half the cherries. Whisk the egg whites in one bowl. Whip the cream in another. Add the egg whites to the cream, then add the custard, diced cherries and candied peel and fold together.

7 Chill in the refrigerator, stirring occasionally, until thick. Rinse out a 1.2-litre/2-pint/5-cup mould with cold water and leave upside down to drain.

8 Make a layer of the custard mixture in the prepared mould and top with four sponge fingers. Continue making layers until all the ingredients have been used, ending with a layer of the custard. Chill until set.

9 Sprinkle a little Maraschino on to a serving plate and turn out the bavarois. Whip the cream with the sugar. Decorate the bavarois with the sweetened cream and remaining cherries.

COOK'S TIP
It is worth paying a little extra to buy the best-quality glacé (candied) cherries and candied peel for this dessert.

Per portion Energy 332kcal/1388kJ; Protein 7.4g; Carbohydrate 32.5g, of which sugars 30.7g; Fat 20.1g, of which saturates 11.7g; Cholesterol 129mg; Calcium 120mg; Fibre 0.5g; Sodium 78mg.

CHEESECAKE WITH SOUR CHERRIES

BELGIANS LOVE SOUR OR MORELLO CHERRIES, WHICH ARE MUCH LESS SWEET THAN STANDARD GLACÉ ONES. THE FRUIT FEATURES IN SAUCES, POULTRY AND GAME DISHES AND MEAT STEWS, AS WELL AS IN DESSERTS SUCH AS THIS CHILLED NO-BAKE CHEESECAKE. THE BASE IS TRADITIONALLY MADE USING BELGIUM'S FAVOURITE COOKIE — SPECULAAS — WHILE THE CREAMY CHEESE TOPPING IS STUDDED WITH CHERRIES AND SPIKED WITH SOME OF THE CHERRY-FLAVOURED KRIEK BEER FOR WHICH THE COUNTRY IS FAMOUS. SERVE IT WITH A GLASS OF KRIEK TOO, IF YOU LIKE.

SERVES SIX–EIGHT

INGREDIENTS
   500g/1¼lb jar stoned (pitted)
    Morello cherries in syrup
   60ml/4 tbsp water
   30ml/2 tbsp powdered gelatine
   150ml/¼ pint/⅔ cup *Kriek* beer,
    such as St Louis or Belle-Vue
   500g/1¼lb/2¼ cups Quark, soft
    cheese or fromage frais
   150ml/¼ pint/⅔ cup crème fraîche
    or sour cream
   200ml/7fl oz/scant 1 cup double
    (heavy) cream
   115g/4oz/generous ½ cup caster
    (superfine) sugar
   90ml/6 tbsp flaked (sliced) almonds,
    to decorate (optional)
For the crust
   200g/7oz *speculaas* cookies (spice
    cookies) or other cookies suitable
    for crumbing
   100g/3¾oz/scant ½ cup
    unsalted butter
   30ml/2 tbsp cherry jam (optional)

1 Make the crust. Crumb the cookies in a food processor or put them between sheets of baking parchment or in a strong, sealed plastic bag and crush with a rolling pin until you have fine crumbs. Transfer into a large bowl.

2 Melt the butter gently in a small pan over low heat.

3 Stir the melted butter into the crumbs with the cherry jam, if using. Mix well, then shape the mixture into a ball.

4 Place the mixture in a 23cm/9in springform cake tin (pan) and press it out to form an even base using your fingers. Cover with plastic wrap (clear film) and place in the refrigerator.

5 Meanwhile, drain the cherries in a colander placed over a measuring jug (cup), reserving the syrup. Chop 115g/4oz/⅔ cup of the cherries and set them aside. Leave the remaining cherries in the colander.

6 Put the water in a cup or small bowl and sprinkle the gelatine on the surface. Leave for a few minutes until spongy.

7 Pour 150ml/¼ pint/⅔ cup of the syrup from the cherries into a pan. Bring to the boil, then remove from the heat and cool for 30 seconds.

8 Whisk in the gelatine until dissolved. Stir in the *Kriek* beer and strain the mixture into a jug (pitcher).

9 In a large bowl, beat the Quark, soft cheese or fromage frais with the crème fraîche or sour cream, and gradually add the gelatine mixture. Fold in the reserved chopped cherries.

10 Whip the cream with the sugar in a bowl, until stiff peaks form. Carefully fold it into the cheese mixture.

11 Spoon the filling over the crumb base and smooth the top with a wetted spoon or spatula. Cover with clear film (plastic wrap). Chill in the refrigerator for at least 4 hours or overnight.

12 Remove the cheesecake from the tin (*see* Cook's tip) and transfer to a serving platter. Sprinkle the flaked almonds over the surface and press some on to the sides. Serve with the cherries.

COOK'S TIP
To remove the cheesecake from the tin, rinse a slim metal spatula or knife under very hot water, dry quickly and run the spatula or knife between the cheesecake and the sides of the tin. Unclip the spring and lift off the sides of the tin. Run the spatula or knife under the cheesecake to loosen it from the base and transfer it to a serving platter.

Per portion Energy 574kcal/2394kJ; Protein 6.5g; Carbohydrate 50.1g, of which sugars 39g; Fat 39.5g, of which saturates 24.9g; Cholesterol 87mg; Calcium 145mg; Fibre 0.7g; Sodium 198mg.

PETIT BEURRE BISCUIT CAKE

THIS EASY NO-BAKE CAKE IS MADE WITH RICH BUTTERCREAM FLAVOURED WITH COFFEE AND LAYERED WITH PETIT BEURRE (LITERALLY 'LITTLE BUTTER') BISCUITS. IN THE 19TH CENTURY, TWO ANTWERP-BASED FAMILY FIRMS, DE BEUKELAER AND PAREIN, PRODUCED THESE BISCUITS, WHICH HAD SUPERIOR KEEPING QUALITIES TO ANYTHING ELSE AVAILABLE AT THE TIME. THEY BECAME SO FAMOUS THAT PEOPLE FROM ALL OVER THE COUNTRY WOULD TRAVEL TO ANTWERP (NICKNAMED COOKIE CITY) TO STOCK UP. FOR BEST RESULTS, MAKE THIS CAKE THE DAY BEFORE YOU INTEND TO SERVE IT.

SERVES FOUR

INGREDIENTS

   250g/9oz/generous 1 cup best quality
     unsalted butter, softened
   150g/5oz/1¼ cups icing
     (confectioners') sugar
   15ml/1 tbsp instant coffee granules
   15ml/1 tbsp coffee liqueur or
     brandy (optional)
   250ml/8fl oz/1 cup creamy milk,
     at room temperature
   20–24 petit beurre biscuits
     (butter cookies)
   chocolate vermicelli (sprinkles), shaved
     chocolate curls or unsweetened cocoa
     powder, to decorate

1 Beat the butter in a bowl until soft and creamy. Gradually add the icing sugar, until completely combined. Beat in the coffee granules and the coffee liqueur, if using, until the mixture is smooth and silky.

2 Pour the milk into a shallow dish. Arrange four biscuits together on a flat serving plate so that they form a square. Spread some of the coffee buttercream on top, keeping the biscuits together. Make another layer of biscuits, dipping each of them briefly in the milk before putting them in position. Spread more buttercream on top.

3 Continue in this fashion until you have stacked the biscuits five or six layers high. When the final layer of biscuits has been added, cover the whole structure with buttercream, spreading it smooth with a spatula or large knife.

4 Sprinkle chocolate vermicelli or shaved chocolate curls over the cake, or dust with cocoa powder. Leave to set for at least 1 hour in the refrigerator. Keep chilled until ready to serve.

VARIATIONS
• It is important to use a biscuit (cookie) that will absorb liquid and soften without disintegrating, so if you cannot locate petit beurre biscuits, substitute another biscuit with similar qualities.
• Jam can be used instead of buttercream to sandwich the layers together.

COOK'S TIP
Do not dip the biscuits (cookies) in the milk for too long, or they will be too soggy to spread with buttercream.

Per portion Energy 974kcal/4066kJ; Protein 7.7g; Carbohydrate 98.5g, of which sugars 59.1g; Fat 63.8g, of which saturates 38.8g; Cholesterol 165mg; Calcium 195mg; Fibre 1.3g; Sodium 716mg.

STRAWBERRY MOUSSE, WAASLAND-STYLE

Several areas in Belgium produce succulent strawberries in the summer, and this creamy mousse provides the perfect showcase for them. One such region is Waasland, which since 1953 has held an annual strawberry festival in Melsele. This is based on a 16th-century tradition, in which the first fruits of the year were offered to the Virgin Mary in the Chapel of Gaverland. The modern festivities include the election of Miss Strawberry, who has the honour of offering the first of the season's crop to the Belgian King and Queen.

SERVES FOUR–SIX

INGREDIENTS
    500g/1¼lb/5–6 cups strawberries
    100g/3¾oz/scant 1 cup icing
      (confectioners') sugar
    400ml/14fl oz/1⅔ cups double
      (heavy) cream
    25g/1oz/¼ cup almond slivers

1 Cut half of the strawberries into quarters. Place them in a single layer in a decorative glass bowl. Sprinkle half of the icing sugar on top.

2 In a food processor or blender, purée the remaining strawberries with half of the cream. Taste and add 30–60ml/2–4 tbsp of the remaining icing sugar, depending upon the sweetness of the strawberries, and process until smooth. Pour over the cut strawberries in the bowl.

3 Toast the almonds over medium heat in a dry, heavy frying pan until golden brown, shaking the pan often to prevent them from burning. Leave to cool.

4 Beat the remaining cream with enough of the remaining icing sugar to sweeten it.

COOK'S TIP
Use freshly picked strawberries. Rinse them lightly before hulling, but do not soak in water or they will become soggy. Pat dry with kitchen paper.

5 Spread or pipe the mousse over the purée. Sprinkle the almonds on top, cover with clear film (plastic wrap) and chill until ready to serve.

Per portion Energy 444kcal/1841kJ; Protein 2.7g; Carbohydrate 23.8g, of which sugars 23.7g; Fat 38.2g, of which saturates 22.5g; Cholesterol 91mg; Calcium 65mg; Fibre 1.2g; Sodium 21mg.

BELGIAN CHOCOLATE MOUSSE

BELGIUM IS WORLD-FAMOUS FOR THE QUALITY OF ITS CHOCOLATE, AND BELGIANS TAKE CHOCOLATE CONSUMPTION VERY SERIOUSLY, SAVOURING IT IN ALL ITS FORMS. EVERY FAMILY HAS ITS FAVOURITE RECIPE FOR CHOCOLATE MOUSSE, USUALLY INVOLVING A COMBINATION OF MELTED CHOCOLATE WITH FRESH EGGS AND CREAM, BUTTER, COFFEE AND LIQUEUR. WHATEVER THE RECIPE CALLS FOR, THE ESSENTIAL INGREDIENT IS THE CHOCOLATE, WHICH MUST BE OF EXCELLENT QUALITY.

2 Leave the bowl in position until the chocolate has completely melted, stirring it occasionally. Remove the bowl from above the water and leave to cool to room temperature.

3 In a clean bowl, whip the cream with 15g/½oz tbsp of the sugar until it stands in soft peaks. Set aside.

4 In a separate grease-free bowl, whisk the egg whites, gradually adding 50g/2oz/ 4 tbsp of the remaining sugar, until stiff.

5 Whisk the egg yolks in a third bowl, gradually adding the last of the sugar, until foamy. Fold the egg yolks into the chocolate mixture.

6 Using a metal spoon, fold in the whipped cream and then the egg whites, taking care not to deflate the mixture.

7 Spoon or pipe the mousse into ramekins, dessert glasses or chocolate cups and leave to set for at least 1 hour in the refrigerator. Serve plain or with any of the suggested decorations.

COOK'S TIPS
• The percentage of chocolate solids in the chocolate influences not only the taste but also the texture of the mousse. The higher the percentage of the cocoa, the firmer the mousse will be.
• It is essential to whip the egg whites while slowly adding the sugar or the whites will separate.

SERVES FOUR

INGREDIENTS
  150g/5oz Callebaut callets
    (semisweet bits) or other
    good-quality Belgian chocolate,
    cut into small pieces
  200ml/7fl oz/scant 1 cup whipping
    or double (heavy) cream
  75g/3oz/6 tbsp caster (superfine) sugar
  2 eggs, separated, at room
    temperature
  chocolate curls or sprinkles, roasted
    almond slivers, strips of good-
    quality candied orange peel,
    unsweetened cocoa powder or extra
    whipped cream, to decorate

1 Put the chocolate in a heatproof bowl that will fit over a small pan. Half fill the pan with water and bring to the boil, then immediately remove from the heat and place the bowl of chocolate on top, making sure it does not touch the water.

Per portion Energy 550kcal/2290kJ; Protein 5.9g; Carbohydrate 44.3g, of which sugars 43.9g; Fat 40.1g, of which saturates 23.8g; Cholesterol 166mg; Calcium 61mg; Fibre 1g; Sodium 50mg.

HEAVENLY MUD

THIS DIVINE MOUSSE, CHRISTENED 'HEAVENLY MUD', IS A COMBINATION OF DARK CHOCOLATE, EGGS AND CREAM. IT IS RICH AND FULL OF FLAVOUR, THE HEIGHT OF SELF-INDULGENCE AND A CLASSIC SWEET IN THE NETHERLANDS. THE ANCIENT MAYAN CIVILIZATION BELIEVED THAT CHOCOLATE WAS THE HEAVENLY FOOD OF THE GODS. SIMILARLY, ALL DUTCH PEOPLE WILL AGREE THAT IF THE MUD IN HEAVEN IS LIKE THE CHOCOLATE IN HEMELSE MODDER, IT TRULY IS PARADISE.

SERVES FOUR

INGREDIENTS
 100g/3¾oz dark (bittersweet)
  chocolate, chopped
 30ml/2 tbsp milk
 4 eggs, separated
 25ml/1½ tbsp light brown sugar
To decorate
 whipped double (heavy) cream
 grated chocolate

1 Put the chocolate and milk in a heavy pan and heat over very low heat, stirring until the chocolate is melted and the mixture is smooth.

2 Beat the egg yolks with the sugar in a large bowl. Stir the mixture into the melted chocolate mixture and warm over low heat briefly, stirring constantly, until slightly thickened.

3 Whisk the egg whites in a grease-free bowl until they are very stiff. Remove the chocolate mixture from the heat and fold it into the egg whites.

4 Divide the chocolate mixture among individual serving dishes and chill in the refrigerator for at least 1 hour, until set. Decorate with whipped cream and grated chocolate.

VARIATION

To make another chocolate dessert called Mud from Gerritje, substitute icing (confectioners') sugar for the brown sugar and add some vanilla and ground cinnamon to the chopped chocolate and milk in the pan. Stir 30ml/2 tbsp brandy into the chocolate mixture just before folding it into the egg whites.

Per portion Energy 226kcal/947kJ; Protein 7.8g; Carbohydrate 22g, of which sugars 21.8g; Fat 12.7g, of which saturates 5.8g; Cholesterol 192mg; Calcium 49mg; Fibre 0.6g; Sodium 75mg.

ICE CREAM SUNDAE <u>WITH</u> CHOCOLATE SAUCE

ORDER A 'DAME BLANCHE' IN BELGIUM AND THE WAITER WILL IMMEDIATELY KNOW WHAT YOU MEAN, FOR THE TERM IS USED BY BOTH FRENCH AND FLEMISH SPEAKERS. THIS IMMENSELY POPULAR DESSERT CONSISTS OF GOOD QUALITY VANILLA ICE CREAM LAVISHLY DRIZZLED WITH A DECADENT WARM BELGIAN CHOCOLATE SAUCE. THE TOPPING IS UP TO THE INDIVIDUAL, BUT WHIPPED CREAM, CHOPPED NUTS, CHOCOLATE SHAVINGS, AND A WAFER CAN ALL BE ADDED. IF YOU USE HOME-MADE ICE CREAM, AS IN THIS CLASSIC RECIPE, MAKE IT AT LEAST A DAY AHEAD.

SERVES FOUR

INGREDIENTS
For the ice cream
  350ml/12fl oz/1½ cups full cream
    (whole) milk
  250ml/8fl oz/1 cup double
    (heavy) cream
  1 vanilla pod (bean)
  4 egg yolks
  100g/3¾oz/½ cup caster
    (superfine) sugar
  sweetened whipped cream, chopped
    nuts, chocolate curls and ice cream
    wafers, to serve (optional)
For the chocolate sauce
  60ml/4 tbsp double (heavy) cream
  150ml/¼ pint/⅔ cup milk
  250g/9oz Callebaut callets (semisweet
    bits) or other good-quality Belgian
    chocolate, cut into small pieces
  15ml/1 tbsp brandy, rum or liqueur,
    such as Grand Marnier (optional)

COOK'S TIPS
• If you have a kitchen thermometer, check the temperature of the custard while heating it. When it reaches 80°C/176°F, the custard will be ready. Do not let it boil or it will separate.
• The chocolate sauce can be made ahead of time, and reheated gently over low heat when required.

1 Make the ice cream. Pour 250ml/8fl oz/1 cup of the milk into a heavy pan. Add the cream. Slit the vanilla pod down its length, scrape the seeds into the pan with the tip of the knife, then heat the mixture. When it is hot, but not boiling, remove it from the heat and leave to stand for 10 minutes.

2 Meanwhile, mix the egg yolks and sugar in a medium bowl and beat for about 5 minutes, until thick and creamy. Still beating, add about a third of the warm milk mixture in a steady stream. Pour in the remaining milk mixture and whisk for 2 minutes more.

3 Return the mixture to the pan and cook over medium-high heat, stirring constantly, for 5–7 minutes, until thick enough to coat the back of a spoon. Immediately remove the pan from the heat and stir in the remaining milk. Strain the custard into a stainless steel or glass bowl set over a bowl of iced water.

4 When the mixture has cooled to room temperature, cover the bowl with clear film (plastic wrap) and chill until cold.

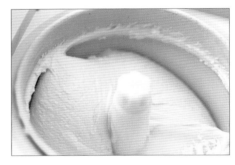

5 Scrape into a freezer container, cover and freeze until firm, whisking two or three times to break up any crystals. If you have an ice cream maker follow manufacturer's instructions, transferring the soft-serve ice cream to a tub and freezing it for 1 hour until scoopable.

6 Make the chocolate sauce. Mix the cream and milk in a pan and heat to simmering point. Remove from the heat and stir in the chocolate until they have have melted and the sauce is smooth. Stir in the brandy or liqueur, if using.

7 Chill glass ice cream coupes or cups. Pour 20ml/4 tsp of the chocolate sauce into each and swirl it around. Top with two scoops of ice cream and more sauce. Pipe whipped cream on top and add nuts, chocolate curls and a wafer.

Per portion Energy 930kcal/3869kJ; Protein 11.2g; Carbohydrate 72.3g, of which sugars 71.7g; Fat 68.2g, of which saturates 40.2g; Cholesterol 324mg; Calcium 229mg; Fibre 1.6g; Sodium 80mg.

CLASSIC BELGIAN CHOCOLATE TRUFFLES

WHEN MADE WITH THE BEST DARK BELGIAN CHOCOLATE, THESE SWEET TRUFFLES ARE THE ULTIMATE INDULGENCE. A SIMPLE GANACHE — A RICH CHOCOLATE AND CREAM MIXTURE — IS SHAPED AND THEN DIPPED IN A VARIETY OF COATINGS, FROM COCOA TO TEMPERED CHOCOLATE. THE LATTER IS PURE LUXURY: A MELT-IN-THE-MOUTH CHOCOLATE ENCASED IN A HARD SHELL. OFTEN FLAVOURED WITH SPIRITS OR LIQUEURS, TRUFFLES ARE AMONG THE MOST POPULAR TREATS SOLD IN BELGIAN CHOCOLATE SHOPS, BUT WITH A BIT OF PATIENCE, THEY ARE EASY TO MAKE AT HOME.

MAKES 30

INGREDIENTS
  250g/9oz good-quality Belgian dark
    (bittersweet) chocolate, such as
    Callebaut, chopped
  150g/5oz/10 tbsp unsalted butter,
    diced and softened
  100m/3½fl oz/scant ½ cup double
    (heavy) cream
  15–30ml/1–2 tbsp brandy or a
    liqueur of your own choice
  15ml/1 tbsp vanilla extract (optional)
  100g/3¾oz/7 tbsp sifted
    unsweetened cocoa powder, icing
    (confectioners') sugar, chopped
    nuts or grated coconut, for coating

1 Melt the chocolate in a heatproof bowl positioned over a pan of just boiled water, stirring until smooth. Stir in the butter until melted.

2 Pour the cream into a medium pan and bring it to simmering point. Remove the pan from the heat and leave to stand for 2 minutes.

3 Pour the cream into the chocolate, stirring with a wooden spoon until the chocolate is completely blended. Stir in the brandy or liqueur, with the vanilla extract, if using. Cover with clear film (plastic wrap) and refrigerate for at least 4 hours, stirring frequently, until the mixture is stiff but still malleable.

4 With a spatula, transfer the mixture to a glass tray or shallow dish and spread it out so that it is 3cm/1¼in deep. Cover with clear film and chill in the refrigerator for 5 hours or overnight.

5 Line two baking trays with baking parchment. Using two teaspoons or a melon baller, shape the ganache into balls and place slightly apart on the parchment-lined baking trays.

6 Cover with clear film and return to the refrigerator to firm up again for 1 hour.

7 To coat the truffles, drop them into separate small bowls of cocoa powder, icing sugar, chopped nuts or grated coconut and roll around until completely coated.

8 Shake off any excess coating, reshape the truffles into balls if necessary with your hands and replace them on the baking parchment.

9 When all the truffles have been coated, serve immediately, while at room temperature, or store in an airtight container in a cool place for up to a week. Allow the truffles to come up to room temperature before serving.

VARIATION
To make chocolate-coated truffles, have ready a baking tray lined with baking parchment, and a fondue fork or skewer for dipping. Use good-quality dark (bittersweet) chocolate with at least 70 per cent cocoa solids. For a glossy coating that retains its shine, temper the chocolate. Melt 100g/3¾oz/1 cup chopped dark chocolate in the top of a double boiler over hot water. When melted, the chocolate will have a temperature of around 42°C/107°F. Stir in 15g/½oz/1 tbsp unsalted butter until smooth, then add an additional 50g/2oz/ ½ cup chopped chocolate. Stir the chocolate constantly and keep checking the temperature. When it registers 32°C/90°F, remove from the heat. Tip the bowl so that the chocolate pools on one side. Spear a truffle and dip it into the chocolate, turning until coated. Let the excess drain off, then put the truffles on the lined baking tray to set for about an hour before serving or storing.

Per portion Energy 101kcal/421kJ; Protein 0.6g; Carbohydrate 6g, of which sugars 5.9g; Fat 8.1g, of which saturates 5g; Cholesterol 15mg; Calcium 7mg; Fibre 0.2g; Sodium 10mg.

COUNTRY LADS AND GIRLS

THESE 'DRINKS', WHICH ARE SERVED IN SMALL GLASSES, ARE A REAL DUTCH SPECIALITY. THE 'LADS', THE BRANDIED RAISINS, WERE A TREAT AT WEDDING PARTIES, ESPECIALLY IN THE NORTH OF THE COUNTRY. THE 'GIRLS' ARE BRANDIED DRIED APRICOTS. TODAY BOTH ARE ALSO EATEN SPOONED OVER ICE CREAM AND MOULDED PUDDINGS. YOU CAN BUY THEM READY-MADE OR MAKE YOUR OWN.

SERVES 15

INGREDIENTS
　　250ml/8fl oz/1 cup water
　　1 cinnamon stick (for the lads)
　　　or thinly pared rind of ½ lemon
　　　(for the girls)
　　100g/3¾oz/generous ½ cup caster
　　　(superfine) sugar
　　250g/9oz/generous 1¾ cups
　　　sultanas (golden raisins) or halved
　　　dried apricots
　　500ml/17fl oz/generous 2 cups
　　　Dutch brandy

1 Put the water, sugar and cinnamon or lemon rind in a pan and bring to the boil, stirring until the sugar has dissolved.

2 Add the washed fruit to the spiced sugar syrup and simmer for 10 minutes.

3 Transfer the mixture into a sterilized 750ml/1¼-pint/3-cup preserving jar (*see* Cook's tip). Leave to cool, then chill in the refrigerator for at least 48 hours.

4 Add the brandy, stir well and seal the jar. Store in a cool dark place for at least 6 weeks before serving.

5 Serve in small wide stemmed glasses with a tiny silver spoon. Once opened, store the jar in the refrigerator and use within 2 weeks of opening.

COOK'S TIP
To sterilize the jar, check for cracks or damage, then wash in hot, soapy water, rinse and turn upside down to drain. Stand on a baking sheet lined with kitchen paper. Rest any lids on top. Place in a cold oven, then heat to 110°C/225°F/ Gas ¼ and bake for 30 minutes.

Per portion Energy 146kcal/614kJ; Protein 0.5g; Carbohydrate 18.5g, of which sugars 18.5g; Fat 0.1g, of which saturates 0g; Cholesterol 0mg; Calcium 14mg; Fibre 0.3g; Sodium 4mg.

BLACKCURRANT LIQUEUR

BLACKCURRANTS GROW VERY WELL IN BELGIUM, AND ARE USED IN A RANGE OF FOODS, INCLUDING JELLIES, JAMS, JUICES, BEERS AND SAUCES, AS WELL AS THIS DELICIOUS LIQUEUR MADE WITH EAU DE VIE OR VODKA. THE LIQUEUR CAN BE MIXED WITH A FRUITY WHITE WINE, AS HERE, OR FOR A REALLY DECADENT COCKTAIL, COMBINE IT WITH CHAMPAGNE TO MAKE A KIR ROYALE.

MAKES 1.5 LITRES/2½ PINTS/6¼ CUPS

INGREDIENTS
   1kg/2¼ lb/9 cups blackcurrants
   500g/1¼ lb/2½ cups sugar
   1 organic unwaxed lemon, sliced
   1 litre/1¾ pints/4 cups eau de vie,
     vodka or other clear alcohol
     (95 per cent proof)
   1 bottle white fruity wine, about
     750ml/1¼ pints/3 cups

1 Rinse the blackcurrants until clean, drain and dry with a clean dish towel. Remove the stems.

2 Spoon a layer of the blackcurrants into a sterilized large preserving jar (*see* Cook's tip on page 214). Add a sprinkling of sugar and a slice or two of lemon.

3 Repeat the layers until all the ingredients have been used, then stir gently to distribute the sugar evenly.

4 Cover tightly and leave for 3 days to allow the sugar to dissolve.

5 Pour the eau de vie or vodka over the blackcurrants, replace the lid and leave for at least 3 weeks or up to 3 months in a cool, dark place. Shake occasionally.

6 Strain the liquid through a fine sieve (strainer) placed over a bowl, pressing the berries with the back of a large spoon to extract as much liquid as possible. Pour into a sterilized bottle, cork and store in a cool place until required.

7 To serve the liqueur as an aperitif, quarter fill a champagne or wine glass with liqueur and top up with chilled white wine.

COOK'S TIPS
• This recipe can be made with thawed, frozen blackcurrants or fresh ones that are slightly past their best.
• Serve topped with chilled soda water for a refreshing summer drink.

Per portion Energy 3930kcal/16485kJ; Protein 0g; Carbohydrate 492g, of which sugars 492g; Fat 0g, of which saturates 0g; Cholesterol 0mg; Calcium 75mg; Fibre 0g; Sodium 180mg.

EGG LIQUEUR

ADVOCAAT IS A LIQUEUR FROM THE PROVINCE OF LIMBURG, BORDERING THE NETHERLANDS, WHERE THE DRINK IS ALSO MADE. THERE ARE TWO VARIETIES: 'THICK ADVOCAAT', WHICH IS SOLID ENOUGH TO BE EATEN WITH A SPOON, AND A MORE LIQUID VERSION THAT CONTAINS EGG WHITES AND IS USED TO MAKE COCKTAILS LIKE THE SNOWBALL — A MIXTURE OF ADVOCAAT, LEMONADE AND LIME JUICE.

MAKES 2 LITRES/3½ PINTS/8 CUPS

INGREDIENTS
   10 egg yolks
   250g/9oz/1¼ cups caster
    (superfine) sugar
   pinch of grated nutmeg (optional)
   5ml/1 tsp vanilla extract or 8g/⅓oz
    sachet vanilla sugar
   397g/14oz can sweetened
    condensed milk
   1 litre/1¾ pints/4 cups grain alcohol,
    brandy or good-quality vodka

COOK'S TIP
The colour of the drink will intensify as the liqueur ages, eventually becoming the familiar pale yellow of the commercial liqueur.

1 Put the egg yolks, sugar and nutmeg, if using, in a very large bowl (so the liquid doesn't spill when you stir it). Mix gently to combine thoroughly.

2 Stir in the vanilla extract or vanilla sugar, sweetened condensed milk and grain alcohol, brandy or vodka.

3 Blend in batches in a blender for 30 seconds. Pour into sterilized bottles (*see* Cook's tip on page 214), cork and place in the refrigerator for at least 2 weeks, shaking occasionally.

4 Serve in shot glasses, use to make liqueur coffee or pour over ice cream.

DIPLOMAT COFFEE

THIS LUXURIOUS DRINK IS A SPECIALITY OF THE KEMPEN, WHERE A GLASS OF ADVOCAAT IS OFTEN SERVED AS AN ACCOMPANIMENT TO A CUP OF COFFEE. THIS RECIPE GOES ONE STEP FURTHER, LAYERING ESPRESSO, ADVOCAAT AND CREAM IN A TALL GLASS. CREAMY AND DELICIOUS, IT IS A FAVOURITE AFTER-DINNER DRINK, OFTEN SERVED WITH A BELGIAN CHOCOLATE PRALINE.

SERVES ONE

INGREDIENTS
   100ml/3½fl oz/scant ½ cup double
    (heavy) cream
   15ml/1 tbsp icing (confectioners') sugar
   45ml/3 tbsp *advocaat* liqueur
   90ml/6 tbsp espresso coffee
   unsweetened cocoa powder or 5ml/1 tsp
    shaved chocolate curls, to decorate

1 Pour the cream into a bowl. Add the icing sugar and whip until stiff.

2 Warm a tall or wide heat-resistant glass, either by filling it with boiling water and letting it stand for 1 minute before draining and drying, or by half filling it with water, heating it on High in a microwave for 30 seconds, then draining and drying the glass.

3 Pour the liqueur into the glass. Carefully pour the coffee on top, trying not to disturb the *advocaat* layer.

4 Top the coffee with the sweetened whipped cream, so that it floats on top of the coffee.

5 Decorate with cocoa or shaved chocolate. Serve immediately.

Egg liqueur per portion Energy 5137kcal/21498kJ; Protein 64g; Carbohydrate 481.6g, of which sugars 481.6g; Fat 95g, of which saturates 40.7g; Cholesterol 2159mg; Calcium 1518mg; Fibre 0g; Sodium 661mg.
Diplomat coffee per portion Energy 701kcal/2902kJ; Protein 1.7g; Carbohydrate 27.6g, of which sugars 27.6g; Fat 60.7g, of which saturates 33.4g; Cholesterol 137mg; Calcium 65mg; Fibre 0g; Sodium 63mg.

COFFEE WITH GENEVER, HASSELT-STYLE

HASSELT, THE CAPITAL OF LIMBURG, IS FAMOUS FOR ITS GENEVER. THIS DRINK IS DISTILLED FROM A MALTED GRAIN MASH AND FLAVOURED WITH BERRIES FROM THE JUNIPER PLANT. IT IS USUALLY DRUNK NEAT AND COLD, OR, AS IN THIS SPECIALITY, MIXED WITH COFFEE AND TOPPED WITH CREAM.

3 Add the genever and crème de cacao liqueur to the warm glass, then pour in the coffee. Stir to combine.

4 Carefully add the sweetened whipped cream, letting it slide down the back of a spoon so that it floats on the surface of the coffee.

5 Decorate the top of the cream with a dusting of cocoa powder or shaved chocolate curls.

SERVES ONE

INGREDIENTS
    100ml/3½fl oz/scant ½ cup double
      (heavy) cream
    15ml/1 tbsp icing (confectioners') sugar
    ½ to 1 shot glass (25–45ml/
      1½–3 tbsp) Hasselt Genever
    1 shot glass (45ml/3 tbsp) crème de
      cacao liqueur
    250ml/8fl oz/1 cup freshly brewed
      espresso coffee
    2.5ml/½ tsp unsweetened cocoa
      powder or 5ml/1 tsp shaved
      chocolate curls, to decorate

1 Pour the cream into a bowl. Add the sugar and whip by hand or with an electric mixer until stiff.

2 Warm a tall or wide heat-resistant glass, either by filling it with boiling water and letting it stand for 1 minute before draining and drying, or by half filling it with water, heating it on High in a microwave for 30 seconds, then draining and drying it.

COOK'S TIP
Ensure the glass is heat-proof, or it could crack when you add the coffee.

Per portion Energy 698kcal/2879kJ; Protein 1.6g; Carbohydrate 12g, of which sugars 12g; Fat 60.7g, of which saturates 33.4g; Cholesterol 137mg; Calcium 57mg; Fibre 0g; Sodium 62mg.

LIÈGE-STYLE COFFEE WITH ICE CREAM

THIS NON-ALCOHOLIC COFFEE, CREAM AND ICE CREAM COMBINATION IS A SPECIALITY OF THE CITY OF LIÈGE IN BELGIUM. ENJOY IT AS AN INDULGENT AFTERNOON TREAT OR SERVE IT AFTER DINNER, AS THE PERFECT WAY TO FINISH OFF A GOOD MEAL, PERHAPS INSTEAD OF DESSERT.

SERVES ONE

INGREDIENTS

- 100ml/3½fl oz/scant ½ cup double (heavy) cream
- 15ml/1 tbsp icing (confectioners') sugar
- 45ml/3 tbsp freshly brewed espresso coffee
- 10ml/2 tsp sugar
- 2 scoops of coffee, mocha or vanilla ice cream
- 2.5ml/½ tsp unsweetened cocoa powder, 5ml/1 tsp shaved chocolate curls, or 3 chocolate coffee beans, to decorate

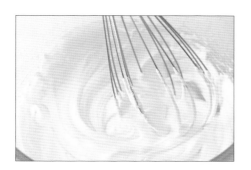

1 Pour the cream into a large, grease-free bowl. Sift over the icing sugar and whip the mixture by hand or with an electric mixer, until stiff.

2 Sweeten the espresso with sugar.

3 Place the scoops of ice cream in a tall or wide heat-resistant glass.

4 Pour over the freshly brewed espresso and top with the whipped cream (you may not need all of it; any that isn't required can be kept in the refrigerator for up to 2 days).

5 Decorate with a dusting of cocoa, a few shavings of chocolate or the chocolate coffee beans. Serve immediately.

COOK'S TIP
Chill the espresso before pouring it over the ice cream, if you prefer.

Per portion Energy 925kcal/3855kJ; Protein 6.2g; Carbohydrate 82.9g, of which sugars 81.6g; Fat 64g, of which saturates 40.7g; Cholesterol 166mg; Calcium 198mg; Fibre 0g; Sodium 97mg.

BAKING AND BREADS

Bread-making and baking in Belgium and the Netherlands has been important since medieval times, and the traditions that were introduced by the monks are still evident in the breads on offer today, such as Abbey Bread, soft Belgian Bread Rolls or The Hague Breakfast. Cakes, cookies, pies and tarts are also popular, and are often lightly spiced and made with dried or fresh fruit, such as apricots, plums or apples, which are used to make the Dutch national pastry, Apple Pie.

BITTER COOKIES

ALMONDS WERE WIDELY USED DURING THE LENTEN FAST LEADING UP TO EASTER IN THE NETHERLANDS, WHEN ALL ANIMAL FOODS WERE FORBIDDEN AND ALMOND MILK WAS USED INSTEAD OF COW'S MILK. SIMILAR IN FLAVOUR TO THE CRISP ITALIAN AMARETTI, THESE COOKIES BECAME IMMENSELY POPULAR AND REMAIN A SAVOURED TREAT. THEY DIFFER FROM MACAROONS, MADE SOLELY FROM SWEET ALMONDS, AS THEY INCLUDE A PROPORTION OF BITTER ALMONDS. THESE CAN BE DIFFICULT TO OBTAIN, SO BITTER ALMOND OIL IS USED HERE IN CONJUNCTION WITH GROUND SWEET ALMONDS.

MAKES 15–18

INGREDIENTS
  125g/4¼oz/generous 1 cup very dry
    blanched almonds
  125g/4¼oz/generous 1 cup icing
    (confectioner's) sugar
  2 drops of bitter almond oil
  50ml/2fl oz/¼ cup egg white,
    lightly beaten

COOK'S TIP
The Dutch tend to not like these cookies when they have dried out and are no longer chewy. When they reach this stage they are generally used in desserts, or even cakes. The cookies can, however, be frozen.

1 Preheat the oven to 180°C/350°F/ Gas 4. Line a baking sheet with baking parchment.

2 Grind the almonds into an extremely fine powder in a food mill or an electric grinder, but do not use a blender.

3 Place the almonds in a bowl, sift in the sugar, add the oil and mix well. Add enough egg white, a spoonful at a time, to knead to a firm dough, then add the remaining egg white to make a very sticky, flabby dough.

4 Using two teaspoons, place 15–18 mounds of the mixture on the prepared baking sheet, spacing them apart. Bake for 15–20 minutes, until lightly browned.

5 Remove the baking sheet from the oven and leave the cookies to stand for a minute, then carefully lift the baking parchment with cookies and place it on a flat surface.

6 Leave to cool completely before removing the cookies from the parchment. These can be stored in an airtight container for up to three days.

Per portion Energy 72kcal/303kJ; Protein 1.8g; Carbohydrate 7.7g, of which sugars 7.6g; Fat 4g, of which saturates 0.3g; Cholesterol 0mg; Calcium 21mg; Fibre 0.5g; Sodium 7mg.

SUGAR COOKIES FROM BRUSSELS

DESPITE THE LOCAL NAME, 'GREEK BREAD', THIS SPECIALITY HAS NOTHING TO DO WITH GREECE AND IS MORE OF AN EXTRA-LARGE COOKIE THAN A TYPE OF BREAD. INSTEAD, THE COOKIES GOT THEIR NAME FROM A BRUSSELS STREET CALLED WOLVENGRACHT, WHERE AUGUSTINE MONKS DISTRIBUTED BREAD TO THE POOR. FROM THERE THE BREAD WAS DUBBED 'DE GRACHT' (BREAD FROM THE DITCH), PRONOUNCED 'GRECHT' IN BRUSSELS DIALECT. DURING THE FRENCH OCCUPATION, THIS WAS TRANSLATED AS 'PAIN A LA GRECQUE', HENCE THE CONFUSION.

MAKES FIVE

INGREDIENTS
250g/9oz/5 cups plain
(all-purpose) flour
100g/3¾oz/generous ½ cup sugar
6ml/1¼ tsp easy-blend (rapid-rise)
dried yeast
pinch of salt
5ml/1 tsp ground cinnamon
30ml/2 tbsp full cream (whole) milk
2 eggs, beaten
100g/3¾oz/scant ½ cup unsalted
butter, cubed and softened
demerara (raw) sugar or Turbinado
sugar, for coating

1 Sift the flour into a large mixing bowl. Stir in the sugar, dried yeast, salt and cinnamon. Make a well in the centre and pour in the milk and beaten eggs.

2 Stir, gradually incorporating the surrounding dry ingredients until the mixture holds together. Add the softened butter, a few pieces at a time, and mix with your fingertips until all of it has been incorporated.

3 Shape the dough into a round and knead on a lightly floured surface for 10 minutes, until smooth.

4 Place it in an oiled bowl, cover with clear film (plastic wrap) and leave to rest in the refrigerator for 1 hour.

5 Divide the dough in five pieces of equal size and roll each piece into a long roll. Using the palm of your hand or a rolling pin, flatten each roll to a rectangle.

6 Sprinkle the demerara or Turbinado sugar on a plate. Press each piece of dough in turn in the sugar until coated all over. Place on a baking sheet lined with baking parchment and leave to rest for 20–30 minutes.

7 Preheat the oven to 190°C/375°F/Gas 5. Bake the cookies for 20 minutes or until golden. Transfer to a wire rack. The cookies will harden as they cool.

8 Serve as an afternoon snack with coffee or tea. They will keep in an airtight container for up to a week.

Per portion Energy 430kcal/1807kJ; Protein 7.6g; Carbohydrate 60.2g, of which sugars 22.1g; Fat 19.4g, of which saturates 11.2g; Cholesterol 119mg; Calcium 103mg; Fibre 1.6g; Sodium 154mg.

JOHN HAIL COOKIE

THIS COOKIE ORIGINALLY CONSISTED OF SMALL DROPS OF DOUGH BAKED TOGETHER. JANHAGEL WAS USED AS A TERM FOR 'RAGTAG AND BOBTAIL' AND THE COOKIE OWED ITS NAME TO THE POORER CLIENTELE WHO BOUGHT IT. HOWEVER, IN THE 19TH CENTURY, THE NAME INSPIRED A BAKER TO PROVIDE THE COOKIE WITH A LAYER OF ALMONDS AND SUGAR THAT RESEMBLED HAGEL, OR 'HAIL'. COMBINED WITH JAN, A COMMON DUTCH FORENAME, THE RESULT WAS AN IRRESISTIBLE SWEET.

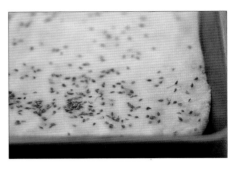

3 Knead the mixture to form an elastic dough then, with floured fingers, press it on to the baking sheet, spreading it out to within 2cm/¾in of the rim.

4 Sprinkle with the almonds and sugar, pressing them in well.

5 Bake for 25–30 minutes, until golden brown. Remove the baking sheet from the oven and cut the pastry into bars.

6 Using a spatula, transfer them to a flat, dry surface to cool. If the undersides of the bars are still soft and pale, turn them upside down on the baking sheet and return to the oven for a few minutes. These can be stored for several weeks in an airtight container.

COOK'S TIP
In the Netherlands, pearl sugar, or *greinsuikerklontjes* is only available at the baker's. You could also use normal sugar cubes crushed into grains with a dough roll, and then sift the finer grains out.

MAKES ABOUT 32

INGREDIENTS
150g/5oz/10 tbsp butter, plus extra for greasing
breadcrumbs, for sprinkling (optional)
250g/9oz/2¼ cups plain (all-purpose) flour, plus extra for dusting
75g/3oz/scant ½ cup caster (superfine) sugar
75g/3oz/⅓ cup Muscovado (molasses) sugar
2.5ml/½ tsp tartaric acid
1.5ml/¼ tsp bicarbonate of soda (baking)
2.5ml/½ tsp vanilla seeds
2.5ml/½ tsp aniseed
2.5ml/½ tsp ground cinnamon
1 egg
To decorate
45ml/3 tbsp flaked (sliced) almonds
45ml/3 tbsp small pearl sugar

1 Preheat the oven to 160°C/325°F/ Gas 3. Grease a 40 x 35cm/16 x 14in baking sheet. Sprinkle with breadcrumbs or line with baking parchment.

2 Sift the flour, sugar, tartaric acid and soda into a bowl. Stir in the vanilla seeds, aniseed and cinnamon. Add the egg, then the butter. Cut with two knives into very small lumps.

Per portion Energy 96kcal/400kJ; Protein 1.2g; Carbohydrate 12.7g, of which sugars 6.6g; Fat 4.8g, of which saturates 2.5g; Cholesterol 10mg; Calcium 19mg; Fibre 0.3g; Sodium 29mg.

CARAMEL WAFFLES

THESE SPLIT WAFFLES WITH A LAYER OF TOFFEE IN BETWEEN ARE A SPECIALITY OF THE CITY OF GOUDA IN THE NETHERLANDS, BUT WAFFLE BAKERS SELLING THEM AT MARKETS AND FAIRS HAVE ENSURED COUNTRY-WIDE POPULARITY. THEIR MANUFACTURE IS NOW A BIG INDUSTRY AND YOU CAN BUY STROOPWAFELS IN EVERY DUTCH SUPERMARKET. HOME-MADE ONES ARE MUCH NICER, HOWEVER, BUT YOU WILL REQUIRE A ROUND ELECTRIC WAFFLE IRON.

MAKES ABOUT 20

INGREDIENTS
    250g/9oz/2¼ cups plain
      (all-purpose) flour
    75g/3oz/scant ½ cup caster
      (superfine) sugar
    pinch of salt
    1 sachet easy-blend (rapid-rise)
      dried yeast
    25ml/1½ tbsp lukewarm milk
    1 small (US medium) egg, beaten
    125g/4¼oz/generous ½ cup butter,
      melted and cooled to lukewarm
For the filling
    225g/8oz/⅔ cup golden
      (light corn) syrup
    150g/5oz/10 tbsp butter
    10ml/2 tsp ground cinnamon

1 Sift the flour into a large bowl, stir in the sugar and salt and make a central well. Pour the yeast in and add the milk. Stir to combine thoroughly. Cover with a clean dish towel and leave to stand for 10 minutes, until the yeast starts to foam.

2 Add the egg and butter and knead until the dough is elastic, adding a little more milk if necessary. Cover with a dampened dish towel and leave to rise for about 1 hour.

3 Shape the dough into 20 balls, cover with a damp towel and leave to stand for at least 15 minutes, until doubled in size.

4 To make the filling, pour the syrup into a pan, add the butter and cinnamon and simmer, stirring constantly, for 10 minutes. Remove from the heat and cool, then keep it lukewarm in a double boiler. The mixture cannot be boiled again or it will separate.

5 Heat a round waffle iron to its highest temperature. If it does not have a non-stick lining, grease it once before cooking the first waffle. Put a dough ball in the iron, press lightly and cook for 1 minute.

6 Remove the waffle from the iron with a knife, place on a board and immediately slice in half with a very sharp serrated knife, starting at the lighter side.

7 Spread the inside with a little of the filling. Put the two halves back together.

8 Make the remaining waffles in the same way. They will keep well for at least 2 weeks in an airtight container.

Per portion Energy 198kcal/825kJ; Protein 1.7g; Carbohydrate 22.7g, of which sugars 13.1g; Fat 11.8g, of which saturates 7.3g; Cholesterol 39mg; Calcium 27mg; Fibre 0.4g; Sodium 118mg.

OLIEBOL

This traditional New Year's treat has outlived all the healthy eating campaigns that tried to limit the number of sweet products in the Dutch diet. Fanatics maintain that if they are prepared properly oliebollen or 'oil balls' do not contain excessive quantities of oil. Sprinkled with sugar, they are believed to symbolize a sweet and everlasting life.

MAKES ABOUT 25

INGREDIENTS
    500g/1¼lb/5 cups strong white
       bread flour
    1 sachet easy-bend (rapid-rise)
       dried yeast
    400ml/14fl oz/1⅔ cups
       lukewarm milk
    2 eggs, lightly beaten
    7.5ml/1½ tsp salt
    vegetable oil, for deep-frying
    icing (confectioners') sugar,
       to decorate and to serve
For the filling
    100g/3¾oz/¾ cup raisins
    100g/3¾oz/scant ½ cup currants
    50g/2oz/½ cup coarsely chopped
       almonds or 50g/2oz/⅓ cup diced
       candied peel
    1 tart apple, peeled, cored and cut
       in small cubes

1 Sift the flour into a large bowl and make a well in the centre. Add the yeast and a little of the milk to the well and mix together. Cover with a dampened dish towel and leave to stand for 15 minutes, until the yeast starts to foam.

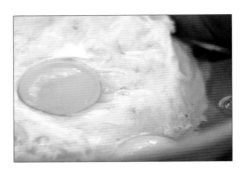

2 Starting from the middle, stir in the remaining milk and the eggs, then mix with a hand-held electric mixer with dough hooks.

3 Add the salt to the mixture and continue mixing until the dough is elastic and comes away from the side of the bowl.

4 Mix in all the filling ingredients until evenly combined. Cover and leave to rise at room temperature for 1 hour.

5 Pour the oil for deep-frying into a pan to a depth of at least 10cm/4in and heat to 175°C/347°F. Have two dessertspoons more oil ready in a cup.

6 Scoop a spoonful of batter from the bowl with one spoon and push the batter into the hot oil with the other. Don't add too many balls at once and allow enough room for them to turn over. Cook for 5 minutes, until golden.

7 Remove the balls with a slotted spoon and drain on kitchen paper. Repeat until you have used all the dough.

8 Pile the balls into a pyramid on a plate, wait for them to cool, sprinkle with icing sugar and serve with more sugar.

Per portion Energy 136kcal/574kJ; Protein 3.5g; Carbohydrate 22.2g, of which sugars 6.9g; Fat 4.3g, of which saturates 0.7g; Cholesterol 16mg; Calcium 60mg; Fibre 1g; Sodium 16mg.

APPLE TURNOVER

ANOTHER SWEET PRODUCT ASSOCIATED WITH THE NEW YEAR CELEBRATION IN THE NETHERLANDS IS THE APPELFLAP *OR 'APPLE TURNOVER'. THIS IS A TRADITIONAL ALTERNATIVE TO THE* APPELBEIGNET *OR 'APPLE FRITTER', WHICH IS NOWADAYS PREFERRED BY MANY BECAUSE IT IS BAKED IN THE OVEN RATHER THAN FRIED IN OIL, MAKING IT A SLIGHTLY HEALTHIER OPTION.*

MAKES 12

INGREDIENTS
　250g/9oz/2¼ cups plain
　　(all-purpose) flour, plus extra
　　for dusting
　2.5ml/½ tsp salt
　90g/3½oz/scant ½ cup cold butter
　5ml/1 tsp white wine vinegar
　500g/1¼lb tart apples, such as
　　Goudrenet or Granny Smith
　45ml/3 tbsp soft brown sugar
　5ml/1 tsp ground cinnamon
　2.5ml/½ tsp crushed fennel seeds
　beaten egg, to glaze
　icing (confectioners') sugar,
　　for sprinkling

1 Sift the flour and salt into a bowl, coarsely grate in the butter and rub in with your fingertips. Using the blade of a knife, gradually stir in 100ml/3½fl oz/ scant ½ cup water and the vinegar. Gather the dough together and shape into a ball.

2 Roll out the dough on a lightly floured surface, then fold the top edge down to the centre and the bottom edge up to the centre and roll out again to a rectangle. Fold in three again, cover with clear film (plastic wrap) and leave to rest in the refrigerator.

VARIATION
You could use store-bought puff pastry instead of making the pastry in this recipe, if you prefer.

3 Peel the apples and grate them coarsely into a bowl. Stir in the sugar, cinnamon and fennel seeds.

4 Preheat the oven to 200°C/400°F/ Gas 6. Line a 30 x 40cm/12 x 16in baking sheet with baking parchment.

5 Roll out the dough on a lightly floured surface to 36 x 48cm/14¼ x 19in rectangle, then cut into 12 squares.

6 Cover the centre of each square with some grated apple and fold over to make a triangle. Press the edges together with a fork.

7 Transfer to the prepared baking sheet and brush with beaten egg. Prick the tops several times with a fork. Bake for about 35 minutes. Remove from the oven and leave to cool, then sprinkle generously with icing sugar.

Per portion Energy 156kcal/658kJ; Protein 2.2g; Carbohydrate 23.9g, of which sugars 8g; Fat 6.5g, lof which saturates 4g; Cholesterol 16mg; Calcium 34mg; Fibre 1.3g; Sodium 47mg.

ST NICHOLAS SLICES

Spicy speculaas is one of the traditional gifts on 5 December, the eve of the Saint's day of Saint Nicholas. The dough would formerly have been shaped in artfully carved wooden moulds, representing themes from daily life, hence the name from the Latin word speculum, meaning mirror. As the modern dough is usually lighter, the dough is baked as a thick layer and then broken. Here is the softer filled version, a favourite nowadays.

MAKES 30–36 PIECES

INGREDIENTS
125g/4¼oz/generous ½ cup butter, softened, plus extra for greasing
breadcrumbs, for sprinkling
250g/9oz/2¼ cups plain (all-purpose) flour, plus extra for dusting
2.5ml/½ tsp baking powder
7.5ml/1½ tsp ground cinnamon
2.5ml/½ tsp ground nutmeg
2.5ml/½ tsp ground cardamom
2.5ml/½ tsp ground allspice
pinch of salt
1.5ml/¼ tsp crushed aniseed
150g/5oz/⅔ cups muscovado (molasses) sugar
60ml/4 tbsp milk, plus extra for brushing
400g/14oz almond paste (*see* Cook's tip)
1 small (US medium) egg
50 split blanched almonds, to decorate

1 Preheat the oven to 180°C/350°F/Gas 4. Grease a shallow 23cm/9in square or 17 x 25cm/6½ x 10in rectangular cake tin (pan) with butter. Sprinkle with breadcrumbs, shaking out any excess.

2 Sift the flour, baking powder, cinnamon, nutmeg, cardamom, allspice and salt into a bowl. Stir in the aniseed and sugar.

3 Add the butter and cut it into the flour mixture with two knives. Knead, adding the milk a spoonful at a time, until the dough is smooth and elastic. You may not require all the milk.

COOK'S TIP
To make almond paste, mix together 200g/7oz/1¾ cups ground almonds, 200g/7oz/1 cup sugar, 1 small (US medium) egg, a drop of bitter almond oil or almond extract and a pinch of grated lemon rind. Knead until smooth, then wrap and chill in the refrigerator until ready to use.

4 Halve the dough and form it into two balls. Roll out one ball on a lightly floured surface to the same shape as the prepared tin but slightly larger.

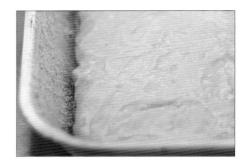

5 Use the dough to line the tin, easing it up the sides and letting it overhang the rim. Roll out the second dough ball in the same way.

6 Mix the almond paste with the egg in a bowl. Spread this over the dough in the tin with dampened fingers.

7 Cover the paste with the second piece of dough, pressing the edges to seal. Trim off any overhanging dough. Brush the top with milk and decorate with the almonds in neat rows. Prick little holes in between the nuts.

8 Bake for 50 minutes, gently flattening any bubbles with the back of a spoon after 30 minutes. Remove from the oven, cover with foil and leave to cool in the tin. Cut into rectangular pieces before serving.

Per portion Energy 126kcal/527kJ; Protein 2.2g; Carbohydrate 16.2g, of which sugars 10.6g; Fat 6.3g, of which saturates 2.1g; Cholesterol 12.7mg; Calcium 0.6mg; Fibre 0.6g; Sodium 25mg.

ALMOND TARTLETS FROM GERAARDSBERGEN

FOOD ITEMS DON'T OFTEN MAKE IT ON TO POSTAGE STAMPS, BUT THESE DELICIOUS DOUBLE-CRUST CURD TARTLETS ARE SO FAMOUS IN BELGIUM THAT THAT THEY DID JUST THAT IN 1985. THE PASTRIES HAVE BEEN MADE IN THE AREA OF GERAARDSBERGEN SINCE MEDIEVAL TIMES. AMONG THEIR MANY DEVOTEES ARE MEMBERS OF THE 'BROTHERHOOD OF THE GERAARDBERGSE MATTENTAART'. ONCE A YEAR, ON MATTENTAART DAY, DEMONSTRATIONS OF HOW TO MAKE THEM OCCUR IN THE TOWN'S MARKETPLACE.

MAKES SIX

INGREDIENTS
    1 litre/1¾ pints/4 cups milk
    500ml/17fl oz/generous 2 cups
      buttermilk
    15ml/1 tbsp white wine vinegar
      or lemon juice
    butter and flour for greasing and dusting
    3 eggs, separated
    5ml/1 tsp vanilla extract
    5ml/1 tsp almond extract
    25g/1oz/¼ cup ground almonds
    115g/4oz/1 cup icing
      (confectioners') sugar
    675g/1½lb puff pastry, thawed
      if frozen
    1 egg yolk mixed with 30ml/2 tbsp
      water, to glaze

1 Make the milk curd (matten) for the filling the day before. Pour the milk into a pan and bring it to the boil. Immediately remove from the heat and stir in the buttermilk and vinegar. Leave to stand for 10–15 minutes, until the mixture has curdled. Pour into a fine sieve (strainer) lined with muslin (cheesecloth). Stand in the sink and leave to drain overnight.

2 Preheat the oven to 220 C/425 F/Gas 7. Grease six 7.5cm/3in loose-bottomed tartlet tins (muffin pans) and dust with flour. Transfer the curds into a food processor and blend until smooth. Scrape into a bowl and stir in the egg yolks, vanilla extract, almond extract and ground almonds. Add half the sugar and mix well.

3 Roll out the puff pastry on a lightly floured surface. Cut out six 7.5cm/3in rounds as lids for the tartlets and six slightly larger rounds for the tartlet cases. Fit the larger rounds into the tartlet tins and prick the base of each lightly with a fork.

4 Beat the egg whites to stiff peaks, gradually adding the remaining icing sugar. Fold the beaten egg whites into the curd mixture, then divide the filling among the pastry cases (pieshells). Fit the lids on top, and press the pastry edges together to seal.

5 Glaze the pastry lids by brushing them with the egg yolk mixture. Using sharp kitchen scissors, cut a couple of slashes in the top of each pastry lid, so steam can escape.

6 Bake for 30–40 minutes or until the pastry is golden. Leave to cool for about 10 minutes, then carefully remove the tartlets from the tins and serve.

Per portion Energy 704kcal/2946kJ; Protein 19.3g; Carbohydrate 73.1g, of which sugars 32.8g; Fat 40.3g, of which saturates 5.5g; Cholesterol 155mg; Calcium 402mg; Fibre 0.3g; Sodium 495mg.

LIMBURG TART

THIS SWEET TART FROM THE SOUTH OF THE NETHERLANDS BOASTS A LONG HISTORY. THERE ARE RECORDS OF THE WORD VLADBECKER, *MEANING 'BAKER OF FLAT TARTS', GOING BACK TO 1338. IN LIMBURG THE TART WAS ORIGINALLY A SPECIAL TREAT DURING A TWICE-YEARLY CHURCH FAIR. NOW IT IS AVAILABLE WIDELY THROUGHOUT THE COUNTRY.*

SERVES SIX–EIGHT

INGREDIENTS
300g/11oz/2¾ cups plain
(all-purpose) flour, plus extra
for dusting
½ sachet easy-blend (rapid-rise)
dried yeast
5ml/1 tsp sugar
100ml/3½fl oz/scant ½ cup
lukewarm milk
25g/1oz/2 tbsp butter, softened,
plus extra for greasing
25g/1oz/2 tbsp caster (superfine) sugar
1 egg, beaten
5ml/1 tsp salt
For the filling
250ml/9fl oz/generous 1 cup milk
¼ vanilla pod (bean)
2 egg yolks
50g/2oz/¼ cup caster (superfine) sugar
25g/1oz/¼ cup cornflour (cornstarch)
For the topping
500–800g/1¼–1¾lb bottled,
canned or prepared fresh fruit,
such as sliced apples, halved
plums, halved apricots or cherries
(do not use berries)
50g/2oz/¼ cup sugar (optional)
To decorate
150ml/¼ pint/⅔ cup juice
15ml/1 tbsp potato flour or sugar

1 Sift the flour into a bowl and make a well. Pour the yeast into the well and add the sugar and a little of the milk. Leave to rest for 10 minutes. Add the remaining milk, the butter, sugar and egg, knead well, then add the salt.

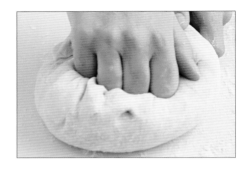

2 Knead well until the dough is no longer sticky and small holes have formed that burst when you squeeze them. If the dough seems too dry, add some extra milk.

3 Cover the bowl with a dampened dish towel and leave the dough to stand at room temperature until it has doubled in size.

4 Preheat the oven to 200°C/400°F/ Gas 6. Grease a 30cm/12in flan tin (pan) with butter.

5 Roll out the dough to a round on a lightly floured surface. Line the prepared tin with the dough round so that it comes about 3cm/1¼in up the side. Prick the base with a fork, cover with a dampened dish towel and leave to rise for about 15 minutes.

6 Meanwhile, make the filling for the tart. Pour 200ml/7fl oz/scant 1 cup of the milk into a medium, heavy pan, then add the vanilla pod and heat the milk gently.

7 Beat the yolks with the sugar and cornflour in a bowl, then stir in the remaining milk and strain into a jug (pitcher). Gradually stir the egg yolk mixture into the vanilla-flavoured milk, then continue to cook, stirring constantly, for a few minutes, until thickened.

8 Remove the pan from the heat, cover the surface with clear film (plastic wrap) to prevent a skin forming and leave until lukewarm. Discard the vanilla pod. Whisk the filling until creamy.

9 Drain the canned fruit, if using, and reserve 150ml/¼ pint/⅔ cup of the juice. Heat the juice in a pan. Mix the potato flour with 30ml/2 tbsp water to a paste in a bowl, then stir into the juice and cook, stirring, until thickened. Remove from the heat and cool.

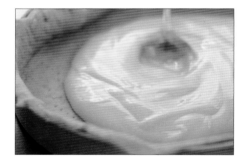

10 Spread the filling over the base of the pastry case (pie shell) and cover with the fruit. If using plums or apricots, place them cut side up. Sprinkle the fresh fruit with sugar.

11 Bake for 30–35 minutes. Remove from the oven and leave to cool. Decorate with the thickened juice or sprinkle with sugar.

COOK'S TIP
For an authentic *vlaai*, always use one kind of fruit and ensure that the rim of the dough is not higher than 3cm/1¼in. It has to be a flat tart, as the name is derived from the Latin word *platus*, meaning flat.

Per portion Energy 265kcal/1123kJ; Protein 6g; Carbohydrate 51.6g, of which sugars 20.2g; Fat 5.3g, of which saturates 2.6g; Cholesterol 59.6mg; Calcium 123mg; Fibre 2.2g; Sodium 46mg.

BREUGHEL'S RICE CUSTARD TART WITH APRICOTS

THIS TART IS DEDICATED TO ONE OF THE GREATEST FLEMISH PAINTERS, PIETER BREUGHEL, WHO IS PERHAPS BEST KNOWN FOR DE BOERENBRUILOFT, A PAINTING THAT DEPICTS GUESTS AT A PEASANT WEDDING, TUCKING INTO THE MANY DIFFERENT TARTS THAT ARE SUCH A FEATURE OF FESTIVE OCCASIONS IN BELGIUM. THIS ALL-TIME FAVOURITE ONE, RIJSTTAART, COMPRISES A YEAST PASTRY CASE FILLED WITH SWEET APRICOT PRESERVE AND CREAMY RICE CUSTARD AND TOPPED WITH CANNED APRICOT HALVES, AND IS SOLD IN ALMOST EVERY BELGIAN BAKERY.

SERVES SIX–EIGHT

INGREDIENTS
   250g/9oz/2¼ cups plain (all-purpose)
    flour, plus extra for dusting
   50g/2oz/¼ cup sugar
   15ml/1 tbsp easy-blend (rapid-rise)
    dried yeast
   2.5ml/½ tsp salt
   1 egg, beaten
   100ml/3½fl oz/scant ½ cup milk
   50–75g/2–3oz/4–6 tbsp unsalted
    butter, softened
For the filling
   500ml/17fl oz/generous 2 cups full
    cream (whole) milk
   150g/5oz/⅔ cup short grain rice
   50g/2oz/¼ cup caster (superfine) sugar
   pinch of salt
   5ml/1 tsp vanilla extract
   2 eggs, separated, plus 2 yolks
   60ml/4 tbsp apricot preserve or
    whole-fruit jam
   400g/14oz can apricot halves, drained

1 Sift the flour into a large mixing bowl. Stir in the sugar, dried yeast and salt. Make a well in the centre and pour in the beaten egg and half the milk.

2 Stir, gradually incorporating the surrounding dry ingredients until the mixture starts to hold together. Add the extra milk, if needed. Add the butter and mix with your fingertips to a soft dough.

3 On a lightly floured surface, knead the mixture lightly, form it into a ball and place in a large, lightly oiled bowl. Cover with clear film (plastic wrap) and leave to rise in a warm, draught-free place for about 30 minutes or until doubled in bulk.

4 Meanwhile, make the filling. Pour the milk into a pan. Bring to the boil, then stir in the rice. Reduce the heat to low, cover the pan and simmer for about 30 minutes, stirring frequently, until all the milk has been absorbed. Stir in the sugar and salt. Leave to cool.

5 Preheat the oven to 180°C/350°F/ Gas 4. Place a baking sheet in the oven. Grease a 23cm/9in springform tin (pan) and dust it with flour.

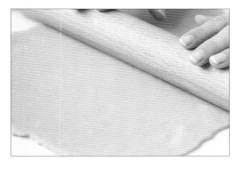

6 Knock back (punch down) the dough. Roll it out on a lightly floured surface and line the springform pan. Prick the base with a fork.

7 Add the vanilla extract and 1 egg yolk to the cool rice mixture. Stir to mix, then beat in the remaining 3 egg yolks one by one.

8 In a clean, grease-free bowl, beat the 2 egg whites until stiff, then fold them into the rice custard.

9 Spread a layer of apricot preserve or jam in the bottom of the pastry case (pie shell). Carefully pour in the rice mixture. Arrange the apricot halves on top, placing them cut side down.

10 Put the pan on the hot baking sheet in the preheated oven and bake for 35–40 minutes.

11 Place on a wire rack until cool enough to handle, then remove the tart from the pan and put it on a plate. Serve at room temperature with coffee, tea or a sweet dessert wine.

Per portion Energy 374kcal/1572kJ; Protein 10.2g; Carbohydrate 59.3g, of which sugars 20.5g; Fat 11.8g, of which saturates 6g; Cholesterol 145mg; Calcium 169mg; Fibre 1.4g; Sodium 106mg.

DUTCH APPLE PIE

The national sweet pastry of the Netherlands is apple pie. Early recipes, dating from the Middle Ages, instructed the cook to sprinkle a lot of spices, such as cardamom, ginger, cloves, mace and cinnamon, over 'golden apples' and the cooking time was measured in the number of paternosters, or prayers, you had to say. Consequently, the outcome was unpredictable. The invention of the oven with heat controls solved this problem. Nowadays, apple pie is displayed in show-cases on bars in cafés and coffee shops. The first cake a Dutch child learns to bake is an apple pie, still best made with the Goudrenet variety.

MAKES ONE 33CM/13IN PIE

INGREDIENTS
  175g/6oz/¾ cup butter, softened,
    plus extra for greasing
  175g/6oz/1½ cups plain (all-purpose)
    flour, plus extra for dusting
  175g/6oz/1½ cups self-raising
    (self-rising) flour
  175g/6oz/scant 1 cup caster
    (superfine) sugar
  1 egg
  2.5ml/½ tsp finely grated
    lemon rind
  pinch of salt
For the filling
  1kg/2¼lb tart apples, such as
    Goudrenet or Granny Smith
  juice of 1 lemon
  60ml/4 tbsp sugar
  10ml/2 tsp ground cinnamon
  30ml/2 tbsp breadcrumbs
  5ml/1 tsp aniseed, crushed
For the glaze
  60ml/4 tbsp apricot jam
  30ml/2 tbsp rum

1 Preheat the oven to 200°C/400°F/ Gas 6. Grease a 33cm/13in springform tin (pan) with butter.

2 To make the filling, peel and core the apples, then thinly slice them into even pieces and place them in a non-metallic bowl.

3 Mix together the lemon juice, sugar and cinnamon, pour over the apples and set aside.

4 Meanwhile, make the dough. Sift the flour into a bowl and stir in the sugar. butter, egg, lemon rind and salt and knead to a dough. Cut off one-third of the dough and set aside.

5 Roll out the remaining dough on a lightly floured surface to a 37cm/14½in round and use to line the prepared tin. If the dough cracks, press it gently together again.

6 Mix together the breadcrumbs and aniseed and sprinkle the mixture evenly over the base of the pastry case (pie shell).

7 Arrange the apple slices in slightly overlapping concentric circles on top of the breadcrumb mixture.

8 Roll out the remaining dough to a 33cm/13in round. Cut into 1cm/½in wide strips and arrange them in a lattice pattern over the apples.

9 Bake for 45–55 minutes, until golden brown. Meanwhile, mix together the jam and rum for the glaze.

10 Remove the pie from the oven and, while still warm, brush the top with the glaze. Carefully lift off the sides of the tin, place a cake dome or upturned bowl over the pie and leave to cool. This pie freezes well.

Per pie Energy 4174kcal/17592kJ; Protein 48.1g; Carbohydrate 672.4g, of which sugars 383.2g; Fat 155.5g, of which saturates 93.4g; Cholesterol 563mg; Calcium 760mg; Fibre 27.5g; Sodium 1431mg.

CINNAMON BUNS FROM WAASLAND

YOU NEED NOT FEAR RABIES IF YOU LIVE IN THE WAASLAND REGION OF EAST FLANDERS FOR THE
SPICY BUNS UNIQUE TO THE AREA ARE ALLEGED TO OFFER PROTECTION AGAINST THE DISEASE. EACH
NOVEMBER 3, ST HUBERT'S DAY, ROMAN CATHOLIC PRIESTS CONFER A BLESSING ON THE BAGEL-
SHAPED BUNS, AND THE POPULATION ARE SAFE FOR ANOTHER YEAR. KNOWN LOCALLY AS MASTELLEN,
THE BUNS HAVE A STRONG CINNAMON FLAVOUR AND TASTE DELICIOUS WITH BREAD AND HONEY.

MAKES ABOUT 16

INGREDIENTS
    1kg/2¼lb/9 cups strong white
        bread flour
    50g/2oz/¼ cup brown sugar
    10g/¼oz easy-blend (rapid-rise)
        dried yeast
    15ml/1 tbsp salt
    500ml/17fl oz/generous 2 cups
        lukewarm milk
    1 egg, beaten
    300g/11oz/1⅓ cups butter, diced
        and softened
    5ml/1 tsp ground cinnamon
    egg yolk, to glaze
    butter, honey, homemade jam or
        Belgian Chocolate Spread
        (*see* page 41), to serve

1 Sift the flour into a bowl. Stir in the sugar, dried yeast and salt. Make a well in the centre and pour in the milk and egg. Stir, gradually incorporating the dry ingredients until the mixture starts to hold together. Add the butter, a few pieces at a time, and mix with your fingertips until all of it has been incorporated.

2 Knead the dough for 5 minutes, then flatten it out, sprinkle the cinnamon over the surface and knead it for 5–8 minutes more to distribute the spice evenly. The dough should be smooth and moist. Place in an oiled bowl, cover with a clean dish towel and leave to rise for 30 minutes at room temperature, or overnight in the refrigerator.

3 Divide the dough into 16 pieces and roll each into a ball, Place on baking sheets lined with baking parchment, leaving enough space between them so they can rise. Cover again and set aside for 15 minutes.

4 Using your thumb or the handle of a wooden spoon, make a deep indentation in the middle of each ball of dough. Glaze the rings with the egg yolk and leave them to rise for 30 minutes more.

5 Preheat the oven to 220°C/425°F/Gas 7. Bake the buns for 10–15 minutes until golden. Cool on a wire rack. Serve with butter, honey, jam or chocolate spread.

Per portion 384kcal/1612kJ; Protein 7.5g; Carbohydrate 53.4g, of which sugars 5.8g; Fat 17.1g, of which saturates 10.3g; Cholesterol 54mg; Calcium 132mg; Fibre 1.9g; Sodium 134mg.

SPICE CAKE

ANY DUTCH TRAVELLER VISITING A MIDDLE EASTERN MARKET IMMEDIATELY FEELS AT HOME AS THE AROMA OF COFFEE AND SPICES REMINDS THEM OF THEIR FAMILIAR SNACK OF COFFEE AND SPICED CAKE. FOR CENTURIES THE SPICE ROUTE RAN OVERLAND, BUT THE SEA ROUTE PROVIDED THE DUTCH WITH EASIER ACCESS TO SPICES. THIS WHEAT FLOUR AND SUGAR RECIPE DATES FROM WORLD WAR II WHEN TRADITIONAL SPICE CAKES, MADE FROM RYE FLOUR AND HONEY, WERE NOT AVAILABLE.

SERVES 20

INGREDIENTS
butter, for greasing
breadcrumbs, for sprinkling
500g/1¼lb/5 cups plain
 (all-purpose) flour
20ml/4 tsp baking powder
5ml/1 tsp salt
350g/12oz/1½ cups muscovado
 (molasses) sugar
10ml/2 tsp ground cinnamon
1.5ml/¼ tsp ground allspice
1.5ml/¼ tsp ground cloves
2.5ml/½ tsp ground nutmeg
1.5ml/¼ tsp ground cardamom
400–450ml/14–15fl oz/1⅔–2 cups milk

1 Preheat the oven to 150°C/300°F/ Gas 2. Grease a 2-litre/3½ pint cake tin (pan) and sprinkle with breadcrumbs.

2 Sift the flour, baking powder and salt into a large bowl.

3 Stir in the sugar, cinnamon, allspice, cloves, nutmeg and cardamom.

4 Gradually stir in the milk, then whisk until the mixture is smooth with a dropping (pourable) consistency.

5 Pour the mixture into the prepared tin and bake for 1½ hours, or until a wooden cocktail stick (toothpick) inserted in the centre comes out clean.

6 Remove from the oven, turn out on to a wire rack and leave to cool.

7 Wrap the cake in foil and store for at least 3 days before eating to allow the flavour of the spices to develop fully.

Per portion Energy 166.5kcal/708kJ; Protein 3.2g; Carbohydrate 39.2g, of which sugars 19.6g; Fat 0.7g, of which saturates 0.3g; Cholesterol 1.2mg; Calcium 80mg; Fibre 0.7g; Sodium 227mg.

FRISIAN SUGAR BREAD

AN EXCERPT FROM A 17TH-CENTURY SERMON SAID THAT '...WERE THEY NOT ASHAMED TO DO SO, MEN WOULD FOUND AN ACADEMY TO WHICH THEY WOULD SEND ALL COOKS AND PASTRY BAKERS'. SUCH SERMONS DID NOT DAMPEN THE DUTCH PASSION FOR SWEETS, HOWEVER, AND THEY STILL INDULGE THEIR SWEET TOOTH AT BREAKFAST. THE ULTIMATE DELIGHT IS THIS FRISIAN SPECIALITY BREAD MADE WITH SUGAR AND SPICES, WHICH IS NOW SOLD ALL OVER THE COUNTRY.

MAKES ONE LOAF

INGREDIENTS
  500g/1¼lb/5 cups strong white
    bread flour, plus extra for dusting
  2 sachets easy-blend (rapid-rise)
    dried yeast
  300ml/½ pint/1¼ cups
    lukewarm milk
  50g/2oz/¼ cup caster
    (superfine) sugar
  pinch of ground cinnamon
  pinch of ground nutmeg
  pinch of powdered saffron
  50g/2oz/¼ cup butter, softened,
    plus extra for greasing
  1 egg yolk
  10ml/2 tsp salt
  sugar, for sprinkling
For the filling
  250g/9oz pearl sugar, or hazelnut
    size pearl sugar, or *grove greinsuiker*
  5ml/1 tsp cinnamon

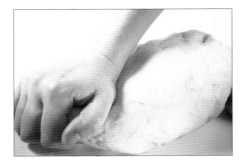

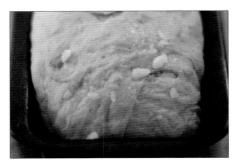

3 Add the cinnamon, nutmeg and saffron to the remaining milk, add to the bowl and mix. Add the egg yolk, the remaining sugar and the butter and knead briefly, then add the salt. Turn out on to a lightly floured surface and knead vigorously for at least 15 minutes, until the dough is no longer sticky and is full of little bubbles. Add extra milk if necessary.

7 Grease a 2-litre/3½-pint rectangular loaf tin (pan) with butter and sprinkle with sugar. Put the dough roll into the tin, with the final fold underneath. Cover the tin with a dampened dish towel and leave to stand at room temperature for about 1 hour, until the dough has just risen above the rim.

8 Preheat the oven to 200°C/400°F/ Gas 6. To prevent the sugar from dripping into the oven, it is advisable to place a sheet of baking parchment underneath the tin.

9 Bake for 30 minutes. If the top seems to be browning too quickly, cover it with foil after 20 minutes. Brush the top of the loaf with cold water and return it the oven for 1 minute. Turn out the loaf on to a wire rack and leave to cool.

1 Sift the flour into a bowl and make a well in the centre. Add the yeast and a little milk and mix to a creamy consistency, incorporating some of the flour. Add 5ml/1 tsp of the sugar.

2 Cover with a clean dish towel and leave to stand for 10 minutes.

COOK'S TIP

If you don't have pearl sugar (*grove greinsuiker*) use small sugar cubes or white cane sugar lumps, which you could cut into small pieces.

4 Form the dough into a ball, return to a clean bowl and cover with a damp dish towel. Leave to stand at room temperature for 1 hour, or until it has doubled in bulk.

5 Toss the sugar with the cinnamon in a bowl, then flour your hands and knead the grains into the dough.

6 Turn out the dough on to a floured surface and push it out into a rectangle 30cm/12in wide. Brush the flour away on both sides. Roll up the rectangle, starting at the top or bottom, wherever the filling is most sparse.

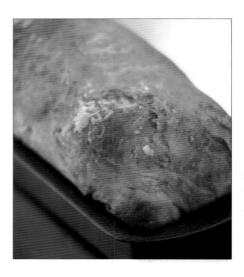

Per loaf Energy 3458kcal/14660kJ; Protein 61.9g; Carbohydrate 716.4g, of which sugars 335.4g; Fat 58.2g, of which saturates 31.8g; Cholesterol 326mg; Calcium 1251mg; Fibre 15.5g; Sodium 474mg.

CHRISTMAS BREAD FROM WALLONIA

THIS TRADITIONAL SWEET CHRISTMAS BREAD GOES BY SEVERAL NAMES, INCLUDING COUGNOU, COUGNOLLE AND COQUILLE. IT IS BAKED IN VARIOUS SIZES BUT ALWAYS IN THE SHAPE OF THE SWADDLED INFANT JESUS. WHEN THE LOAVES APPEAR IN BAKERIES AT THE END OF THE YEAR, THEY ARE OFTEN BOUGHT AND PRESENTED AS GIFTS. GENEROUS AMOUNTS OF BUTTER, EGGS AND RAISINS GIVE THE BREADS A CAKE-LIKE QUALITY, AND THEY ARE OFTEN HIGHLY DECORATED.

MAKES TWO SMALL BREADS

INGREDIENTS
250g/9oz/1½ cups raisins
1kg/2¼lb/9 cups unbleached strong
  white bread flour
50g/2oz/¼ cup sugar
5ml/1 tsp easy-blend (rapid-rise)
  dried yeast
5ml/1 tsp salt
4 eggs, beaten
250ml/8fl oz/1 cup lukewarm milk
250ml/8fl oz/1 cup lukewarm water
250g/9oz/generous 1 cup unsalted
  butter, cubed and softened
1 egg mixed with 5ml/1 tsp water,
  to glaze

1 Put the raisins in a small bowl and pour over water to cover. Set aside to plump up.

2 Sift the flour into a large mixing bowl. Stir in the sugar, dried yeast and salt.

COOK'S TIP
The dough can be made in a mixer fitted with a dough hook, if you have one. Put the dry ingredients in the bowl, add the eggs, milk and water and beat on low speed until the flour is moist. Leave for 5 minutes, raise the speed and gradually work the butter into the dough. Work the dough for 5 minutes more, then add the drained raisins and continue until the dough forms a ball. Remove and knead by hand for 3 more minutes. Proceed as in the recipe.

3 Make a well in the centre of the dry ingredients and pour in the beaten eggs, the milk and half the water.

4 Stir with a wooden spoon, gradually incorporating the dry ingredients and adding more water if necessary, until the mixture holds together.

5 Add the softened butter, a few pieces at a time, and mix with your fingertips until all of it has been incorporated. Knead the dough for 5 minutes. It will be very soft and moist.

6 Drain the raisins and add them to the dough. Knead them in until evenly distributed, then remove from the bowl and knead it on a floured surface for 5–8 minutes more, adding a little more flour if needed.

7 Place in an oiled bowl, cover and leave to rise for 30 minutes.

8 Gently knock back (punch down) the dough, return it to the bowl and replace the cover. Leave to rise for 1 hour at room temperature or overnight in the refrigerator.

9 Divide the dough into two equal halves. Leave to rest for 5 minutes, then mould each dough ball into the shape of a baby wrapped in a blanket. To do this, mould the top third into a round for the head, then shape the remainder into an oval, tapering at the base.

10 Place the shaped loaves on two baking sheets lined with baking parchment.

11 Brush half the egg-and-water mixture over the loaves, cover with a clean dish towel and leave to rise for 1 hour or until doubled in bulk. Preheat the oven to 240°C/475°F/Gas 9 shortly before the end of the rising time.

12 Glaze the loaves with the remaining egg mixture. Introduce steam into the oven by spraying it lightly with water from a spray bottle. Bake the loaves for 10 minutes, then reduce the oven temperature to 230°C/425°F/Gas 8 and bake them for 20 minutes more until golden brown.

13 Remove the loaves from the oven, leave to cool on the baking sheets for about 15 minutes, then transfer to wire racks to cool completely. Serve plain or with butter and jam.

Per large bread Energy 3278kcal/13799kJ; Protein 67.3g; Carbohydrate 507.9g, of which sugars 126.9g; Fat 123g, of which saturates 70.6g; Cholesterol 654mg; Calcium 1001mg; Fibre 18g; Sodium 1043mg.

CURRANT BREAD

FOR MANY CENTURIES THE STAPLE BREAD EATEN BY DUTCH COUNTRY PEOPLE WAS DARK RYE BREAD. WHITE BREAD WAS A REAL LUXURY, HENCE THE DUTCH EXPRESSION WITTEBROODSWEKEN, *WHICH LITERALLY MEANS 'WHITE BREAD WEEKS', FOR A HONEYMOON. EVEN MORE LUXURIOUS WAS THIS WHITE CURRANT BREAD. BAKERS ALL OVER THE COUNTRY STILL TAKE GREAT PRIDE IN BAKING IT, ESPECIALLY FOR THE WEEKEND AND FESTIVALS SUCH AS CHRISTMAS AND EASTER. MUCH LONGER CURRANT BREADS ARE BAKED IN THE REGION OF TWENTE, SITUATED IN THE EASTERN PART OF THE COUNTRY, WHERE THE BIRTH OF A BABY IS CELEBRATED WITH A 1.5–METRE/1 1/2–YARD LOAF.*

MAKES ONE LOAF

INGREDIENTS

    500g/1 1/4 lb/generous 5 cups
      strong white bread flour,
      plus extra for dusting
    2 sachets easy-blend (rapid-rise)
      dried yeast
    250ml/8fl oz/1 cup lukewarm milk
    50g/2oz/1/4 cup white caster
      (superfine) sugar
    pinch of ground cinnamon
    pinch of ground nutmeg
    pinch of powdered saffron
    1 egg yolk, lightly beaten
    50g/2oz/1/4 cup butter, softened,
      plus extra for greasing
    10ml/2 tsp salt
For the filling
    150g/5oz/2/3 cup currants
    150g/5oz/1 cup raisins
    50g/2oz/1/3 cup finely diced glacé
      (candied) citron peel
    50g/2oz/1/3 cup glacé (candied)
      orange peel

VARIATION

Before rolling up the dough at the end of step 3, shape 200g/7oz almond paste into a roll, place on the dough rectangle, roll up and continue as per the recipe.

1 Sift the flour into a bowl and make a well in the centre. Add the yeast and a little of the milk to the well and mix together, incorporating some of the flour. Add 5ml/1 tsp of the sugar, cover the bowl with a clean dish towel and leave to stand for 10 minutes.

2 Add the cinnamon, nutmeg and saffron to the remaining milk, add to the bowl and mix well. Add the egg yolk, the remaining sugar and the butter and knead briefly, then add the salt.

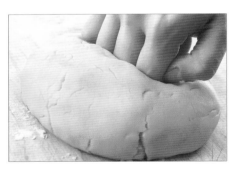

3 Turn out the dough on to a lightly floured surface and knead vigorously for at least 15 minutes, until the dough is no longer sticky and is full of bubbles, adding a little extra milk if necessary.

4 Shape the dough into a ball, return to a clean bowl and cover with a damp dish towel. Leave at room temperature for 1 hour, until it has doubled in bulk.

5 To make the filling, poach the currants and raisins in simmering water for 10 minutes. Drain and pat dry in a cloth.

6 Turn out the dough and knead in the dried fruit and both types of glacé fruit peel. Dust the dough and work surface with flour and roll into a rectangle 30cm/12in wide. Roll up the rectangle, starting wherever the filling is most sparse.

7 Lightly grease a 30 x 10 x 10cm/12 x 10 x 10in loaf tin (pan). Place the dough roll in the tin, with the final fold underneath. Cover with a dampened dish towel. Leave at room temperature for about 1 hour, until the dough has just risen above the rim. Preheat the oven to 200°C/400°F/Gas 6.

8 Bake the loaf for 35 minutes, then brush the top with cold water and return to the oven for 1 minute. Turn out on to a wire rack and leave to cool.

Per loaf Energy 3375kcal/14303kJ; Protein 57.3g; Carbohydrate 705.8g, of which sugars 324.8g; Fat 55.2g, of which saturates 28.6g; Cholesterol 308mg; Calcium 1098mg; Fibre 26.2g; Sodium 4651mg.

THE HAGUE BREAKFAST

THESE SOFT WHITE BUNS SPRINKLED WITH SEEDS ARE DELICIOUS AT ANY TIME OF DAY AND ARE ALWAYS A BIG SUCCESS AT CHILDREN'S PARTIES, ESPECIALLY IF YOU ALLOW THE CHILDREN TO MAKE THEM THEMSELVES. THEY ARE ALSO A GOOD ADDITION AT PICNICS AND BARBECUES, AND ARE IDEAL FOR A FESTIVE BREAKFAST. THEY CAN BE MADE WELL IN ADVANCE AS THEY FREEZE WELL — SO IT'S WORTH KEEPING A BAG IN THE FREEZER FOR UNEXPECTED VISITORS.

4 Turn out the dough on to a lightly floured surface and press out into a square, then cut into 40 equal pieces. Cover them with a damp dish towel.

5 Working with one piece of dough at a time, roll each piece into thin strips on a dampened surface.

6 Form the strips into shapes such as knots, snails, figures of eight, pretzels and plaits (braids). Cover with a dampened dish towel and leave to rise for 30 minutes or until doubled in bulk.

7 Shortly before the end of the rising time, preheat the oven to 220°C/425°F/ Gas 7. Grease a baking sheet with butter.

8 Transfer the bread shapes to the baking sheet, brush with the egg yolk and milk and sprinkle some with poppy seeds, some with sesame seeds and others with caraway seeds. Bake in the preheated oven for 15–20 minutes, until golden brown. Leave to cool slightly before serving.

MAKES 40

INGREDIENTS
    500g/1¼lb/5 cups plain (all-purpose)
      flour, plus extra for dusting
    1 sachet easy-blend (rapid-rise)
      dried yeast
    2.5ml/½ tsp sugar
    300ml/½ pint/1¼ cups lukewarm milk
    25g/1oz/2 tbsp butter, softened, plus
      extra for greasing
    10ml/2 tsp salt
    1 egg yolk, beaten with 5ml/1 tsp milk
    poppy seeds, sesame seeds, caraway
      seeds, to decorate

1 Sift the flour into a large mixing bowl and make a well in the centre. Add the yeast and sugar to the well and stir in a little of the milk. Leave to stand for 10 minutes.

2 Add the remaining milk and the butter and knead together, then add the salt. Knead well to a smooth elastic dough, adding a little more milk if necessary.

3 Shape into a ball, cover with a dampened dish towel and leave to rise at room temperature for about 1 hour, until doubled in bulk.

Per portion Energy 53kcal/222kJ; Protein 1.5g; Carbohydrate 10.1g, of which sugars 0.6g; Fat 0.9g, of which saturates 0.5g; Cholesterol 7mg; Calcium 27mg; Fibre 0.4g; Sodium 8mg.

BELGIAN BREAD ROLLS

These bread rolls are a favourite Sunday morning treat in Belgium. People often order them in advance from their local baker, along with other breakfast treats such as koffie koeken (coffee pastries) and sweet or fruited breads, and carry them home, still warm, to their waiting families. It is even more rewarding to bake the pistoleetjes yourself, however, as they will infuse the house with the intoxicating aroma of newly baked bread.

MAKES SIX–EIGHT

INGREDIENTS
    500g/1¼lb/5 cups strong white
        bread flour, plus extra for dusting
    2.5ml/½ tsp sugar
    6ml/1¼ tsp easy-blend (rapid-rise)
        dried yeast
    5ml/1 tsp salt
    300ml/½ pint/1¼ cups
        lukewarm water
    10ml/2 tsp vegetable oil or
        softened butter
    poppy, sunflower, flax or sesame
        seeds for topping (optional)
    butter, honey, home-made jam
        or Belgian Chocolate Spread
        (*see* page 41), to serve

1 Sift the flour into a large mixing bowl. Stir in the sugar, dried yeast and salt. Make a well in the centre and pour in the water. Stir, gradually incorporating the surrounding dry ingredients until the mixture holds together.

2 Add the oil or softened butter, a few pieces at a time, and mix with your fingertips until it has been incorporated. Knead for 5–10 minutes, until the dough is smooth and elastic.

COOK'S TIP
The amount of water will vary, depending on the absorbency of the flour and the type of bread required. The dough for these rolls may be a little wet and sticky, but this makes the rolls moist.

3 Transfer the dough to an oiled roasting tin (pan) or similar container. Fold it like a blanket, cover with clear film (plastic wrap) and leave it to rest in the refrigerator overnight.

4 Divide the dough in six or eight pieces and shape each into a ball. At this point the rolls can be coated by rolling them in a damp towel, then dipping them into the chosen seeds.

5 Leaving room for expansion, place the rolls on a large baking sheet lined with baking parchment. Using an oiled skewer, make an indent in the centre of each roll.

6 Cover with a clean dish towel and leave the rolls to rise at room temperature for 30 minutes or until doubled in bulk.

7 Preheat the oven to 220°C/425°F/ Gas 7. Introduce steam into the oven by spraying it lightly with water from a spray bottle. Put the baking sheets in the oven and spray briefly with water once more.

8 Bake the rolls for 15 minutes or until the tops are golden brown and the base of each roll sounds hollow when tapped. Cool on a wire rack.

Per portion Energy 239kcal/1013kJ; Protein 5.9g; Carbohydrate 48.9g, of which sugars 1.3g; Fat 3.6g, of which saturates 0.5g; Cholesterol 0mg; Calcium 88mg; Fibre 1.9g; Sodium 2mg.

ABBEY BREAD

In medieval times, abbeys and convents in Belgium baked every day and distributed it to the poor and the sick. Many abbeys still make breads, as well as beer and cheeses, according to artisan methods. Until the 19th century, only rye flour was available in Belgium and all bread was therefore 'black'. When cheap wheat arrived from America, paler bread was preferred. A combination of the two produced this nutritious multigrain loaf, which has become very popular. Start making it the day before baking.

MAKES TWO LOAVES

INGREDIENTS
　75g/3oz/½ cup linseeds, plus water
　　for soaking
　250g/9oz/2¼ cups strong white
　　bread flour
　250g/9oz/2¼ cups wholemeal
　　(whole-wheat) flour
　250g/9oz/2¼ cups rye flour
　15ml/1 tbsp salt
　15ml/1 tbsp easy-blend (rapid-rise)
　　dried yeast
　300ml/½ pint/1¼ cups
　　lukewarm water
For the poolish
　75g/3oz/⅔ cup strong white
　　bread flour
　75g/3oz/⅔ cup rye flour
　2.5ml/½ tsp easy-blend (rapid-rise)
　　dried yeast
　150ml/¼ pint/⅔ cup water

COOK'S TIPS
• Poolish is a pre-fermentation method, which gives bread a richer and more complex flavour and enhances shelf-life.
• Linseeds, which are also sold as flax seeds, give the bread a nutty flavour and are a good source of omega-3 fatty acids. Soaking them makes them easier to digest.

1 Make the poolish. Mix the dry ingredients in a bowl. Stir in the water with a fork to make a smooth paste. Cover the bowl and leave the mixture to stand for 8–12 hours at room temperature.

2 Put the linseeds in a bowl and pour over 120ml/4fl oz/½ cup hot water. Leave to stand for at least 1 hour.

3 Put the flours into a mixing bowl. Add the salt and yeast. Make a well in the centre and add the poolish, with the water. Mix, gradually incorporating the surrounding flour mixture, until the mixture comes together to form a dough. Transfer to a lightly floured surface and knead the dough for 10 minutes.

4 Drain any free water from the linseeds, then knead them into the dough until well distributed. Continue to knead for about 2 minutes more. Transfer the dough to an oiled roasting tin (pan) or similar flat container.

5 Pat it out, then fold it over like a blanket, cover with clear film (plastic wrap) and leave to rise in a dry place until it doubles in volume, about 1 hour.

6 Knock back (punch down) the dough, then divide it into two equal pieces. Shape each into a ball or a loaf shape and place in bread tins (pans) or in coiled proofing baskets. Cover and leave to rise for 30–60 minutes, until the loaves have doubled in bulk.

7 Preheat the oven to 230°C/450°F/Gas 8. Introduce steam into the oven by spraying it lightly with water from a spray bottle. Remove the breads from the tins or baskets, score with a knife and transfer to a baking sheet lined with baking parchment. Put them in the oven and spray again with water.

8 Bake for 40 minutes or until golden brown and they sound hollow when tapped on the base. Cool on wire racks.

Per loaf Energy 1711kcal/7251kJ; Protein 52.1g; Carbohydrate 328.9g, of which sugars 5.2g; Fat 29.9g, of which saturates 4.3g; Cholesterol 0mg; Calcium 579mg; Fibre 38.3g; Sodium 1001mg.

DUTCH WHOLEMEAL BREAD

EVERY COUNTRY HAS ITS OWN FAVOURITE TYPES OF BREAD. THE DUTCH SHARE THEIR PREFERENCE FOR LOAVES BAKED IN A TIN WITH THE ENGLISH, ALTHOUGH THE SHAPE AND INGREDIENTS DIFFER SLIGHTLY. THIS RECIPE IS FOR A TRADITIONAL DUTCH WHOLEMEAL LOAF, WHICH HAS A LOVELY CHEWY TEXTURE AND NUTTY FLAVOUR FROM THE WHOLEMEAL FLOUR.

MAKES TWO LOAVES

INGREDIENTS
800g/1¾lb/7 cups wholemeal
    (whole-wheat) flour, plus extra
    for dusting
40g/1½oz/3 tbsp golden caster
    (superfine) sugar
40g/1½oz/3 tbsp butter, softened
450ml/¾ pint/scant 2 cups
    lukewarm water
25ml/1½ tbsp salt
melted butter, for brushing
For the starter
200g/7oz/1¾ cups wholemeal
    (whole-wheat) flour
3 sachets easy-blend (rapid-rise)
    dried yeast
200–300ml/7–10fl oz/scant 1–1¼ cups
    lukewarm water

1 For the starter, mix together the flour and yeast in a measuring jug (cup). Stir in the water, a spoonful at a time.

2 Cover with foil and leave to stand until the mixture has foamed up to measure 1 litre/1¾ pints/4 cups.

VARIATIONS
• You could add a selection of seeds, such as sesame seeds, pumpkin seeds and sunflower seeds to the dough mixture, or you could brush the top of the loaves with water and sprinkle with sesame or poppy seeds before baking them.
• For a lighter loaf, substitute strong white bread flour for half the wholemeal (whole-wheat flour).

3 Put the flour, sugar and butter in the bowl of an electric mixer. Add the starter and the lukewarm water and knead slowly with the mixer fitted with a dough hook. Add the salt after a few minutes, then increase the speed of the mixer and knead for about 15 minutes, until the dough comes away from the side of the bowl. Alternatively, knead the dough by hand on a lightly floured surface for 20 minutes.

4 Transfer the dough to a very large bowl (4.5 litres/8 pints/4¾ quarts). Cover with damp muslin (cheesecloth) and leave to stand until the dough has risen just above the bowl rim.

5 Preheat the oven to 220°C/425°F/Gas 7. Brush two 30 x 10 x 10cm/12 x 4 x 4in loaf tins (pans) with melted butter.

6 Turn out the dough on to a lightly floured surface and with floured hands shape it into a rectangle 30cm/12in wide. Using kitchen scissors, cut the rectangle in half widthways. Dust both with flour and brush off any excess.

7 Roll up both dough rectangles and place in the prepared tins, with the folds tucked underneath.

8 Slash the surface of the loaves diagonally with a large, sharp knife. Cover with dampened dish towels and leave until the dough has risen well above the rims of the tins.

9 Bake for 20–25 minutes, but do not allow the crusts to become too dark. Brush the tops of the loaves with cold water and return to the oven for 1 minute. Turn out the loaves on to wire racks and leave to cool.

Per loaf Energy 1933kcal/8198kJ; Protein 47.2g; Carbohydrate 409.5g, of which sugars 28.5g; Fat 23g, of which saturates 11.4g; Cholesterol 43mg; Calcium 715mg; Fibre 15.5g; Sodium 1120mg.

SUPPLIERS

Mail-order food and equipment:
www.fantes.com/tools.htm#bakeware
www.dutchvillage.com/DVShoppingfolder/
    dvfood/
www.dutchmarket.com/sckit.html
www.hollandbymail.nl
www.hollandsbest.com
www.typicaldutchstuff.com
www.holland-at-home.nl
www.dutchshop.co.uk
www.belgianfoodonline.com
http://shop.belgianshop.com
www.belgianfood.com
www.belgianfries.com/bfblog/?page_id=283
www.friteshop.com

Australia:

The Dutch Shop
(Dutch coffee shop, food)
85 Market Street, Smithfield
Sydney NSW
Tel: (02) 9604 0233
sydney.citysearch.com.au

De Hollandse Winkel
(Dutch supermarket)
1 Alfred Street, Blackburn
1330 VIC
Tel: (03) 9894 0288
ourhouse.ninemsn.com.au

The Belgian Waffle Shop
(Belgian waffles)
Manly Wharf, Manly
Sydney, NSW 2095

Canada:

The Dutch Market
(Dutch food, equipment and recipes)
6 Indian Creek Road East
Chatham, ON N7M 4H1
Tel: 1(866) 355-1351 (toll-free)
    or (519) 352-2831
www.dutchmarket.com

Holland Store
(Dutch food, equipment and recipes)
2542 Weston Road, Toronto
ON, M9N 2A6
Tel: (416) 247-8659
www.come.to/hollandstore

Fritz European Fry House
(Belgian fries)
718 Davie St
Vancouver BC
(604) 684-0811
www.fritzeuropeanfryhouse.com

Belgian Chocolate House
(Belgian chocolates)
2455 Queen St E, Toronto
ON M4E, CA
Tel: (416) 691-1424
www.orderline.com/chocolate/

France:

Bizen
(Dutch food, drink, kitchen utensils)
Le Grand Vallon,
01100 Apremont
www.bizen-shop.com

Holland Snack
(Dutch kroketten, bitterballen)
Quai Mistral/Avenue de Provence
26000 Valence
Tel: (0)4 75 71 47 84
www.hollandsnack.com

Germany:

De Hollandse Winkel
Semperstr. 2 (am Goldbekplatz)
22303 Hamburg-Winterhude
Tel: 040-27 80 03 71
people.freenet.de/nl-ham/hwinkel.htm

The Netherlands:

Culinaire-Plaza
(Dutch food)
Breedestraat 47
6983 BX Doesburg
www.holland-shopping.com/shop

De Belg Waterloo
(Belgian fries)
Moesstraat 12
9717JW Groningen
Tel: 0505730438
www.debelgwaterloo.nl

Fred de Leeuw
(Amsterdam onions)
Vrijheidslaan 78, Amsterdam
www.freddeleeuw.nl

Holland Products Shops
(Dutch food, drink)
Ir. J.P. van Muijlwijkstraat 25–1
6828 BP Arnhem
www.holland-products.com

Just Dutch
(Dutch food, drink, kitchen utensils)
Dreef 62,
6996 BC Drempt
Tel: +31 313 655136
www.justdutch.biz

Realdutchfood.com
(Dutch food, drink, kitchen utensils)
Aresstraat 13-01
5048 CD Tilburg
info@realdutchfood.com
www.realdutchfood.com

New Zealand:

The Windmill, the real Dutch Stores
(Dutch food, gifts)
10 Hillary Square
Orewa, Auckland
Tel: +64 09 427 8477
www.orewa-beach.co.nz/home/windmill.htm

Karikaas Natural Dairy Products
(Dutch cheese)
156 Whiterock Road
Loburn-Rangiora
RD 2, North Canterbury
Tel: + 64 33 128 708
www.karikaas.co.nz

Spain:

The Food Hall
Paseo del Embajador 59
Ciudalcampo 28707
San Sebastian de los Reyes
Madrid
info@thefoodhall.es;
www.thefoodhall.es

United Kingdom:

Home Sweet Holland
(Dutch food, kitchen utensils)
46 Broom Avenue
Manchester
M19 2UD
Tel: 0161 612 8192
www.homesweetholland.co.uk

Leonidas
(Belgian chocolates)
37 Victoria Street
London SW1H 0ED
Tel: 020 7222 7337
www.leonidasbelgianchocolates.co.uk

The Belgian Food Company
(Belgian waffles and chocolates)
369 Oxford Street,
London W1C 2JW

83 Oxford Street,
London W1D 2EX

Belgian beer guide
(on-line guide to where to buy Belgian
   beer, and some restaurants)
www.belgianbeerguide.co.uk/pubguide.
html

United States:

A Touch of Dutch
(Dutch food and utensils)
23 NW Front Street
P.O. Box 1395, Coupeville
WA 98239, Whidbey Island
www.atouchofdutch.com

Best Dutch Store
(Dutch food, cookies)
3845 Rivertown Pkwy, Ste 300
Grandville, MI 49418
Tel: 1-800-826-6841
www.bestdutch.com

Dutch Village
(Dutch food and other items)
12350 James Street
Holland,
Michigan 49424
Tel: (616) 396-1475
www.dutchvillage.com

www.godutch.com
(on-line guide to Dutch food and shopping
   in North America)
www.godutch.com/directory/
index.php?tagcategory=4

Holland American Bakery
(Dutch food, cookies)
246 Route 23
Sussex, NJ 07461
Tel: 973-875-5258
   or 888-401-9515
www.hollandamericanbakery.com

Gourmet Food Store
(Belgian chocolates and desserts)
Tel: (877) 591-8008
www.gourmetfoodstore.com

The Dutch Market
(Dutch store and café)
257 Park Avenue,
Rochester, NY 14607
www.dutchmarketusa.com

Marky's
(Belgian chocolates and
   Dutch cheese)
687 NE 79th Street
Miami, FL 33138
Tel: (305) 628-4650
www.markys.com

Bruges Waffles & Frites
(Belgian waffles and fries)
336 West Broadway
Salt Lake City,
Utah 84101
Tel: (801).363.4444
info@brugeswaffles.com

Fritz Belgian Fries
(Belgian fries)
45 Main Street,
Keene NH 03431
Tel: (603) 357-6393
www.fritzbelgianfriesrestaurantnightlife.com/

Pommes Frites Inc.
(Belgian fries)
123 2nd Ave.
New York
NY 10003
Tel: 212-674-1234
www.pommesfrites.ws

Publisher's acknowledgements:
All pictures © Anness Publishing Ltd,
apart from the following: t = top; b =
bottom; r = right; l = left; c = centre:

Alamy 6tr (Julien Robitaille/Alamy); 8tl
(Picture Partners/Alamy); 8bl (Picture
Contact/Alamy); 8br (Alan Collins/Alamy);
9br (Robert Harding Picture Library Ltd/
Alamy); 11 (The Print Collector/Alamy);
13bl (Sam Bloomberg-Rissman/Alamy);
13tr (LOOK Die Bildagentur der Fotografen
GmbH/Alamy); 14bl (Eddy Linssen/Alamy);
15bl (Mary Evans Picture Library/Alamy);
16tr (David Noble Photography/Alamy);
16bl (Tibor Bognar/Alamy); 18tl (Andrew
Critchell/Alamy); 18tr (Helene
Rogers/Alamy); 20tr (Stephen Roberts
Photography/Alamy); 20br (Picture
Contact/Alamy); 21tr (Cephas Picture
Library/Alamy); 23br (Peter Titmuss/
Alamy); 28bl (Arco Images GmbH/Alamy);
30t (Chris Howes/Wild Places Photography/
Alamy); 32br (Art Kowalsky/Alamy); 40bl
(Peter Horree/Alamy).

Bridgeman 10b (Rafael Valls Gallery,
London, UK/The Bridgeman Art Library)

Corbis 11bl (Christie's Images/Corbis);
12bl (Hulton-Deutsch Collection/Corbis);
14tr (John Van Hasselt/Corbis); 15tr
(Owen Franken/Corbis); 19 (Francis G.
Mayer/Corbis); 25br (Ariel Skelley/Corbis);
34b (Yves Forestier/Corbis Sygma); 43br
(Craig Aurness/Corbis).

iStock 6bl (Jarno Gonzalez Zarraonandia);
7tl (Nataliia Kasian); 7br; 17tl (Stan
Rippel); 23tl (Nathan Wajsman)36l (Tarek
El Sombati); 38tr (Raoul Vernede); 42tl
(Frank van Haalen); 43tr (Gertjan Hooijer).

Rex Features 24tr (Ilpo Musto/Rex Features).

Suzanne Vandyck 21bl; 22bl; 24bl; 25tl.

INDEX